NINE WEEKS

NINE WEEKS
a teacher's education in Army Basic Training

Rich Stowell

© 2009 Rich Stowell.

Cover design copyright 2009 Dramatic Design Photo by Paul R. Wade.

All rights reserved.

PREFACE

Have you ever stood in a room with 50 relative strangers, all naked, on display so that a man who is not your doctor can examine you for ticks? It's pretty awkward.

Basic Training was strange in so many ways, though. It was stranger for me than for almost anyone else in the Army I speak with about it, although most people did roughly the same things, irrespective of when they went or where.

I was inspired to join the Army out of a sense of patriotism and duty to my country, which I love. That love has not waned. To the contrary, in my nearly three years now as an enlisted Soldier, it has grown stronger and deeper. I have met countless Soldiers who are as honorable, selfless, and committed as I could ever hope to be. They inspire me.

After Basic, inspiration of another sort struck. The ten weeks I spent at Fort Sill for Basic Combat Training were filled with experiences that were funny, exhausting, maddening, rousing, frustrating, and above all, rewarding. But the educator in me was badly disappointed with the quality of training, and felt compelled to put my thoughts to paper.

Since the moment I left my house I kept a meticulous journal. I wrote home to my wife as often as I could, and I perspicaciously observed everything that happened at Basic. I was so aware because it was so new and difficult for me. Films like *Full Metal Jacket* don't exaggerate; oh to God that they did. Imagine the four minute-long boot camp scene from *Forrest Gump*, and multiply it by 6,816. That's how long the real-life scene played, each frame more vivid and deteriorating than the one before.

In this book, I hope to convey the range of feelings that were so vivid and intense during that summer. It was bewildering: I had an entirely new language and culture to learn. The curve was steep and price for failure steeper.

The reader, too, may feel overwhelmed with the myriad abbreviations and military jargon. Imagine a new recruit trying to gather it all in among the infinite other worries he has. But the point of reading this is entertainment, so, instead of a drill sergeant yelling and making you do push-ups, I have listed abbreviations in Appendix I, in order of appearance and also alphabetically.

A few other notes on conventions are in order. For all rank references, I have used the three-letter Army abbreviations which is more elegant than the cumbersome AP Style. They are indicated in Table 2. Military time is also generally used, to give the sense of confusion that we often felt trying to figure out when lights out was. Dates are likewise written as they generally are in the Army, as 12 SEP 2009, or 12 September. Finally, although I capitalize "Soldier" in my other writing, as I do in this preface, throughout the book you'll see that I don't. Partly it's because the frequency of the word renders it problematic, but mainly I reserve the title of "Soldier" for those who have gone out and served beyond the Basic Training environment.

The audience I had in mind for this book was non-military. I thought that the public at large ought to know about, and would be interested in, how the American Soldier is made. I have found since writing it that Soldiers enjoy it too, finding pieces of their own experiences within.

At the very least, this work will be a record for my son of what I did the year before he came into this world. It is my hope that many others will enjoy it and learn from it as well.

CONTENTS

"This Week Doesn't Even Count"   1
WEEK 0

"Foxtrot Battery's Lost Their Mind"   28
WEEK 1

"Ate Up Like a Football Bat"   58
WEEK 2

"Shovel it Down, You Can Taste it Later"   86
WEEK 3

"Front-Leaning Rest Position, MOVE!"   114
WEEK 4

"We're Heading to The Range"   138
WEEK 5

"A Master's Degree in Moronism"   162
WEEK 6

"Win Me A Streamer"   186
WEEK7

"You Think You Already Graduated"   208
WEEK 8

"We'll Cancel Family Day and You Won't Graduate"   228
WEEK 9

Epilogue

Appendix

Acknowledgements

About the Author

To my wonderfully patient and supportive wife

WEEK 0

"This Week Doesn't Even Count"

As the bus pulled off Interstate 44 onto the wood-lined road, I noticed the sign that read, "Welcome to Fort Sill, the best post in the Army." Not a moment later, the bus driver proclaimed over the PA: "Welcome to Fort Sill, your life as you know it is over."

My life was as a 30-year old-high school teacher who had recently joined a fraternity of 17- to 20-year olds for a hellish summer camp at Fort Sill, Oklahoma. Aside from the irony of becoming peers with the kids like those I had been in charge of in my civilian high school teaching career for the previous seven years, I wasn't really ever excited to play Army like all the other guys I had ever met in the military.

For one thing, leaving my wife was the toughest thing I could have done at that point in my life. Having waited until my thirtieth year to marry, I suppose I was independent by some estimation. Yet, I must have surrendered some manly compulsion to live on my own, because I could barely face the fact that I would spend nearly an entire summer without her. It was late May; my college sweetheart, Esther, and I were wed the previous year, and since then we hadn't spent more than two nights apart. It was a strange goodbye.

"See you in nine weeks, love you."

So much was left unspoken, and I regretted it as soon as she drove off from the Military Entrance and Processing Station in San Jose. I was a broken man at that moment, never having felt so lonely. Though I am sure lots of other recruits do the same, I made several trips to the restroom to just sit in the stall and cry. And I *bawled*. We had been apart for mere minutes and I was already regretting my enlistment, making promises to myself to treat her like a queen forever when I got back.

My time at the MEPS was an eternity. I first visited the place with my recruiter the previous December to take the Armed Services Vocational Aptitude Battery test and get a full physical to determine my service eligibility. I felt a little offended that, as a seemingly healthy and intelligent man with so much more to lose at this stage in my life by joining the military than I had to gain, that they would even call into question my fitness to join. After seeing some of the others who were knocking on Uncle Sam's door, I understood perfectly why. The good folks at MEPS were the gatekeepers, and though it sounds superficial, there was a sizeable element that needed to be kept out.

The Military Entrance and Processing Station is the latest iteration of the Induction Centers of the Vietnam era. Once the civilian doctors hired by the military (MEPS inducts for all branches of service) certified me worthy for Army service, I signed a six-year contract with the California Army National Guard. My wife was present when I raised my right hand and swore the oath of enlistment:

"I, Richard Stowell, do solemnly swear that I will support and defend the Constitution of the United States and the State of California against all enemies, foreign and domestic; that I will bear true faith and allegiance to the same; and that I will

3 | "This Week Doesn't Even Count"

obey the orders of the President of the United States and the Governor of California and the orders of the officers appointed over me, according to law and regulations. So help me God.

Back in January, that oath represented largely why I had decided to join. Fulfilled by a successful teaching career among the underserved of Oakland, my wife and I decided I could do something more. In the National Guard I could dedicate myself to a higher purpose, to defend my country and serve the people of my state. As a teacher-turning-soldier, I thrust myself into a new world where my former career gave me a unique insight. It was meant to be an educational experience of the richest kind, one that any lover of real learning should relish. Now, four months later, confronted with the prospect of being in Oklahoma for nine weeks, I was unsure—scared to be more precise.

There were five of us going to Fort Sill from San Jose that day; three had prior military service, so they would begin Warrior Transition Course once they arrived on post. The WTC guys were cool and confident. One of them could tell that I was shaken, and took pity on me. We got to talking about our families—we had much in common—and we hung out throughout the trip to Oklahoma, which ended up being quite long: a delay at Minetta San Jose, another one in Dallas, and a night in Oklahoma City, made up the 36 hours between my former life and my arrival at Sill. The delays were like immersion into a cold swimming pool one painful step at a time, each one reminding you a little more than the last how comfortable you had been to stay in the dry.

A charter bus took us from the sooner state capital to the military facility 80 miles to the southwest. It might as well have been the moon. Fifty miles north of the Texas border, Sill seemed to be in the midst of endless rolling hills, but it all looked so foreign to me, befitting my apprehension and feeling of helplessness.

Established as a fort for US troops engaged with Oklahoma tribes in the 19th century, Fort Sill represented the last Army outpost on a disappearing frontier. Cavalry troops defended white settlers in the region from the time the fort was staked in 1869 until it became the home of the US Field Artillery in 1902. The symbol of white advancement and progress a hundred years ago was more backward and stale than any place I had yet been.

The bus wound through the post past a hospital and various modern buildings. Eventually we rolled up into a section of the base that too many decades had ignored. Wooden barracks, slathered mercilessly in the same dull color, stretched in both directions—a monochromatic wasteland where even the grass and sky took on a depressing hue. Our charter bus, which happened to be top-of-the-line in comfort and style, was like a time machine depositing us in a different era, where time stood still. We disembarked in front of one building that looked like all the others, except this one was adorned with a placard, whose foot-high letters read, "Soldiering starts here!" One final word of reassurance from a WTC soldier, "Don't believe all the hype."

The hype was that the Basic Combat Training experience would be the most grueling I could imagine, and that those in charge—the infamous drill sergeants—were intimidating beyond measure.

We were shouted into a room to begin processing. After some pretty bad sack lunches we were given "line numbers" to identify us. I was not "Rich," as I had been for 30 years. Nor was I "Stowell," as my recruiter called me. I wasn't even "last four 0474," as the processing command had identified me. Here, on my first day of BCT I was christened "117," "one-one-seven," which, in the military, is very different from "one seventeen." The latter would make you sound like a fool.

I and the other 150 or so young men who had made the bus ride that day made up Second Platoon in the 95th Adjutant

5 | "This Week Doesn't Even Count"

General Battalion—"Reception Battalion," for short. A few dozen more would join us over the next few hours and to be the most recent 200 soldiers to begin training in This Man's Army. That day some clothing was issued to us and we were moved into our barracks, where I was introduced to my new "Battle Buddy." His name, as fate would have it, was 118. Before he arrived at Sill he was Matthew Beal, a simple guy from North Carolina who knew three things: that his mama loved him, that Jesus died for him, and wrestling.

It seemed like everyone was from North Carolina. Or Mississippi. Or any state that at any point in history had raised arms against the union. I could count on two hands the privates without a drawl.

The WTC soldiers had been channeled off into their own group, so the rest of us were all newbies, privates mostly. Almost entirely we were deer in the headlights, except for several young men who had already been to BCT. These soldiers were on post for Advanced Individual Training. AIT soldiers had already been through Reception once, and became the experts for everyone who wanted to know what was happening.

Soldiers who enlist in the United States Army get shipped off to one of the five Basic Training Posts in the country: Fort Jackson, South Carolina; Fort Benning, Georgia; Fort Leonard Wood, Missouri, or Fort Knox, Kentucky; or Sill. One wonders whether the geography of training operations has determined recruitment demographics or vice versa. The last BCT facility west of the Rockies was Fort Ord, California, on the Monterrey Bay, which saw its final Basic Training graduates in 1976.

After Basic, soldiers move up the in the Initial Entry Training pecking order to AIT. Most AIT courses run between five and fifteen weeks, depending on the job. Fort Sill has been the home of the Field Artillery for over 100 years, so any soldier whose MOS (Military Occupation Specialty) was in the artillery would do advanced training here.

High schoolers hoping to start their Army careers early often choose the "split option" contract. That is, they split their IET over two summers, the first half of which they train at a Basic Combat Training facility during the summer after their junior year in high school. After graduation, they move on to AIT to complete their Initial Entry Training. As a high school teacher, I joined the National Guard on the condition that I would be able to likewise split. I may have been the oldest split-op in the history of Fort Sill.

That evening two drill sergeants, Davis and Clayton, officially welcomed us to Reception. Davis's main piece of advice was, memorably, to "wash our ass." In a nutshell, that's what Reception was all about—getting us cleaned up for Army service. It didn't need to be pretty, it just needed to get done. And the Army needed a few days to do it. Haircuts, uniform issue, vaccinations, dental and optical exams, and payroll processing. All these things took time, and we couldn't start BCT until they were done.

"Reception Battalion sucks," conceded Drill Sergeant Schlotthauer, who was brutally honest and somewhat prophetic. He would be in charge of making sure these important things happened so that we could ship off "downrange" in a timely manner. He explained that we couldn't begin our real training until every last one of us had been properly processed. Rumors were already spreading that our countdown to BCT graduation didn't start until after Reception. There is no way, I thought, that an institution as honorable as the United States Army would tolerate such an unjust practice as keeping me away from my family any more time than I was promised. After all, my contract clearly stated that my training period would last exactly nine weeks. I already had plans for the end of July!

The schedule on the leaflet we received indicated that all the necessities of reception would take three days. At least we could

7 | "This Week Doesn't Even Count"

hurry and get the real stuff started by Sunday. I was willing to hurry, if everyone else was. My delusions were spectacular.

That's what DS Schlotthauer was for. He shattered my delusional reasoning. "This week doesn't even count," he said. I was crushed. I already felt gypped for having to spend four hours at MEPS. Now this guy was telling me that an entire week of my precious time away from home wasn't going to count? The first thing the most fearsome Army in the world taught me was to surrender. For the next nine, or maybe ten or eleven, weeks, it wasn't my life. I might as well get used to it. I could move through the system like a product on an assembly line, a piece replaced here, a bolt tightened there, painlessly, or I could spend valuable time and energy feeling sorry for myself and my complete loss of agency.

Not only was Schlotthauer straightforward and honest, but funny too, and the soldiers all liked him. He had a knack for combining the two characteristics. Stern and direct, he left no doubt as to exactly what he wanted to communicate, and he guaranteed that you'd remember it because you'd be laughing about it with your pals the next day. He also understood the degree to which trust factored into obedience, and that obedience was the corollary to leadership.

Hanging on the wall in our barracks was a framed poster, with the words of Major John M. Schofield:

"The discipline, which makes the soldiers of a free country reliable in battle, is not to be gained by harsh or tyrannical treatment. On the contrary such treatment is far more likely to destroy than make an Army. It is possible to impart instructions and give commands in such a manner and such a tone of voice to inspire in the soldier an intense desire to obey, while the opposite manner and tone of voice cannot fail to excite strong resentment and a desire to disobey...

As I pondered these words, an intense feeling of respect for Schlotthauer came over me. He practiced the principles that guide effective leaders. I thought about how the examples of my new leaders could shape my work as a teacher. Schlotthauer was an exemplary noncommissioned officer, part of a corps whose duty was to train, mentor, and lead new soldiers.

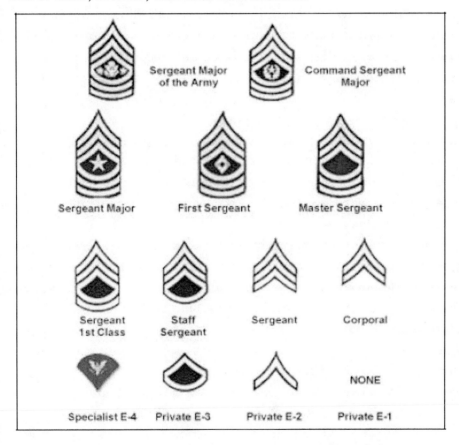

As our senior NCO and platoon drill sergeant, it was Schlotthauer's job to make us understand how important BCT was, and how impossible it was to leave prematurely. He didn't do this by yelling (though he did yell at select moments.) He helped us to understand it by explaining it in an entertaining way. He once gave us a speech congratulating us on choosing to come to

9 | "This Week Doesn't Even Count"

BCT for the summer instead of "chasing pussy." He also threw in some warnings: "You can't go home, no matter what," was his message.

Not that some privates didn't try. The shock that BCT delivers to the individual is severe, and usually drives inductees to familiar things: prayer, letter-writing, camaraderie with like-minded peers. Keeping photos was a common way for one to cling to the well-known in a natural effort to temper the effects of the unknown. For some, the shock drove them to do outrageous things, like run away illegally. One private in our platoon attempted such an illegal escape the first night. According to rumors he ran off with little more than the shirt on his back in whatever direction he guessed might offer the best chances. So he ran and ran, until, in the dark of the night, fell in a ditch and broke his arm. Military Police eventually caught up with him and after some medical treatment he was right back in Reception, where he would have to remain until his arm healed.

Indoctrination of the futility of such an act of desperation was a constant effort. It was explained to us several times that leaving one's battle buddy or platoon area for any reason constituted the crime "Absence Without Leave." A soldier who is AWOL for more than 30 days is deemed a deserter, a more severe offense. Furthermore, since we were enlisted during a time of war, the penalty for desertion could be death. (Desertion is merely an absence from which the absent party does not intend to return to military service, and is most certainly punishable by death during time of war. The last deserter punished by death was PVT Eddie Slovik in 1945[1]).

Apparently, one of the cleverer methods for seeking escape

---

[1] The case of PVT Slovik is a particularly disgraceful one for the Army. Slovik, who claimed he was afraid to fight on the front lines in Europe, turned himself to his superiors. He never actually deserted, he only refused to fight. He was the only U.S. soldier executed for that crime since the Civil War.

was to challenge the military's time-honored "don't ask, don't tell" policy on homosexuality. The Army is hip to this, and Schlotthauer gave us fair warning that, if any one of us pulled the "homo card," we would be required to kiss our battle buddy as proof. Even then, one probably wouldn't get discharged, just punished and mercilessly humiliated.

To show his more sensitive side, he also warned against the dangers of suicide, as if it needed explanation. "If you plan on hurting yourself, come and tell me," he said. "I will order your battle buddy to stay with you at all times." As wise as they were, Army drill sergeants clung to amazing delusions themselves, like suicidal privates giving their leaders fair warning. His remedy continued, "He will be with you when you take a shit, he will be with you when you shower, pointing out your nut sack and saying, 'hey, you missed a spot.'"

Schlotthauer was tough and funny; other NCOs had their own endearing qualities. Davis was a broad-shouldered and crusty African-American who fit perfectly the image I had of a prototypical drill sergeant. Davis was soft-spoken, but he spoke with authority. Clayton rounded out our drill sergeant cadre. She was a Louisianan in her thirties who struck me and just about everyone else as adorable. Clayton established herself early in a brisk attempt to overcome her god-given obstacle.

"Jess because you think I am a fee-male don't mean you kin ge-et over awn me."

She had another glaring potential impediment: her height. She stood about an inch over five feet, had a small frame and large hips, all of which only added to her aura as a delight. Her uniform was identical to every other soldier, except for her female drill sergeant hat.

Male drill sergeants wore the campaign hat, with its distinctive "Montana Peak", referring to the four dimples on the crown. Most privates would recognize it as a Smokey the Bear hat. Drill

11 | "This Week Doesn't Even Count"

Instructors sometimes refer to it as a "brown round," but usually it was simply a drill sergeant hat. Basic Training instructors in the United States Armed Forces have donned the campaign hat since the 1960s, following an absence of the hats in service. They were worn by U.S. soldiers in WWI and the decades following, though the style had been slightly modified. Its use was discontinued in 1939, until it was revived for training NCOs. On the front of the hat worn by U.S. Army Drill Sergeants is a golden disc, upon which is emblazoned the Great Seal of the United States.

The female drill sergeants wore a slightly different headpiece. Forest green, instead of the cocoa brown of their male counterparts', it was a variation on a woven Australian bush hat with its brim cocked on the side and fastened to the crown. The first female drill sergeants entered the corps in 1972; Clayton was only one of several at Fort Sill during my reception, even though the fort only trained young men[2]. She was one of the feistiest among them, no doubt, but she didn't have the temperament to order men around; it wasn't because of her gender—she wouldn't have fared any better with females under her charge. In fact, she probably would have done worse. No, she just wasn't unpleasant enough to fit the role.

As if to downplay the most obvious difference between every male private and her she would highlight it: "Sound off like you gotta pair, soldier!" It was her subtle way of letting them know that they deserved her best attempt at imperiousness and she expected that they could return the compliment. It usually came across as cute, and almost every private gave her the benefit of the doubt, since she was, in a drill sergeant kind of way, adorable.

She could sound off, too. As we marched, we would hear the familiar "left, left, left, right, left" that goes without mention. To

---

[2] Field Artillery occupations, along with infantry, are available only to males. Fort Benning, Georgia, home of the infantry, is also an all-male Basic Training center.

break the monotony, drill sergeants call out, or sing, cadences to help keep step. Clayton was a singer, and we would dutifully repeat each line as loud as we could:

Uh oh! Oh no!
I gotta leave I gotta go!
This Army life is not my style,
It's got me, it's got me, it's got me lookin' like Gomer Pyle!
Uh oh! Oh no!
I gotta leave I gotta go!
This Army life is all messed up,
It's got me, it's got me, it's got me lookin' like Elmer Fudd!

"Singing" serves two main purposes—it raises troop morale and *esprit de corps*, but primarily it helps the less-coordinated to keep in step. For some reason that I could not fully understand, many soldiers were unable to put their left foot down on the call of "left." Having banged my own head trying to inculcate the plainest truths to my own students, I felt for the sergeants who had to teach the dexterously-challenged the simple march.

Davis was nearly the exact opposite of Clayton in every way, not least of all in manner. He seldom raised his voice above a pitch necessary to communicate to 200 soldiers at a time, and I never saw him get right in a private's face. If Clayton tried to prove herself brawny enough to be a drill sergeant in This Man's Army, then Davis seemed to try to appear gentle enough to mentor young men into soldierhood, and was prone to some endearing moments himself.

He lavished upon us the wisdom he had earned by making lots of mistakes in his youth. On one occasion, he passed the wait time at the dining facility (not unusually up to an hour) with a drug-prevention course. Speaking of a bygone era when marijuana, for instance, was "extra strength," he exhorted us to forswear the vices that had plagued so many servicemen of his

13 | "This Week Doesn't Even Count"

generation. I appreciated his attempt at constructive counseling; everyone else enjoyed the humor with which he delivered it.

A little overwhelmed after the introductions of those who would have complete dominion over us for what seemed to be an eternity, we rendezvoused at the barracks. We unloaded our gear, mostly our civilian attire, into our wall lockers. I slept on the top bunk above Beal, next to me was 119, a hyperactive extrovert from Pennsylvania named Miller.

Aside from his hyperactivity, Miller was exceedingly competitive. He was a star high school athlete and took every opportunity to demonstrate his prowess—physical and otherwise. He would challenge others to push-up contests, and never lost. One evening, he gathered the entire barracks section around the drinking fountain to take monetary pledges for a feat he was about to perform—he had caught a moth, and, unprovoked, set about to establish his daring by eating it. He refused to eat it without reward, though; he asked ten dollars each from several soldiers. After settling for a total of twenty, he proceeded to devour the moth. I can only imagine the dusty flapping wings challenging his ability to chew and swallow, but he struggled through it, fought to keep from gagging, and took his cash. Such were the conditions that dictated our amusement in the barracks.

Miller quickly became one of the favorites in the barracks. He always seemed to be in a jovial mood. Those first few days I felt oppressed by the weight of the United States Army embodied in the drill sergeants. Miller, on the other hand—who quickly embraced his new military name, 1-1-9—would laugh behind their backs. He represented the sort of young man that the Army relies on: aggressive, somewhat foolhardy, yet eager to perform. He taught me that even grueling experiences include opportunities to be amused.

The combination of my age and my personality shaped my reactions to the events going on around me in ways different from the younger recruits. I adapted much slower to circumstance than my new peers, and I had difficulty accepting the fact that I was, for all intents and purposes, just another 18-year old. On the other hand, I had the perspective and experience that age often bestows. When we would meet outside of the barracks, as we did every time the drill sergeants excused us to go inside, we would often be ordered—

"Front-leaning rest position, MOVE!"

—to do push-ups (got "smoked," "dropped," or "dusted off," alternatively) as a platoon for any number of reasons. Ostensibly the grounds were tardiness, talking, or generally poor appearance. Privates would groan and complain, assuming that if such and such rule hadn't been violated, then we would be off scot-free enjoying free time without a face to face encounter with the sidewalk. I recognized that the drill sergeants were merely testing our reaction. It didn't matter why they dropped us, only that we would drop without complaint. We rarely did, at least on first request, which only resulted in more push-ups.

Miller didn't mind pushing, he very much enjoyed it. He also enjoyed testing the limits of the adults in charge of him, something he undoubtedly did in high school where he was just days before. I, on the other hand, hated testing boundaries. I respected them, maybe too much. Such allegiance to the order was almost painful to me, because it made me surrender all the equity that I had gained from it in my civilian life. PVT Miller, who had no maturity or world experience, had an enthusiastic come-what-may attitude that made it enjoyable for him. In contrast, I was wise to the game, wrapped up in a strange anxiety toward the experience. So I found myself in the odd position of looking up to an 18-year-old who may have well been my bane in one of the classes I taught. Such was the topsy-turvy world into which I had thrust myself.

A few yards away from our barracks entrance was a steel

15 | "This Week Doesn't Even Count"

canopy that sheltered a concrete pad about 30 feet by 60 feet. This was a general purpose meeting place where we received briefings throughout our time at Reception.

"Briefings" are the fine print of "things you should know." Our leaders had all sorts of things that they didn't want to be held liable for, so they put them out (in slipshod fashion) in mass briefings. Our first sergeant gave his debut briefing that first day. He referred to everyone as "*Highspeed.*" I quickly learned that "highspeed" was an all-purpose nickname that could be either complimentary or derisive. Another thing I quickly learned was to never fall asleep or appear to be asleep during a briefing. I thank the Lord I did not learn it through direct experience. PVT *Highspeed* experienced it for me.

"Come 'ere, *Highspeed!*" snapped the first seargent. The dozing private quickly complied.

"Give my brief," directed the NCO. PVT *Highspeed* stood there with an understandably dumb look on his face. He had already warned a different soldier; PVT *Highspeed* picked the wrong time to appear to be nodding.

First sergeant continued to make his point: "Why aren't you talking? You obviously know what I was going to say, so give my brief," he repeated. PVT *Highspeed* stood there with a stupid look on his face, but he played it as smart as he could have. In his situation there were no right answers, and the safest course was to remain quiet. Many soldiers revert to habits learned in school: negotiating, excusing, and trying to talking their way out of tight spots. They didn't get any tighter than this. Here was the highest-ranking soldier we had been introduced to demanding something quite impossible for *Highspeed* to deliver in front of over 300 trainees (another platoon had joined us for the briefing.) The one in the fishbowl stood pat.

"If you didn't know what I was going to say, then you wouldn't have fallen asleep, right?"

Direct questions demanded answers, even if the query disguised something else. Losing patience, he ordered a third time, "Give my brief!"

I felt for this kid, but it had the desired effect. Two-hundred-ninety-nine backs straightened up a bit, and every pair of eyes opened a bit more, scared to death of falling asleep. Over time that fear would wax and wane, but the lesson generally stuck.

Sleeping was for the barracks at designated times; lights went out at 2030, and we were to be unconscious by 2130. That usually gave us a half-hour for the "3 Ss:" Shit, Shower, and Shave. My nightly ritual included the aforementioned, plus dental necessities, however many letters I could write, a journal entry, some scripture reading, and a very long prayer. I rarely prayed harder in my life than those first nights at Reception, and crying usually put me to sleep.

Was I ashamed to cry? Hell no, though I did my best to hide my therapeutic sobbing in my pillow. It is hard to describe the emotional agony of those first few nights at Fort Sill. I slept well, but wake-up always came too soon. Dressed, we met outside with the other sections and awaited further orders. Our uniform was a combination of the reflective physical training (PT) shirt and shorts and army green socks pulled tightly to the top of the calf. One could determine exactly how many days a trainee had been on post by looking at his socks, wearing them loose or bunched was asking for trouble, naturally.

We had much to accomplish, and we did so with the zest of a slug waiting for a turn at the salt lick. The deadlines were arbitrary, and not ours. Ironically, nearly every private would scheme to get ahead in the 200-long line. Waiting is painful, and at some point in our evolution, man developed an instinct to move up in a line or get out of it. The Army's plan was to get us combat-ready by purging this instinct. Besides, less time waiting on the front end simply meant more on the back. No matter how we

17 | "This Week Doesn't Even Count"

tried, though, we couldn't speed up the lines. So we waited.

In fact most of our time at Reception was spent waiting... in line...holding still...and it was Oklahoma...and summer...and hot. There were several lines: one for a cash card; another for eyeglasses; still another to enter the mini Post Exchange (PX); and a final one for that ritual of all Basic Trainees, the barber. The civilian barbers had little sympathy for the tender scalps of their customers. All my hair was removed within 40 seconds, and I wasn't the only one who left the barber chair with a bleeding mole. Nearly every private was disappointed with his new style, not realizing that he looked only as silly as everyone else.

That same day I got a new eyeglass prescription, as the ones I arrived with were not approved for training. The ones I chose looked quite stylish, a departure from the BCG that they had issued just a year previously. "BCG?" I asked one soldier who had the thick, plastic-rimmed, vintage Charles Nelson Reilly specs. "Basic Combat Glasses," I assumed. He politely corrected: "No, *Birth Control* Glasses."

We also had to buy supplies to get us through the communal living arrangements of a Basic Trainee: deodorant, soap, toothpaste, floss, and the like. I had come prepared, but in true Army fashion, was told that no matter what I had come with, I needed to buy everything on the list anew. The sameness axiom was inescapable, even in the realm of personal hygiene preferences.

On the second day, we were off to the medical section, where we were to have blood drawn to determine which vaccinations we needed. Needles didn't bother me, and I looked forward to getting pumped full of the latest preventative medicines free of charge. It was also a final amnesty—everyone was given the opportunity to disclaim any previously unmentioned disqualifying conditions to a civilian doctor.

The word "civilian" was music to our ears, as we were quickly learning that military personnel were not the friendliest. We were disappointed to find, however, that the civilians working in this particular installation were often just as unpleasant as the most bad-tempered NCO. Whether we were getting our blood drawn or our teeth x-rayed, the civilians were downright rude. To them, we were paperwork; on any given day the dental personnel had to x-ray and complete paperwork for 400 privates. There were probably five of them working at one time, so their workload was substantial, to say the least.

They were typical government workers, way down on the totem pole. It was a DMV where yelling at customers—young men who were voluntarily sacrificing much more than desk minions—was the convention. No customer service surveys were in sight. It was in stark contrast to the women who took our pictures. Also civilians, these ladies had to process the exact same enlistees through their photo service. They were as genial as could be, because they were selling. Their livelihood correlated directly with the mood of the privates. The forces of the free market were on full display even in this soviet-style summer camp. (As courteous as the picture ladies were, I passed on the T-shirt with my photo emblazoned on the front, same with the coffee mug, big items among soldiers. I did succumb to the pressure to buy a simple photo package.)

Pictures were taken on our last full day in Reception. Before we got to that privilege, we had to get the boring stuff out of the way. Most boring was our time spent at the administration building, finalizing the paperwork that would follow us to the other side of the tracks, and which would ensure that we were dealt with properly. This included getting paid, which was becoming a priority for me.

I hadn't enlisted for extra income, but the experience was so fitfully difficult that extra money became a salve more than a necessity. It was also mildly comforting knowing that others were aware of my marital and housing status and rank, all of which translated into higher pay. Living in the Bay Area is expensive, and to its credit, the Army recognizes the fact and compensates active duty soldiers for housing costs based on ZIP code. As a married man not living as a dependent, I received the Basic Allowance for Housing (BAH). Being away from my wife also qualified me for separation pay.

On the first Saturday away from home we slept in until 0500. We cleaned barracks nearly all morning. It became clear, as I wiped down my bed posts for the 16th time—that the training staff had no real plan. We got the place as spotless as a run-down, 30-year-old building could get. We washed showers, toilets, swept several times, dusted, and practiced the time-honored art of military bunk-making, with their hallmark hospital corners. After lunch, we cleaned the grounds around the Reception Battalion, which consisted of a central parade field of grass, the concrete drill pad, five buildings on the field's perimeter, and the network of paths connecting the buildings.

There is no such thing as military efficiency, only military thoroughness. The plan for tidying up the Reception grounds was an elegant example: 200+ soldiers were ordered to form a single line facing the breath of the grounds, an arm's length from the next man. In such a formation we were told to walk to the other side of the compound, picking up any trash. Our instructions from DS Davis were clear, "If it don't grow, pick it up."

We made our way through the grounds; when a building or a bush got in our way, we collapsed the line, squeezing in tighter on either side. It was a task that any competent group could complete in three or four minutes, tops, but we had several hours to kill. Inevitably, almost every private laid claim to a spot of ground and ensured that it was immaculate. We were content to station ourselves in the sun, basking in its warmth, which seemed to protect us from the drills sergeants' scrutiny.

However, the sun posed a problem. Blazing solar rays and scalps that hadn't seen them in years were a terrible combination. We were given an abundance of sunscreen, almost exclusively for use on our bright white domes. Schlotthauer threatened to punish anyone who ended up with cranial sunburn. The charge? Damage to government property.

Water was a commodity that wasn't taken for granted. "Drink WA-TER!' the drill sergeants shouted, never as a request or suggestion. Although we stood or sat idly most of our time at Reception, the heat would quickly sap our bodies of moisture.

Standing was grueling, both physically and mentally. I couldn't believe how much of our time was just spent waiting in line, usually planted on two tired feet. It was demanding of our bodies because we were to stand at "parade rest." In such a position, our feet were shoulder-width apart, "resting the weight of the body equally on the heels and balls of both feet," as the Army manual states. Our hands were "at the small of the back and centered on the belt," and "fingers of both hands extended and joined," thumbs interlocked "so that the palm of the right hand is outward." Needless to say it is a silent position.

My arms, after twenty minutes or so, would become tight and sore, requiring steady use of muscles just to maintain them at such an unnatural position. Staring straight forward put a strain on my neck. My feet throbbed at the heels, shooting pain up my legs. It was a sight to see, though. The only movement at times was a private collapsing—having fainted from standing too long with knees locked. *That* certainly wasn't in the manual.

I could hardly bear the sharp pain, and would steal a quick shift in weight or roll my ankles to relieve the pressure on my heels, all while trying not to draw the attention of the NCOs. My hands would sink down past the small of my back to rest on my butt or hang all the way until the only thing keeping them from my sides was the clasp of my hands. I gave in to the temptation

21 | "This Week Doesn't Even Count"

to roll my neck to release the stress and tightness. These were my great sins at Reception.

I saw them as faults, too. I had decided to give myself almost completely to the Army program—doctrine, physical demands, attitude, and all—at least for the coming nine weeks. I could endure it, and it was worth my time on the chance that it actually would make me a better man. Even just standing there might improve me, I thought. How could I claim to be self-disciplined—an attribute worthy in any field of endeavor—if I couldn't stand still for a few minutes?

A few hours was more like it. One way to relax was to "get smart." Reading the "*Smartbook*" or drinking water were the only two acceptable alternates to standing fairly like statues. The *IET Soldier's Handbook*, or *Smartbook*, colloquially, was among the first items we received at Fort Sill. It was our ticket out of parade rest while in line. After "Front-Leaning Rest Position, MOVE!" and "Drink WA-TER!" the most common command given was "Get Smart!" the cue to open the book and pretend to read.

I developed a peculiar idiosyncrasy at some point in my life: once I began to read a book, I couldn't stop until I had completed it. So I was, cursed with the task of reading the 318 pages of instructions for new recruits, as told by the writers of TRADOC, (short for Training and Doctrine), from which I learned such useful nuggets of information as origin of the "Caisson Song" (later renamed "The Army Goes Rolling Along."), the causes of trenchfoot and the "effects of striking the groin." Lest TRADOC be accused of leaving anything to assumptions, the *Soldier's Handbook* confirmed that "Bathing prevents hygiene-related diseases such as scabies, ringworm, athlete's foot, skin infections, and pinkeye."

That Sunday I looked forward to Church like I had never looked forward to Church before. Earlier in the week we were told that we wouldn't have the opportunity to worship at the LDS service, as it was held too far away for us to travel while in Reception. After a long, boring Saturday, I was elated to hear that the LDS guys would be allowed to go to our service after all, which was at 0830 hours.

By 0600 the rain was pouring and we trudged off in our PT uniforms: shorts and all, draped in a forest camouflage poncho. There were four of us ready and willing to count ourselves as Mormons; being ushered to the head of the chow line in order to catch our ride to the service site was only an incidental benefit. We were told to remind the NCOs in charge that we were to go in to eat first, but even that required tenacity and perseverance, perhaps to test one's sincerity of faith.

At any rate, PVT Blakeman, a 17-year-old Idaho Guardsman, and I dogged the sergeant on duty into letting us into the dining facility as promised. Once inside, we grabbed our food, ate quickly, and stepped outside where we went after every meal, waiting for someone with rank to tell us where to go next.

It was an unwritten and often-spoken rule that if a private needed to know anything, an NCO would tell him. We were passive objects, not capable of formulating practicable information and certainly not encouraged to actively seek it. I took it on faith, this Sunday morning, that a concerned NCO would inform Blakeman and me where to go. We learned in this case that genuine concern was in short supply.

We stood steadfastly in the rain, the heavy drops seeming to test our resolve. After 25 minutes without a clue, we decided to take the proactive route, and headed back inside to inquire. The NCO on duty erupted in rage.

"You mean to tell me that you knew you had to go to an early church service, and you thought you could eat bacon and eggs and the whole thing? Get out of my face!"

Not sure what that meant, we hustled back to the drill pad, hoping that we hadn't missed the ride, somehow knowing that we

23 | "This Week Doesn't Even Count"

had. Another drill sergeant told us, in the most sensitive way, that the Army didn't say we couldn't go to our church service, but that circumstances prevented us from attending.

Righteous indignation swelled inside me and I cut in, "Nobody told us where to go." I recounted our experience waiting patiently in the rain. He could sense that frustration and disappointment had overcome me in a serious way, and he apologized again, then dismissed us. We tried to conduct our own worship service in the barracks, but the NCOs put the kibosh to that, on the grounds that we weren't part of the team if we were worshipping individually. Individuality had no place in the Army.

Trying to turn it into a learning experience, I decided that for the next nine weeks I would hound NCOs until I had very specific directions. When it came to church, this would prove a lesson well-learned. I also realized that attending church was a privilege at Basic Training, one that I hadn't appreciated as a free man, and one that I would relish as a basic trainee.

So my first Sunday away from home began in dismal fashion, and my mood quickly soured further. It was 3 June, my wife's birthday, and I began to feel more depressed than the day I left her. I turned to God, having no one else with whom to talk. I recorded the following in my journal: "I prayed and tried very hard to have a good attitude. The combination worked because, by the time I called Esther at 1830 I felt great." I wrote to her:

"*My Sweetheart Esther:*

Your name sounds so beautiful to me. Things continue to go well for me, but I still miss you very much. I just got off the phone with you and I feel great. I can't wait for us to have a face to face conversation again. I think about that drive to San Jose last week, and it makes me so sad. When I see you again, it will be the opposite feeling.

The next day excitement built upon contentment when we got

Nine Weeks | 24

The moisture wicking tan t-shirt or cotton t-shirt is worn underneath the coat and is tucked inside the trousers at all times.

Army chaplaincy religious denomination pin on insignia is the only branch insignia authorized on the ACU. It is worn 1/8 inch above and centered on the nametape.

The U.S. flag insignia is worn on the right shoulder pocket flap of the ACU coat.

The former wartime service shoulder sleeve insignia is centered on the hook and loop-faced pad on the right sleeve of the ACU coat.

Name and U.S. Army tapes are 5 inches long and are worn immediately above and parallel with the top of the slanted chest pocket flaps. The background can be either olive green or the universal camouflage pattern.

A maximum of two pin-on identification badges may be worn centered on the ACU coat pockets.

The embroidered rank insignia is 2 inches high and 1 3/4 inches wide, and worn centered on the front hook and loop-face pad of the ACU coat for all ranks. The background of the rank insignia can be either olive green or the universal camouflage pattern. The rank insignia background will match the background of the name and U.S. Army tapes.

Army combat boots are made of tan rough side out cattlehide leather with a plain toe and tan rubber outsoles. The boots are laced diagonally with tan laces, with the excess lace tucked into the top of the boot under the bloused trousers, or wrapped around the top of the boot. Metal cleats and side tabs, and sewn-in or laced-in zipper inserts are not authorized.

Skill badges will be worn in order of precedence 1/8 inch above and centered on the U.S. Army tape. Two badges require a 1/4 inch space between them. Up to five badges may be worn with the first four in two rows of two and the fifth on top.

Skill tabs will be placed centered on the shoulder pocket flap on the left shoulder of the ACU coat in order of precedence with a maximum of three worn at one time. There are only four authorized skill tabs (President's Hundred, Special Forces, Ranger, and Sapper).

Tabs that are part of unit organizational patches such as the airborne or mountain tabs, are worn with the shoulder sleeve insignia below the shoulder pocket flap.

Shoulder sleeve insignia is centered on the hook and loop-faced pad on the left sleeve of the ACU coat.

The coat is normally worn outside the trousers, and the trousers are worn with a belt. The coat will not extend below the top of the cargo pocket on the trousers and will not be higher than the bottom of the side pocket on the trousers.

Sleeves will be worn down at all times, and not rolled or cuffed.

The knee pouch for internal knee-pad inserts and the bellowed calf storage pocket on the left and right legs will be worn closed at all times.

The trousers will be tucked into the top of the boots or bloused using the draw string at the bottom of the trousers or by using commercial blousing devices. They should not extend below the third eyelet from the top of the boot.

25 | "This Week Doesn't Even Count"

our clothing issue, which was possibly the chief motivation for many of these young men to join. Who could hardly blame them? After walking around for the past several days in the Improved Physical Fitness Uniform (IPFU) sporting our thigh-length shorts and knee-high socks, it was exhilarating to finally slip on the vaunted ACU—Army Combat Uniform. In all we were each issued over $1000 in clothing: four sets of ACU jackets and pants, an all-weather field jacket, hats, gloves, sweats, cold-weather undergarments, name tapes, and two pairs of boots.

The uniform of a United States Soldier comes with responsibility. Immediately we all felt more distinguished and manly. We were also aware that our comportment was held to a higher standard while in uniform; the clothes themselves seeming to elicit such behavior—standing up straighter, being more polite to others, and generally acting more dignified. The final touch was my specialist rank insignia, which I attached front and center on my chest.

Tuesday was our final full day at Reception. After going through the motions of a final PT assessment in the morning, and packing in the afternoon, Schlotthauer gave us a final motivational discourse and a phone call. Supervision was spottier than previous days; we were told to keep it under three minutes, but the only check on us was the soldier behind us in line waiting his turn. Having thought it through, I went to the payphone station that was at the opposite corner of the parade field and safely out of hearing range of all the NCOs. As I waited in line, I laughed with another soldier, reminiscing our few days at Reception and the life we were looking forward to after Basic. Eventually, we got our turn on two adjacent phones, long after the allotted three minutes for the privates ahead of us. We didn't mind.

I was talking to my wife when a pair of soldiers passed by who clearly felt they were more important than we. One of them caught the private on the phone next to me with his hand down the back of his shorts and corrected him. The private wasn't that interested, and brushed him off as politely as he could. He had more pressing things on his mind, and talking on the phone to a loved one took priority over just about anything else. I had a different perspective, and noticed the look of self-importance on the passing soldiers' faces turning to irritation. I was fully engaged on the developing situation, and quickly losing track of what my wife was saying. The soldier repeated himself forcefully, indicating that a hand down the backside of one's shorts was a no-go.

"Oh, sorry man," the offender said innocently, acknowledging a soldier trying to help him do the right thing.

"How about 'sergeant,'" scowled the soldier. ("Man" is a word verboten in the U.S. Army.)

So I realized that (a) this guy was probably still in some type of training, (b) he was an NCO, and (c) the private's response wasn't measuring up to the *Smartbook's* definition of proper military courtesy. The sergeant waited for a second attempt, but the newby was lost in his conversation. I gave him my best non-verbal message that this guy wanted more.

"Oh," he stammered, "You're a sergeant?"

"Yeah, how 'bout you address me properly and stand at parade rest?" He began walking away somewhat satisfied that he had met his obligation to dutifully scold the young private.

"Sorry, *sarge*," he replied in what could have been an audition for the lead role in a reprise of *Gomer Pyle, U.S.M.C.*

By now the tension had been cracked with my laughter. Although I assumed that "sarge" wasn't standard protocol, either, I guess the soldiers who started the affair weren't so confident after all. The taste of being unnecessarily aggressive with a new recruit had satisfied them sufficiently to end the matter, and they left us to finish our conversations. A "happy birthday" and an "I love you" and it was back to the barracks. We still had to

27 | "This Week Doesn't Even Count"

pack, and sergeants would pay us a visit to remind the wannabe frat boys that we were not going home yet, but the end of the beginning was upon us.

The next morning we would wait for the buses to take us to our new home for the coming nine weeks.

At least now we could start counting.

WEEK 1

"Foxtrot Battery's Lost Their Mind"

I CARRIED MY two duffle bags containing everything I owned, efficiently packed, outside to wait under the awning. After breakfast our highly-trained NCOs alphabetized us and directed us to the parade lawn at 95th, doing what we had been trained best to do: wait.

And we waited.

Our leaders had divided us into four groups; I was in the fourth, along with everyone else from Ray to Zaccardi. So for five hours we sat atop our luggage to make our way to the "other side of the tracks," a euphemism for the real Basic Training of which soldiers spoke so ominously. It was an awkward wait, most of us just sat there. Others feigned bravado in the face of the unknown.

After several hours our reception cadre figured out that we were, indeed, in alphabetical order all along, and we were allowed to visit the latrine. By noon the drill sergeants from the other side had arrived.

We were on our feet for a quick handoff ceremony, and as quickly as it ended, the new drills were ordering us to the trucks.

29 | "Foxtrot Battery's Lost Their Mind"

The "real" Basic thus began, and all privates were intent on complying quickly. In the June Oklahoma heat, we ran at top speed, carrying two or three duffle bags each, and, whipped along by the barking of 11 new drill sergeants.

It was like the first day of school, and the teachers were trying to make an impression as strict disciplinarians. It reminded me of the advice I had been given as a teacher when welcoming a new set of student to my high school classroom: "don't smile till Christmas."

The rest of Fourth Platoon was seated around me in the air-conditioned Cadillac. It was quite literally a long cattle car converted into a soldier transport. The silence was shattered on our first stop, as we were again raucously herded off the Cadillac and onto some bleachers under a steel canopy, eerily reminiscent of the one at 95th.

It was our beginning of school assembly: a high-speed soldiering extravaganza that excited and motivated us. Several basic trainees, obviously from a class that was near graduation, put on a spectacle of things we would learn over the course of the next nine weeks. They, along with their drill sergeants, drove up in a military transport and stopped when a simulated IED exploded on the roadside, earning oohs and aahs from the crowd.

The soldiers, donning helmets, bullet-proof vests, shaded goggles, knee- and elbow-pads, and, of course, carrying weapons, broke into two teams and began moving toward their target: a two-story building occupied by several men wearing robes and headdresses. It was going to be entertaining watching these Americans take it to the Taliban or Al Qaeda or whomever was supposed to be in the building firing at the truck. To those training at Fort Sill, they were generally referred to as, "Haji," Our enemy wasn't "Charlie" anymore.

"Haji" (*hadji*) is an Arabic honorific applied to a Muslim who has made the pilgrimage to Mecca. Its recent use by U.S.

servicemen is somewhat pejorative, and trainees were never allowed to utter it at Basic. The cadre of Foxtrot Battery didn't use it excessively, either, but when they did, we understood that they were talking about Arab-looking, terrorist-like enemy combatants. At any rate, the soldiers in this demonstration needed targets, and they might as well have been *haji*.

The teams advanced in choreographed precision, firing on their targets as they reacted to commands shouted by their drill sergeants. Eventually, as we expected they would, the Americans overtook the building, either killing *haji* or taking him prisoner.

After the demonstration, we met our Battery Commander, Captain Carl E. Warren, who welcomed us to Foxtrot Battery, First of the 40th Field Artillery Battalion. In Army organization, a battalion is anywhere from 300 – 500 soldiers, grouped into three to five batteries, companies, or troops. The basic unit of army hierarchy is the platoon, consisting of usually between 30 and 50 soldiers, divided into four squads. Squads can be subdivided into teams. A company comprises four to six platoons. From bottom to top, then: team, squad, platoon, battery (or company or troop), battalion, and brigade, the largest unit in the Basic Training section.

Since Fort Sill is the home to the Field Artillery, we belonged to a battery instead of a company. The nomenclature derives from the formation of guns and other artillery pieces grouped for battle, siege, or defense (a battery of guns). By the 19th-century, field units operating such weaponry were grouped into organizational units under the same name. "Battery" also referred to the place where our unit met.

So that's where the Cadillacs took us after the demonstration. We hauled our bags with a ferocity matched only by the disorder with which they were haphazardly strewn about the battery area, and there we met our new drill sergeants, Jackson and Robertson. DS Jackson seemed to be the senior of the two, though both were staff sergeants. DS Robertson circulated our formation and glared, piping in when emphasis was needed on this or that instruction. His contribution was to put his face as close as possible to his target, hissing insults and threats while pointing his hand to underscore his determination to see that things got done his way. Jackson seemed more concerned, at least at this point, that we understood instructions clearly.

Thus the duo led us—Jackson spouting instructions, making sure we knew what to do; Robertson making sure it got done quickly and efficiently. Other platoons had three drill sergeants; ours made up for their dearth with an increase in intensity.

We stood outside on the drill pad for several minutes in such a manner, the other platoons likewise formed in their respective areas within the battery. Our battery area occupied one-eighth of the entire building, called the "Starship." The starship looked somewhat like a bloated tic-tac-toe board from the bird's eye, each protruding wing housing a battery.

The battery areas all looked the same, to describe ours would be to describe them all. The view from a marching private entering the area was that of an alleyway, three stories rising up on each side. Straight ahead were a set of stairs that led to a balcony from which drill sergeants could keep watchful eyes on us. The ground level was open space, interrupted by eight pillars that sometimes afforded us a respite from the drill sergeants' attentive stares.

Often times when we would mill around the drill pad, waiting for our next orders, an NCO or officer would happen by. Military courtesy dictated that we publicly recognize such, at which time everyone would jump to their feet. If it was a drill sergeant or other NCO, the first junior enlisted man to see him or her would say, in a thunderous voice, "At ease!," prompting his fellow soldiers to stand at parade rest. Having been duly rendered his deserved courtesy, the NCO would reply, "As you were," relieving the soldiers of inferior rank the obligation of maintaining a formal stance. NCOs who suffered from chronic unpleasantness or aversion to IET soldiers would wait as long as possible to relax the troops. It wasn't uncommon for a drill sergeant to neglect to put troops backs at ease and exit the area entirely, leaving the soldiers to wonder, silently at first, and then cooperatively, if they could break their ridiculous pose.

Officers were almost always more polite. Protocol was similar for recognizing them, and NCOs were under the same obligation to render the courtesy. Upon entry to the area or room, an officer of any rank would expect to be greeted with a single shout of "Battery [or group or platoon], atten—SHUN!" All enlisted personnel within earshot would spring bolt upright, and the one who made the call would salute on behalf of the group.

We became very used to calling "at ease" for NCOs, but there was always something about announcing officers that made privates nervous. It was a certain amount of risk that, perhaps the soldier arriving was not an officer, that he was present all along, or that someone else had already announced him. All possibilities would have rendered foolish a loud pronouncement by a junior enlistee. To make such a public declaration of the rightness or wrongness of your position that every single soldier in the battery should heed, carried an incredible amount of pressure. Yet, there was some odd thrill that accompanied a successful announcement, and it seemed to be the goal of everyone to do it. Like asking for a first dance at a junior high ball, elbows would encourage someone to do it as the officer approached. Then, jubilant congratulations were heaped on the soldier for doing it correctly after the officer blessed the effort with a "carry on."

Though at times solemn and staid, Army etiquette could also be downright juvenile. Our education paired reverential manners with comical chants and grunts. Of course we sang as we marched, and recited creeds and oaths. In Foxtrot, "carry on" was followed by, "*Woosah, Falcons!*"[1] We didn't understand what we were supposed to say, but by God we were to say it loud! Few others knew exactly *what* we were saying, but everybody knew what it *meant*. Often drills from other batteries would glide by and put us "as we were," which elicited the mysterious phrase, then move along mumbling "what the fuck did they say?"

At any rate, in the case of recognizing officers, a false positive was far better than a negative. That is to say, the risk of missing a call to attention was far greater than that of calling it needlessly. Thus, our attention was often directed to the Charge of Quarters, from where officers and NCOs alike were likely to appear.

The Charge of Quarters, or "CQ," was to the right of the grand staircase, from our vantage point. Inside was CPT Warren's office, that of his executive officer, 1LT Henley, 1SG Gulliksen, and the battery training NCO, SGT Stevenson.

Stevenson was a piece of work. When we met in an auditorium-style classroom to complete some very important paperwork on our first day in Foxtrot (so important, in fact, that they provided enough copies for only some of the privates to fill out), Stevenson let loose on one of the privates from Fourth Platoon who didn't get a certain slip of paper. PVT Rogers (for whom there was no love lost from me) let a few drops leak from his canteen onto some cards that were being distributed as he leaned over to pass them down the table. Stevenson caught a glimpse of what happened and he exploded.

"You owe me, Rogers!" He said it with a look of sincere disgust and anger, his eyes piercing his verbal victim. They bespoke an eerie anticipation to the day he could impose some creatively diabolic punishment on this poor private for wetting cards that meant nothing to either of them. As Stevenson made his way to the front of the room, he turned his neck to send a glare back to

---

[1] *From Bad Boys, the Will Smith, Martin Lawrence cop movie.*

Rogers to make sure the private had got the message. Why was he so angry? Why did he obviously hate Rogers so much, having only just seen him for the first time? I thought we were all on the same team. I was quickly learning that was not the case.

Immediately upon making our way to our new home for the next nine weeks, the barracks, we commenced the most standard of Army rituals—paperwork. To fill out the ostensibly necessary forms, we sat like second-graders in front of our bunks, cross-legged on the hard laminate tile floor, following instructions like 50 eager schoolchildren.

Army paperwork is a crapshoot. It is almost a sure bet that once a form is successfully completed, one or more of four things will happen. One, filling it out anew will be required at some future date. Two, it will be filled out "incorrectly." Three, it will be lost. Four, it will be the wrong form. And making an honest mistake could ignite the violent fury of an NCO, like Stevenson's rage against PVT Rogers. On this day, however, there were greater sins.

To preempt such a drastic error, I raised my hand to ask a simple question. Though annoyed, DS Robertson helpfully answered.

"Thank you, drill sergeant."

DS Robertson put his perfectly shaven face two inches away from mine, and said without unclenching his teeth, "Give me ten, private." I was always a private to DS Robertson.

"Don't thank me," was the mantra, "Thank your recruiter." If only I could make the phone call.

We found on our bunks a ration of necessities for communal living: a roll of toilet paper, a stick of lip balm, a miniature bottle of hand sanitizer, anti-fungal foot powder, and a four inch cord with eight blue beads. The water beads, we were informed, had a dual purpose; first, they were a tool to track how much water we drank daily. We had a standing order to drink eight quarts each

35 | "Foxtrot Battery's Lost Their Mind"

day. Every time we finished a quart, we slid one bead down the cord, helping ensure we got our share of the good stuff. The beads were worn on the collar, and were color-coded by platoon, ours a Wolfpack blue, helping NCOs to identify and group us, thus fulfilling their other function.

The bay was swimming in blue to constantly remind us of our affiliation with Fourth Platoon. Wall trim was blue, floor tiles were blue, latrine doors were blue, and there was a blue podium at the head of the bay. Underneath the podium was an eight foot-wide re-creation of the Department of the Army Emblem, a colored near-replica of the Army Seal, adopted in 1778. DS Jackson called the area the "Kill Zone."

The original seal was used to designate official documents of the War Department; in 1947, Congress amended the seal and authorized it for public display to identify the Army.

In the center of the emblem is a Roman cuirass, or breastplate, obscuring an unsheathed sword pointing skyward. Beneath the cuirass is the date 1775, atop the sword is a red Phrygian cap (looks like a stocking). Crossing behind the cuirass are a spear and a musket with fixed bayonet; the weapons are black and the cuirass gold.

To the right of center is the Star-Spangled banner, leaning outward and draped over a drum. In front of the drum is a cannon and a stack of three cannon balls. Opposite the American flag is a banner of the Revolutionary War period (blue image on white background), in front of which is a mortar carriage. In front of the carriage are two bombshells.

Above the cap at the very top of the image is a rattle snake coiled around a scroll which reads, "This We'll Defend." The words, "Department of the Army" and "United States of America" encircle the emblem on top and bottom, respectively.

Though we trod the art piece countless times, its poignant symbolism was never revealed, much less discussed. But what business was it of ours? We were merely privates; if it didn't interest the NCOs, it shouldn't have interested us.

But it should have: the cuirass is representative of strength and defense; the sword, spear, musket, cannon, mortar carriage, and ordnance, of American weaponry. The drum symbolizes the Army's public notification of its purpose and intent to serve the nation and its people. The Phrygian cap signifies liberty; the rattlesnake was often used as a revolutionary symbol indicating the American People's constant readiness to defend country.

Yet the beautiful imagery had no place in BCT. We were to

37 | "Foxtrot Battery's Lost Their Mind"

keep off the Kill Zone, and that was that.

Our first night in the battery we were called to a "classroom formation," whereby we were to find a piece of real estate within a distance no less than six feet and no greater than 30 feet from the drill sergeant, who typically sat in a leather office chair that he rolled just outside his office. The formation was used to get administrative tasks done quickly, and on this night DS Jackson sat us through two hours of paperwork that he had to complete.

"Who's in the Regular Army?" Hands shot up in the air. DS Jackson counted and scribbled away on his packet.

He asked about injuries from heat stroke to deviated septum. Then he moved on to religion, and got a quick poll. "Who's a Latter-day Saint?" I raised my hand proudly and was excited to see several others in the platoon do likewise.

Everyone was eager to answer questions in the affirmative. We were all so apprehensive at this point that we thought, since they were asking, the questions were terribly important and of some consequence like, say, earning a trip anywhere away from our battery. For example, certain soldiers seemed almost boastful of the fact that they had a heart murmur, thinking it might disqualify them. Frankly at this point I felt like a prisoner and if anything merited my release I would have been ecstatic and relieved, knowing that I had done all I could to serve. (It wasn't my fault that my heart murmured!)

I became particularly enthused to get questions about marital status and education level. I was the only married man in the platoon (and the only one with a college degree), and I assumed it would garner some sort of prestige. When I raised my hand to indicate that I did have a degree, DS Jackson clarified, asking if I had a masters.

"Yes, drill sergeant."

"What in?"

"'Teaching Mathematics,' drill sergeant."

"What's the name of the degree, knucklehead?"

"'Teaching Mathematics,' drill sergeant."

With a reluctant smile he nodded and said, "OK."

Jackson was amazingly relaxed and warm, even helpful. He briefed us on the proper making of a bunk, wall locker organization, and the procedures for going to sleep and waking up. I half expected him to show me the Army procedures for brushing my teeth and wiping my ass. But then again, I hadn't finished reading the *Soldier's Guide*.

That's not to say that such intimate matters were outside the drill sergeants' purview. DS Robertson wanted to know why my underwear was different. I had to explain to him that, as a faithful Mormon, I wore a special kind of underwear. It was made from the same fabric as the issued pairs, only knee length, instead of banana hammock. He was irritated, but that pesky freedom of religion thing had him stifled.

The first night we also learned who our official battle buddies would be. I was a little disappointed to have been placed with Yeidder. He was nice, and smart, but he just wasn't cool. The dynamics of living among pre-college males was quickly rubbing off on me. "Yeti" to DS Robertson, Yeidder was also quite portly, one characteristic sure to attract unwanted attention. Though I'd rather have had a more athletic, interesting companion, I nevertheless made good friends with him. We cooperated better than most other privates and finished organizing our lockers early. At the end of one of the most chaotic and jarring days of my life, I was ready for a nice shower and bed.

The nice shower would have to wait. At 2030, we were ordered to disrobe and form a line in one aisle of the barracks. Wearing shower shoes and a towel, and carrying only a bar of soap, we would wait in line for our turn in the showers while DS Jackson timed us.

"Foxtrot Battery's Lost Their Mind"

The role of scholar gave way to that of inmate. In a single-file line, 54 naked soldiers stood stinking, waiting for a minute of warm water to wash in. I waited, trying to avoid eye-to-eye or eye-to-any other body part contact with my comrades. By the end of our Basic Training, privates would be slapping each other on the ass and masturbating in the bathroom, but for now, we just didn't know each other that well.

The whistle blew once every sixty seconds. With eight shower stalls the task took less than ten minutes, and, though I had to devise a mental plan for getting vital parts lathered and rinsed within the allotted time, I was fairly clean and ready for bed by 2100 hours.

A fireguard roster was posted on the whiteboard near the office. The fireguard is a true throwback, evidence of the Army's refusal to let some traditions go. In some earlier era, fires would warm barracks , and someone had to be posted continually to ensure that the fire was stoked yet under control. As the Army modernized, the need for constant vigilance remained, thus the all-night guard.

Shifts were covered by two soldiers at a time, beginning at lights out, 2130. The duration and rotation of shifts were flexible, but the standard was one hour, so by wake up at 0430, 14 soldiers had covered a shift. Our *Smartbooks* specified that we would "have the opportunity for seven hours of continuous sleep per night" barring any watch duty. The anguish of a 0230 wake up shake from a soldier seeking relief from fireguard is nearly unbearable. Once posted, soldiers were responsible for counting heads and logging any unusual activity.

There was never anything that got recorded in the fireguard book aside from shift changes and drill sergeants checking in. That is not so say that nothing noteworthy ever happened, but we were at least smart enough to realize that reporting such activity would mean nothing but trouble for the entire platoon. If one private fell asleep on fireguard, then it was going to be 54 privates getting smoked.

"Toes on line!" was the first thing we heard in the morning. We all went forward to a natural line created by the tiles, and stood at attention. Like the opening scene from *Full Metal Jacket*—our posture made possible a full group inspection and easy delivery of instruction, and put us vulnerable to any insult our tormentors wanted to hurl.

Sometimes they would make us do physical exercise, simply because they could. Usually, they would simply give us instructions for the morning. A typical a.m. would consist of some personal hygiene time—no showers—and barracks "maintenance" until 0515, when we were expected to report to the first sergeant for first call.

Our first week in Foxtrot involved lots of yelling, and we found ourselves in classrooms quite a bit. When I first joined, my recruiter had told me that we would be in classes during Basic. As a teacher and college graduate, that excited me. The more class, the better, I thought. I had visions of erudite lectures, note-taking, question-answer sessions, studying, and tests. Those are the things at which I had excelled.

To my disappointment and everyone's frustration, Army Basic Training classes were nothing of the sort. What really happened is that the entire battery would file in to an auditorium with folding chairs, take seats, and listen to scripted lectures, sometimes for several hours at a time. The lectures often accompanied PowerPoint presentations that any moron could have read, yet drill sergeants and the other NCOs paraded around with pomp as if they had just delivered the greatest lecture ever. We usually caught barely a word.

Ironically, the science of effective instruction began in the military. In the 1950s, military training commanders were concerned with the amount of information a cold-war soldier, with a greater number of more technical jobs needed to be filled, could master. Warfare in this new age had more in common with public relations campaigns than the bloody battles of the past, and begged a new question: How can the soldier learn to perfection the new demands placed upon him? A new field of study was born trying to answer that question.

Instructional Design answered it pretty well. Eventually its principles were adopted by industry, then public education. The premise is simple: start with the end goal, determine the intermediate steps that need to be taken in order to achieve that goal, and design instructional courses, or modules, that ensure the student's ability to take each step. Backwards design, the instructional experts call it. School teachers employ it in varying degrees in classrooms across the country.

Though it sounds logical, backward design is counterintuitive. At least it's counter-instinctive. Most instructors present information to students who do their part by asking questions. Those queries tend to guide a lecture and choice of examples to illustrate a point. Often students share their understanding of material to enrich the class. When students have learned enough, the teaching stops and the testing begins.

Modern instructional design flips that model on its head. Under the new model, a set of standards or performance objectives are defined. Instructors decide what needs to be demonstrated in order for those objectives to be indisputably performed to perfection. Thus, objectives need to be clearly defined so that even the most casual observer can state without ambiguity whether a student meets the objective. Moreover, the approach is decidedly behavioral. Students are expected to "do" more than to understand. In a theoretical sense, though, understanding is very important because it helps a student do things better.

Drill sergeants didn't care whether we understood. They had their checklists of extensive performance objectives, upon which they marked the appropriate one of two boxes, "Go" or "No Go."

One can only imagine that the training NCOs had their performance evaluated by such checklists, so they were satisfied that the PowerPoint presentation was merely delivered. We were "instructed" to follow along and learn it, but it was apparent that nobody in charge really knew how to ensure that actual learning occurred. So we sat, ready to do whatever we needed to cope. They expected us to take notes at lightning speed and without desks, on pocket-sized notepads. Any questions? Of course not. Questions were evidence of not paying attention when the information was first disseminated.

The classroom experience at Basic caught me by surprise, but the routine we learned during the first week would be followed for the remainder of the cycle. Veritable kindergarteners, we "formed up" outside the classroom door. The formation was an elemental act in BCT.

On the command, "fall IN!" one soldier began formation by standing at attention—facing the leader of the element. The first soldier and the three who lined up directly behind him were the first men in the four "ranks."

The term "rank and file" comes from this long-lasting military (from Napoleonic days) nomenclature. Once the element—in this case, our battery—was in column formation, the NCO can give a facing movement and a marching command. "Left, FACE!" prompted every soldier to turn to his left, using proper footwork. At this point, the four "ranks" were now "files."

"File from the right, column RIGHT!" tells the far-right file to go right—every soldier marching forward to the "pivot point" and making a right turn into the classroom. We would thus enter the classroom in grand style, filling in the rows of chairs orderly and silently. Only when the entire battery was in the room, standing

43 | "Foxtrot Battery's Lost Their Mind"

in front of his chair at attention, would we be given the command, "take, SEATS!"

But we wouldn't take our seats. The command, "take, SEATS!" was merely the cue to sound off with the battery motto, which we had just "learned:"

Foxtrot Battery's lost their minds, up in here, up in here!
Hardcore soldiers you will find, up in here, up in here!
Hold up, everybody stop, somebody's left the gate unlocked!
Regulators where you at? (Regulators only) up in here, up in here!
Reapers where you at? up in here, up in here!
Crusaders, where you at? up in here, up in here!
Wolfpack, where you at? up in here, up in here!
(Whistle down as we fall to our seats)
...BOOM! Artillery!

Two-hundred pairs of buttocks would hit the seats as the room shook with the vocal "boom" of the artillery call. What had I got myself into? I would have never thought so many people could be convinced that this was cool. Those in charge were the ones most thoroughly convinced. Drill Sergeant Eppinghaus, a hyperactive airborne artilleryman who acted more like a college frat boy than an NCO in charge of dozens of privates, began dutifully reading the PowerPoint. There are two types of officers in the Army: commissioned and non-commissioned. Non-commissioned officers hold the rank corporal and up (sergeant, staff sergeant, and sergeant first class, all greeted with "sergeant;" master sergeant, first sergeant, sergeant major, command sergeant, command sergeant major, and sergeant major of the Army). When addressing an NCO, the enlisted soldier will stand at parade rest, and always begin and end sentences with the NCO's title.

Commissioned officers are the management of the military. They outrank enlisted Soldiers, NCOs included, and are often commanders of units. They are the lieutenants, captains, majors, lieutenant colonels, colonels, and generals of the army.

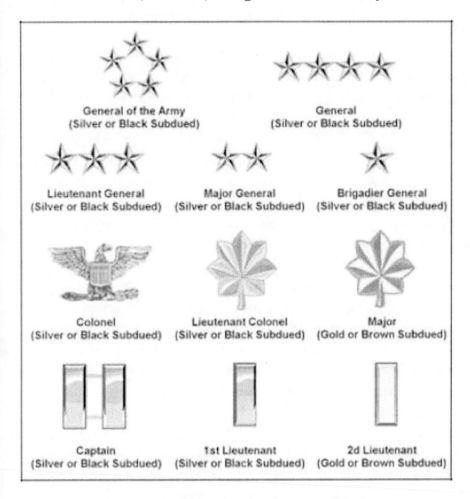

Due to the responsibility and prestige of the officer ranks, soldiers address them in a more respectful manner. When speaking to them, Eppinghaus informed us, junior ranking soldiers always stand at the position of attention. There are various rules governing when and where to render a salute, and, as we already knew, we were to call attention when officers entered a room.

45 | "Foxtrot Battery's Lost Their Mind"

As if we thought that drill sergeants fell from the sky, Eppinghaus explained to us that they went to school, too. Drill sergeants heaping abuse upon future drill sergeants. It may have been a terrible ordeal to go through, but they used it as a club; the treatment they suffered justified the incompetency with which they beat us. The inmates weren't running the asylum, but recent parolees were. At least they had the advantage of knowing what it was all about, being able to see the big picture.

So far we really only saw one part of the picture, the part where we got yelled at a lot. We sat through the yelling—they claiming it was world class teaching. Within an hour of having "learned" how to address officers, we got the opportunity to put it into practice when our Battalion Commander, Lieutenant Colonel Pastore stood before us for a briefing.

All of us were very impressed with the commander when he dismissed the drill sergeants. My guess was that he wanted the privates to be able to speak freely; we were all still green and made the mistake of playing along.

Sitting upright in our seats, we waited to hear what this man who had the power to order around drill sergeants, would have to say to us. The first thing was, "relax." Was he serious? Our ability to relax had already been purged. He repeated, more seriously, "relax."

Wondering if this was some sort of cruel trick we hesitantly relaxed, finally getting comfortable in our chairs for the first time in about a week. I guess he thought it made us respect him more, that he had the authority to tell us to do anything in the world, and he chose to tell us to relax. We hung on his every word, he was a very engaging and dynamic speaker: funny yet serious. Commanding, yet calm, the commander communicated well to junior enlisted personnel. He had commissioned after several years in the enlisted track, and now this field-grade officer had been given command over the 1/40 Battalion at Fort Sill.

LTC Pastore said two things that made quite an impression upon me. First, we were all "killers." I found it interesting that he had chosen that word. I hadn't joined the Army to become a killer, though I was quickly discovering that I was expected to act like everyone else. The leaders in BCT couldn't have given two shits about my ASVAB score or my elite MOS. With my test score and taste for the exceptional, I had chosen the most unique job description I could find from the list of over 200 occupations that my recruiter presented me several months earlier. I was his first 46-Romeo, and he never missed an opportunity to brag to fellow recruiters. Now I was a grunt, just like all the mechanics and artillerymen around me. We were soldiers first. Killers.

The second thing the commander said was that he was concerned about the trends indicating that trainees were not retaining information. He admonished us to ask lots of questions, especially "why." He asked us to remind our drill sergeants to conduct After-Action Reports. AARs would be the safety valve on all the pent-up mental frustration that goes with learning vast amounts of technical information in such a high-stress environment.

During an AAR we could ask the drill sergeants "why?" Why are we doing this? Why does it work? "Why" questions get to the heart of learning. If a student can feel safe enough to ask why, it is reasonable to assume that the necessary synapses are functioning. Moreover, the answers to those why questions helps cement the information into the mind. This guy was giving me hope where just moments before there was none. It was apparent that LTC Pastore was serious about training effectively, and he knew what needed to be done.

Unfortunately for us, neither the lieutenant colonel nor any other concerned commanders were involved in the day-to-day training operations. That job was left to the NCOs—drill sergeants. A reminder of that reality was thrust in our faces immediately,

"Foxtrot Battery's Lost Their Mind"

when the drill sergeants reentered the room, toward the end of the briefing, during the question-answer session. Of course, upon their return they caught us in the act of obeying the commander's order to relax. We were ripped relentlessly. They couldn't drop us right there in the class room, but the drill sergeants had tricks, one of which we learned as soon as Pastore was gone.

"On your feet!" Eppinghaus blurted out. "Sit down!"

"On your feet! Sit down!"

"On your feet! Sit down!" It went on for several minutes. After a while, Eppinghaus even got tired of saying it, so he simply motioned with his hand: arm extended toward us, index finger pointed up, followed by a snap of the wrist to put us down.

The punishment was exquisite—the physical task of standing and sitting was difficult enough, but the absolute control he wielded over us was priceless. The drill sergeant demands unqualified obedience to even the most absurd orders. The scene would last several minutes, and, like so many other occurrences in Basic, we would want to laugh were it not for the fact that we were on the losing end of the situation. The other NCOs partook in more than enough laughter to go around. I had a feeling we wouldn't be having many AARs.

While we waited in lines for meals and latrines, drill sergeants would take turns teaching us in the most condescending ways. DS Jones gave us the secret to BCT success.

"Three things you need to know," he told us while we stood at ease. He instructed us to write them down: "One: Do as you're told." Sounds simple, I thought.

"Two: Do as you're told."

"Three: Do as you're goddamned told!"

It is difficult to express the seriousness and severity of the advice. The Army had found the most intimidating soldiers to serve as drill sergeants. Ours were doing a good job scaring the shit out of me. I was at least as old as some of them, yet inexperienced in the ways of the Army, and my personal confidence was ebbing. I was out of my element, and regretting having joined. What did any of this have to do with serving my country?

Jones also enlightened us on proper handling of weaponry. During our first week, we had been issued items that seemed to be pretty important for warriors: weapons and body armor. We filed through the supply room, located opposite the CQ, and Mr. Biskins handed each of us a real-life, honest-to-goodness M16 rifle. At that moment, I felt like I was really in the Army. It was exhilarating to carry the weapon that defined the U.S. infantryman from Vietnam to the present. With great power comes great responsibility: each was accountable for his rifle at every moment, 24 hours a day.

The first thing we learned about our weapons was what they were not: "guns." ("This is my rifle; this is my gun. This is for shooting; this is for fun.") Beyond that, the facts got more complicated: The Mike 16 Alpha Deuce is a "gas-powered, air-cooled, magazine-fed, lightweight, shoulder-fired weapon capable of firing five types of rounds: ball, tracer, dummy, blank, and plastic."

Then Jones regaled us about the feminine qualities of our rifles. Jones was a man who loved to hear himself talk. He could have been a preacher, were it not for his foul mouth and overactive libido.

"Your weapon is like a girl. You treat her right, and she will serve you well. You mistreat and abuse her, she'll… You gotta keep her clean…This trigger here…this is like a little clit… sensitive. You gotta be gentle." To validate his last point, he cocked the rifle, took off the safety, and dropped it butt-first not more than two inches from the stage, where it hit without even tipping out of his loose grip. The bolt slid forward, clicking ominously. It was true, that rifle reached climax like, well…the

"Foxtrot Battery's Lost Their Mind"

metaphor seemed apt.

Jones wanted the analogy to take full root in our barren minds, so he ordered us to write a letter. At first we dismissed it, but one night back at the barracks, we shrewdly used the task to justify writing letters when it was expressly forbidden. I rushed off some b.s. because our drill sergeants wanted the proof that we were writing our current girls, not our flesh and blood ones back home:

"*Estee Baby* (we had orders to name our rifle)*:*

We have only known each other for a short while, but I'm already falling in love. I can tell this is going to be a beautiful relationship. You have all the qualities I look for in a lover: consistency, firmness, boldness, and you are a joy to hold. During our time together, I look forward to getting to know you intimately. I am willing to take it slow, though, so we can get to know each other before we go all the way. In the meantime, I promise to love you, protect you, and treat you with TLC.

"Who's good at computers?"

I spotted the opportunity immediately. If I could help out, then there ought to be something in it for me, not least of which was the recognition that my intellect was above a third-grade level, or what drill sergeants credited the average basic trainee.

Seeing my hand raised, Jackson called me forward. "Come on, Mr. College Graduate." I, along with PV2 Ryan Snider, was the newly ordained platoon House Mouse, the teachers' pets of our new school. As such, Snider and I did routine clerical tasks: filing, data entry, and errands for the drill sergeants. Our first task was to transfer records from paper to computer. We spent a lot of time in the office. Though menial, our work was a reprieve from the often boring and even more menial life in the barracks. We were the brain workers of the *Animal Farm* in Fourth Platoon.

We also relieved the drill sergeants from the encumbrance of creating a nightly fireguard roster. The first night that I posted the new rotation, simply following the alphabetical order of platoon members' last names, DS Jackson caught a of glimpse of my name in the 0130 slot.

"House Mouse don't pull fireguard."

Enough said. I wasn't one to argue anyway, so Snider and I effectively gained 40 extra hours of sleep over the course of our training.

It came at a cost, though. First, we had to endure the constant complaints of all the privates who thought our fireguard assignments were unjust. It was, in fact, more complicated than going in alphabetical order. For one thing, every fourth night our platoon was in charge of CQ duty, in which we would man the charge of quarters, answering the phone and directing inquiries to the proper personnel. CQ shifts began in the afternoon and continued until 0630 the next morning, and also had to be done in pairs. Thus, certain soldiers would miss fireguard since they had covered a CQ shift.

We also had endless management duties, including keeping track of where everyone was, assigning tasks, and acting as drill sergeant-trainee liaison.

Nevertheless, the House Mouse title was a way to separate myself from the pack. I didn't have any grand illusions of my own status, but I did expect to be treated differently than the teenagers in my battery. I think Jackson agreed. When we were alone, we spoke more like adults, though I always rendered him proper military courtesy; likewise, he acknowledged that I wasn't exactly like the others. Right off the bat, he gave me added responsibility, like Mail Clerk: I was responsible for depositing outgoing mail before first call. OK, it wasn't exactly *The Apprentice*, but it was something. I was also put in charge of assigning jobs for barracks cleaning ("maintenance," euphemistically) which was to be conducted every morning.

"Foxtrot Battery's Lost Their Mind"

Cleaning the bay was not rocket science, but we could sooner build a space bound vehicle than get the bay clean enough for our NCOs. Sure, we knew what to do—sweep and mop, ensure bunks were properly made, scrub the showers, toilets, and sinks, and take out the trash. Yet every morning the drill sergeants would arrive to a cluttered bay. Try as we might, we (the handful of us who were sincerely interested in doing our duty and pleasing our drill sergeants) couldn't ever get 54 privates to accomplish all of that. As a result, Jackson and Robertson were perpetually peeved at our platoon. A peeved drill sergeant very quickly becomes a pissed off drill sergeant. Rare was the morning that we could make it to breakfast without a public declaration that we were the worst platoon in the Army.

While they were certainly tougher on us than I would have liked at the time, their frustration was understandable. They were professional babysitters. We were never manly enough for them, and they let us know it. Once "knuckleheads" to DS Jackson, we soon became "bitches."

"Good morning bitches."
"Come 'ere, bitches."
"Fall in bitches"
"Hey bitches."
"Listen up, bitches."
"Shut the fuck up, bitches."
"Good night bitches."

Our behavior reinforced his image of us as womanly and childish. Yet their behavior fed the frustration and disappointment. They had to be present nearly all the time to supervise; the irony was the more they were there, the more we grew to depend on their governance for survival. We were like battered women, growing accustomed to the abuse, and proportionally more attached and needy. Every insult increased our desire for acceptance in their eyes. "Bitches" became a term of endearment, one that we were proud of, sadly.

Our masters had other terms for us. Sometimes of ignorance, other times from laziness, and often from wanton meanness, drill sergeants would devise funny nicknames for the privates. Unlike a coach or teacher who looks for something interesting about a person and cleverly invents a name that the subject could take some pride in, a drill sergeant would just say the first thing that came to his mind. Yeidder was Yeti; Snider was Nader. Vadney was Vaginal, because in some lame sophomoric sense, it was funny, but only if no one was around willing to keep our terrible senses of humor in check. Then there was Tucker. Not Tucker, but Crazy Tucker.

One evening some non-descript private, alongside his dutiful battle buddy, knocked on drill sergeant's office door. Non-descript private was hyperventilating, and his battle-buddy informed DS Robertson that he may have been having a panic attack. After long (and unsatisfactory) explanations, DS Robertson was left with no other choice than to drive him to the hospital. We didn't hear from non-descript private for some time, but saw that his bunk was unoccupied. Word was that he was taken to the psychiatric ward for evaluation.

Non-descript private was Tucker, as was his battle buddy. We had several pairs of same surname soldiers in our platoon: Privates Tucker and Tucker, Privates Scott and Scott, Privates Rogers and Rogers, Privates Sanders and Sanders, and Privates Walker and Walker. Clearly, we needed secondary identifiers, so after Tucker's breakdown, he became "Crazy Tucker." His companion, who was slightly larger, was "Big Tucker." Big and little seemed adequate descriptors absent anything more obvious, so there was "Big Rogers" and "Little Rogers," "Big Sanders" and "Little Sanders," "Big Walker" and "Fat Walker," who was not particularly big or little, but substantially stouter than "Big Walker." One thing you did not want to call Fat Walker was

53 | "Foxtrot Battery's Lost Their Mind"

"Walker Texas Ranger," as tempting as it was. Walker, a Missouri high school state wrestling standout, was one tough son of a bitch who looked for opportunities to prove it.

Though boyishly friendly, Fat Walker was also highly emotional, prone to goofing around, and really quite lazy. In Reception, he was rumored to have urinated into another soldier's canteen. He vehemently denied it, but it was the platoon consensus that he had it in him. Nonetheless, I became somewhat fond of Walker, and for some reason dismissed his shortcomings more readily than those of others.

Living in close quarters had the obvious effect of drawing us close together. In a letter to my wife I wrote, "There are 54 privates in my platoon. I don't have any particular reason to like any of them, but I can tell we are going to be like family, for better or for worse."

Some privates took the calling a bit too far, though. Sanchez, for instance, would prowl around after lights out stalking his victims, whom he'd sneak up on and position his crotch in front of. Pulling down his pants and displaying his testicles, he would wake up the private whose first perplexingly dreadful sight would be a ball sack mere inches away.

Our second day at the battery we called home. DS Robertson had us that day, and he was insistent that he wasn't obligated to let us use the phone, like a jerk-off cop telling you that he was only going to cite you for 13 mph over the limit instead of the 16 you were driving. Playing the part of hapless motorists, we let him think that we were deeply appreciative.

Robertson explained to us, as if he were reading SAT instructions, the procedures for making the call. We stood in crisp files with our backs to the ten payphones on the CQ wall. At the thirty second warning, the next person in each line would turn around to face it, toes on a line about 15 feet away. We were only to approach the phone on his "go."

Once on the phone, we stood at parade rest—no leaning on the phone, no hands resting on the phone box. We would be strictly timed—three minutes. Since we were using phone cards, the conversation may only run two minutes after dialing (and in some truly unfortunate cases, misdialing) the 15-digit account number and PIN. At times some phones lost a connection. Tough luck. Some soldiers' parents didn't answer the phone. Too bad.

The joy of hearing my sweet Esther's voice was incomparable. I felt as giddy as the day I first asked her out, excited to just be on the phone with her. The distress of not being allowed to talk to her for days at a time was far surpassed by the reward of finally making the connection. I have no recollection of what we talked about those short 180 seconds, but the tears streaming down my cheeks told my drill sergeant that I loved every last one of them.

As each group of soldiers finished their calls, they made way to the bleachers to wait. At the conclusion of the 20 minutes it took for the entire platoon to finish, DS Robertson grumbled something about our mamas' titties in a halfhearted attempt at motivation. Of course when he went through Basic he never missed home, nor was he allowed a phone call, to hear him speak of it.

Three days in to my life at the battery, and I was all ready to go home, eager for the day I would leave this crazy life and reunite with my bride and home. The next day I penned my first letter to her since we had been in Foxtrot:

> "*I have cried at least once a day thinking of you (I am crying right now.) I don't mean to discourage you or make you feel sorry for me. Instead, I tell you that so that you'll realize how much I need you. This is the hardest thing I have ever done in my life, and when it almost has me broken down, there is only one thing that keeps my spirit up enough to continue. It's not all the reasons that I joined: to serve my country, to challenge myself, to learn new skills, or to have adventure. The thing that*

"Foxtrot Battery's Lost Their Mind"

makes me want to succeed is to think about how proud you will be of me for graduating.
Just 70 days to go...

As excited as I was to do the stuff that the Madison Avenue types want the public to think happened in Army Basic Training, it was still some time away. A new requirement—we were the first cycle for which it was mandatory—was the Combat Life Saver course. CLS is a valuable skill set that included such battlefield necessities as dressing a wound, applying a tourniquet, checking for injuries, and initiating a saline lock for an intravenous infusion. Any one of these remedies might be necessary in the event of an enemy ambush or deadly debris from a roadside explosive. We found out that at BCT, the biggest risk to a soldier's life was to be bored to death in CLS classes.

Drill sergeants were not expert in CLS tasks, so we were handed off to SGT Stanley, a mild-mannered combat medic who knew his subject matter, but was dull and unenthusiastic. He droned on monotonously about all sorts of incredibly important stuff, yet it was a battle to simply stay awake. Note taking was a strategy for staying lucid more than to learn.

Needless to say, dozing off in class was an abominable sin. Usually, drill sergeants would tell a sleepy private to stand off to the side; if there were dunce caps available, they would have absolutely been employed. After a short grace period, however, we were highly encouraged to remove ourselves from the chairs and impose the consequence with reflective initiative. I had to stand up from my chair several times in order to keep from collapsing on my battle buddy.

We endured—not hyperbole—a four-hour block of instruction on the first day of CLS. I remember several key concepts from the interminable slideshows: first, that pigs are used to simulate humans in demonstrating how to treat grave wounds; second, that pigs bleed a lot when you sever their femoral arteries; and third, that watching a pig nearly bleed to death has a tendency to wake one from a daze. To augment the slideshows and videos, each of us was issued a yellow, paper-bound CLS study guide. The letter-sized book was to be carried on our persons at all times, its enormity protruding from our left cargo pockets.

"Is that CLS book in your right cargo pocket, private? Get in the front-leaning rest."

During days when we weren't scheduled to be in a classroom, tortured by PowerPoint, we had to practice staying awake while pretending to study. Very soon we were to be tested in old-fashioned, multiple-choice style, the results of which would determine our eligibility to graduate. Since we were the first cycle subject to the CLS requirement, the drill sergeants of Foxtrot were not going to leave anything to chance. They gave us hours on end of study time. They neglected to realize, however, that effective study was impossible while having to do push ups throughout the session. We began our study session with no guidance other than: you have your book, the test is next Friday.

All of Fourth Platoon looked toward me to rescue them; since I had teaching experience, I would obviously be able to teach them something I knew nothing about, with little effort on their part. I did my best to organize study sessions, but I was fighting my own fatigue and that of my platoon mates, while DS Robertson did his best to prevent us from cramming.

Not that he didn't want us to learn, but we got the distinct idea that Robertson wasn't exactly a scholar. According to his account, he had joined the Army just after his senior year in high school, in the summer of 2001. To his delight, war broke out just before he had graduated BCT, and he has been an infantry killer ever since. Studying out of books just wasn't his thing. He favored actual drill and practice, with a healthy share of physical punishment thrown in. With or without realizing it, he undermined our best, albeit

57 | "Foxtrot Battery's Lost Their Mind"

feeble, efforts to learn the mind-numbingly tedious material in the CLS course book.

"Why is Weir asking me questions? Front-leaning rest position, MOVE!"

We all dropped to the floor instinctively. To DS Robertson, following orders, learning our place in the pecking order, being humiliated, and getting physically fit were all more important than studying.

He just wouldn't allow us to get in a routine to learn the CLS information. At one point, he gave us an impossible choice: we would be given uninterrupted quite study time on the condition that all 54 soldiers in Wolfpack remained silent, stayed awake, and kept on task. Robertson would patrol the barracks at random intervals. We might as well have all gone to sleep right then to take advantage of the few precious minutes before his first circuit. After all, it was a hopeless proposition to stay awake out of sheer will, what with only six and a half hours sleep, followed by strenuous physical training, a heavy and complete breakfast, and several taxing hours in the classroom. Besides, it was not unlikely that our fatherly drill sergeant was only looking for an excuse to work us over, whether someone was dozing or not. It could have been, as was usually the case, that even a minor infraction, or the perception of one, that earned us a call to the front-leaning rest.

Before long we were in our familiar position, face down to the tile floor, CLS handbook to our sides, unstudied and unlearned.

Week One was drawing to an end, and we ended most days in that familiar position.

Foxtrot Battery's lost their minds? Give me a few more weeks like this, and it was guaranteed.

WEEK 2

"Ate Up Like a Football Bat"

PRIVATES TRICKLED OUT from the stairwell and laundry room and found their spots in formation. Once assembled, we waited like statues for DS Jackson to march us off somewhere. But before long, we were in a full-blown family argument. It would start with one soldier making a comment, inducing someone else to tell that private to shut up. Of course the first man would have to defend or explain himself, at which point several others would jump in trying to quiet the first two or take sides. The reaction was thus unleashed, everyone trying to solve a problem that they didn't realize they were a part of. The noise would reach a crescendo just as the drill sergeant appeared.

"Open ranks, MARCH!"

The first rank took two steps forward, the second stood pat. The third and fourth ranks stepped backwards. We needed a bit of extra space for…you guessed it.

"Half-left, FACE!"

Each Soldier pivoted 45 degrees, and on command we punitively pushed.

We ought to have learned that our drills were very serious about standing at attention in formation. We didn't. Invariably, the platoon formation degenerated into a place to argue, mingle, joke, or scold someone for doing one of the former. So daily we were smoked for being idiots in formation.

"You are the worst bunch of privates I have ever had!"

We had presumably earned his respect for joining the Army during a time of war, but, as DS Jackson explained, we hadn't showed him much else that he could be proud of.

I guess he would have known, he spent enough time with us those first couple of weeks. One evening he entered the bay carrying a box and called us to a classroom formation. Like prepubescents on Christmas morning, we hustled into formation anxiously awaiting our first mail call.

"Stowell." He flung an envelope in my general direction.

"Stangler. Stowell. Stowell. Stowell."

I received four letters that night, all from my wife. They had finally broken through the bottlenecked Fort Sill mail system all at the same time. I was the envy of all, and it was elevating to have something to read from Esther—letters were the valuable oxygen as we suffocated for lack of communication. I sucked in everything she had written, and the pictures, too. I took comfort looking at the photos to match my thoughts about our first year of marriage while marching around, standing in line, and lying in my bunk for the brief moments of consciousness each night.

During Week Two we increasingly traveled separately from the other platoons. This gave us opportunities to move as a platoon team and get to know each other. More importantly, it was a chance for DS Robertson to smoke us on our own merits. Our smoke sessions were usually the consequences of one of two types of infractions: off-task behavior in the barracks, or improper decorum in a formation.

"Let's get in on like Donkey Kong," he said, indicating that it was a veritable game to him ordering us to do the most grueling of exercises with little rest and less sympathy. It didn't matter where we were; public or private, it served his point: to get us to do everything with lightning speed. Forming up was the most repetitive and elemental task we had.

Lining up in proper ranks and files is simple (although at least one soldier could always be counted on to mess it up). Once a soldier's position is established, though, things complicate a bit. He must stand still at attention until given a new command. DS Robertson was a Jedi Master of the position, and made it his mission to imbue his expertise to everyone in Wolfpack.

"Bring the heels together sharply on line, with the toes pointing out equally, forming a 45-degree angle. Rest the weight of the body evenly on the heels and balls of both feet. Keep the legs straight without locking the knees. Hold the body erect with the hips level, chest lifted and arched, and the shoulders square. Keep the head erect and face straight to the front with the chin drawn in so that alignment of the head and neck is vertical. Let the arms hang straight without stiffness. Curl the fingers so that the tips of the thumbs are alongside and touching the first joint of the forefingers. Keep the thumbs straight along the seams of the trouser leg with the first joint of the fingers touching the trousers.

Quoting entire portions verbatim from the manual, DS Robertson cemented in our feeble minds the magnitude of Army Field Manual 3-21.5. The command was unambiguous—stand at attention and don't frickin' move. In Robertson's words, there were three circumstances under which we were allowed to move while in the position of attention: in obedience to a command so indicating, to drink water, and if a meteor was approximately six inches from our face, no more. Violators of the provisions of FM 3-21.5 were usually not punished at the scene of the crime.

Rather, after dinner chow when we had some "soldier time" or "DS contact time" we could count on paying the piper for all the mistakes of the day. And they were legion.

We were, in the parlance of Basic Training, "ate up."

Ate up is a bad thing. To many observers, we were "ate the fuck up." Obviously, some privates were more ate up than others, but it was a general consensus among Foxtrot's drill sergeants that Fourth Platoon was the most ate up of all.

The formation was sacrosanct to a stable Army organization. It was how we traveled and how we waited. We even put our stuff in formation. Each soldier lined up to the man on his right; the right-most soldiers from those to their front. This places a god-like power in the one private at the front-right position.

He is the First Squad Leader—the soldier at the far right of the first rank. But long before our platoon was assigned squad leaders *per se*, the soldier in this position was responsible for ensuring a formation's healthy development. On the command, "dress-right, DRESS!" he would stand pat. In time, all others lifted their right arms in kung-fu fashion, "fingers extended and adjoined," level with the ground, pointing directly to their right, simultaneously snapping their heads to the left. Thus, proper lateral spacing was achieved, as each soldier shuffled his feet around until he was exactly an arm's, a hand's, and a middle finger's length away from his comrade. "Ready, FRONT!" was the cue to lower arms and look forward.

Often, we had to set things down and leave them behind, such as our rifles at meal time, or combat gear on the range. In such instances, we would place our belongings "dress-right dress," meaning that our items would be arranged in the same military order that our persons were. Dress-right dress is a command and an adjective.

Take for instance our quarters. The bunks and lockers were, of course, dress-right dress. From bedding to pillows to the ways our towels and washcloths hung from their racks. Our rifles and shoes were dress-right dress on the tops of our lockers. Our combat gear was supposed to be stowed under our bunks dress-right dress. Presumably, this was so that each soldier could grab his or a battle buddy's gear on a moment's notice. In reality, it was a metaphor for how we were expected to mold into one unit. One vest turned around? One helmet's chinstrap undone? Not dress-right dress; ergo, ate up.

"Front-leaning rest position, MOVE!"

Week One was for learning the basics, Week Two was for refining. Our drill sergeants had a unique refining process that made us stronger. As we struggled to find a place in their estimation, we also had to begin thinking about combat training. It might have been an opportunity for us to excel, but more likely just another factor in our leaders' low assessment of us.

Within a few days of having been issued our rifles, we needed still more essential equipment: the armor and gear that would allow us to march long distances and encamp away from garrison. Our destination for these items was CIF: Central Issue Facility.

The entire battery was herded—not figuratively—onto buses and Cadillacs, for a quick ride, though every second off our feet was a respite we relished. Nevertheless, after fewer than ten minutes en route, the caravan halted in front of a nineteenth-century railroad loading dock attached to a warehouse.

The ex-Marine in charge conducted his symphony of soldiers gearing up with bags full of Army equipment. His pit was a large steel awning protecting 200 trainees from the sizzling sun.

Having learned that we were little more than sheep, we did our best to find a spot in the shade, knowing that we couldn't go anywhere without express orders. It seemed simple to me, but simplicity was too complicated for our shepherds, to my dismay. More than four ranks was too many, according to formation protocol, so all the soldiers at the end of the alphabet, including yours truly, got stuck outside the canopy. Drills bellowed for us to extend the line—we all absorbed the pounding of NCOs screaming at us for being stupid enough to think we could fit under the canopy, then a select few of us absorbed the pounding of hot sunrays for several hours.

My biggest frustration was that nobody seemed genuinely interested in solving the problem, i.e. getting Foxtrot organized for the equipment issue. The main goal, it appeared, was yelling at us. I really didn't understand why, because they all seemed so angry and unhappy when they did it. Why not eliminate the stress, accomplish the task more quickly, and teach privates more effectively all at the same time? I had to consider tentatively that they were either stupid, or they enjoyed the more stressful option.

In retrospect, the likely explanation is that, in the Army, NCOs get approval, whether overt or tacit, from looking like they are leading. True leadership is sometimes hard to detect, but ordering people around is easily observed. Our NCOs were men of action! They ordered about loudly, in hopes that their first sergeant or colleagues would say to themselves, "gee, that fellow sure is a doer. Look at him getting it done."

As it turned out, we ended up in three long ranks, half of the platoon under the hot sun instead of the awning, and doomed to spend hours there. Once so "organized," we filed through two buildings, in assembly-line fashion, to load up on the goods. We emerged from the building with body armor, digital camo vest, helmet, and TA-50[1], so named for the individual equipment listed in the Common Table of Allowance 50. Of course we had no idea what it was called...to us it was a belt, some suspenders, poncho, mud boots, wet weather suit, sleeping pad, knee pads, etc.

---

[1] The Common Table of Allowances is an authorization of clothing and equipment for soldiers. Our allowance consisted exactly of: a rucksack, a dual layer sleeping bag with wet weather cover, a sleeping mat, a load-bearing vest, two one-quart canteens, with pouches and cups, a first aid kit, two ammunition pouches, rain slicker, rain trousers, a poncho, and mud boots.

As a battle-hardened young infantryman, DS Robertson took it upon himself to see that we looked like hot shit when we geared up. He was quite particular in his style of going "full battle rattle." We fitted our vests with the Kevlar plates and customized our LBEs, or "load-bearing equipment," vests to attach canteens, ammunition pouches, and a first aid kit. We organized our rucksacks and made sure they could be properly and quickly donned without straps dangling about. And we fitted our Advanced Combat Helmets with padding, camo cover, and chinstrap. It was exhilarating to wear, I must admit. Like six-year old girls playing dress-up, we paraded about, puffing our chests, and posing in front of battle buddies and mirrors.

The price we paid for the privilege to wear the uniform of a United States Soldier was steep.

"Privates," Robertson began. "You will have exactly 75 seconds to remove all your battle gear and place it dress-right-dress under your bunks. Go."

We rarely met such strict expectations; so naturally, drill sergeant would decrease our time standard! The result of our failure, again: "correction through physical exercise."

"I've never had a bunch of privates as fucked up as y'all."

The refrain was constant. At first jarring, its persistence rendered it fairly hollow. We became, reasonably quickly, anesthetized to the comments that would downright hurt anybody not in Basic Training.

"You ain't worth a goddammed thing!"
"Your daddy should have squirted you on the shower wall!"
"Fuck you!"

And they convinced us that they meant every word of it.

Sometime during my third week at Fort Sill, our drill sergeants had had it. Both Robertson and Jackson retired to their office, effectively sending us the message that not even they, with their

"Ate Up Like a Football Bat"

mighty drill sergeant power, divine patience, and never-ending desire to see us succeed, could mold us into Soldiers.

While we continued with our evening routine, DS Lanka from Third Platoon came over to try his magic.

DS Lanka couldn't have been born under a better surname. He was tall and, for lack of a better, less-obvious word, lanky. He walked like the Big Friendly Giant, each step a long, deliberate lunge, in concert with his arms dangling like ropes in the wind. He had beady eyes and a permanent grimace. He spoke with a deep voice that sounded like he was trying to speak in an even deeper voice; the baritone syllables rolled out methodically, commanding attention at all times.

Lanka's appearance in our bay signaled our own drill sergeants' surrender. He called us forward as a platoon as he sat down in the rolling office chair. He began to explain to us, in a paternal way, how it was time that we get it together. "We don't expect you to be perfect," he said reasonably. "But we don't expect you to be complete fuck-ups, either."

He led us in a sort of Socratic seminar about what the Army demanded, and the importance of teamwork. As the words poured out of his mouth, a private farted. Without missing a beat, Lanka matter-of-factly said, "Whoever did that better give me 20 four-count pushups."

In equal rhythm, the offender flipped to his chest and counted them off.

The sergeant's sermon attempted to teach us why we were so ate up. We all knew what "ate up" meant, but Lanka elaborated anyway. We then got a lesson on Army metaphors. "Ate up like a football bat" were we. A football bat, you see, is useless. Get it? We were good-for nothing. Sort of like a "soup sandwich"—another metaphor that Lanka taught us that night.

These terms, "football bat," and "soup sandwich" were obviously the only way to describe how hopeless we were. Fourth

Platoon was quickly earning, deservedly or not, a reputation of being a bunch of losers. Admittedly, we had our share of weaklings: one private couldn't march; another was a thief and a smuggler; we had a fourth-try recycle whose chronic injuries actually outpaced the drill sergeants' ability to mock them.

For a time we held out the hope that our diminutive status was part of the propaganda campaign waged by our drill sergeants. It wasn't, we were truly the worst. To match, Fourth Platoon had the baddest NCOs. They were proud of it and sought every opportunity, at least with us, to emphasize the fact.

"The other drill sergeants hug their privates," Robertson would complain. Meanwhile, we were doing daily, on average, 45 – 60 minutes of "correction." Privates from Second Platoon, right below us, would remark how they could hear the thuds of our bodies hitting the floor during our evening smoke sessions. One private in our platoon kept count of the push-ups we did and arrived at a figure of 2,200 for the first three days alone.

There were several sources of our drill sergeants' disappointment, some of which were more or less correctable, but others of which were completely out of our control. Of the former, our bunks were rarely dress-right dress, which is to say that one or two of the bunks were off line up to a complete inch. No exaggeration was beneath DS Robertson. "Why are these bunks so fucked up? They're like a mile off, completely crooked!"

Drill sergeants wanted—nay, expected—to see perfectly straight lines of bunks up and down the bay. The rails on the head boards and footboards (which were reversibly identical) ought to have created long dashed lines twenty bunks long, parallel to one another. It was never pointed out in perfection, only detected in deficiency.

We also had a less-than-stellar track record on fireguard. One night, I was enjoying a comfortable dream, when the lights blazed suddenly.

"Ate Up Like a Football Bat"

"Toes on line!"

Reflexively I hopped out of my bunk and stood, half awake, as if a drill sergeant was about to inspect me. Privates were still fast asleep, and the order was repeated. Drill Sergeant Orozco from First Platoon was on the floor, and he was mad. He circulated through our bay explaining that nobody had been posted at the guard desk, which was no small problem. He left us with a warning that night, but it was not the last time our guards would fall asleep on their shift.

Our sins were apparent, but there were many things for which we were punished that were beyond our power, supreme among them: our floors. Not that it mattered to us, we could keep the floors clean enough. What bothered us to the extreme was that we were constantly punished for the imperfections inherent to our bay. Nothing mattered more to inspecting NCOs than the glimmer of the floor, and ours attracted the disdain of all who saw it.

We were taught how to wax the floors, which we did consistently, though it required a monumental effort. Each waxing needed three coats, and in order to apply it smoothly, we needed to remove all the furniture from huge sections of our barracks. Such a task necessitated the cooperation of nearly everyone. Buffing followed waxing, and our floors always looked better after the endeavor, but never sparkled to the drill sergeants' satisfaction. So, we were ate up because of our floors.

Our restroom was another problem. Members of Wolfpack collectively spent an inordinate amount of time in the latrine. We had six stalls, and they seldom seemed to be enough. Aside from the smell that logically emanated from an overused head, the absence of privates on the barracks floor was conspicuous. We were often punished more because someone was not available for a face to face rebuke.

Perhaps there was a correlation between latrine usage and actual illness. If there wasn't, then we suffered from a huge coincidence of having either the sickest or the weakest privates in the battery. Weekly, our platoon sent more soldiers to sick call than any other, sometimes by ratios of four to one.

"Sick call" was the soldier clinic. As the sick call roster manager for Wolfpack, I did my absolute best to talk the privates out of going. Often it was unavoidable: pink eye, fevers, or obvious bodily injury required a trip to the medic.

On my second Sunday in Basic, a private mentioned to me that my eyes looked infected, offering his diagnosis that it was pinkeye. Fantastic, now I was going to have to miss training. I checked in with DS Jackson mostly so that he would know it was inescapable.

"You got the crusties?"

Yes, I had the crusty eye boogers that were a symptom of the highly-contagious infection.

"Yeah, you gotta go to sick call."

Our *Smartbooks* warned that 90 percent of trainees succumb to some type of respiratory illness during BCT. I had been suffering from such an illness since before I was a resident of Fort Sill, with a brief period of improvement during Reception. Since my first week, however, I endured a chronic sore throat, coughing, and runny nose. Along with over half of my platoon. Nevertheless, I avoided sick call until the pinkeye appearance. Early that Monday morning I filled out the appropriate form and headed down to the drill pad, where soldiers from the other three platoons would report by 0445 hours.

We signed in and were marched to another building where a medic evaluated and sorted us. Having determined that I may indeed had pinkeye, he sent me to the Troop Medical Clinic (TMC). A drill sergeant marched us over, stopping by a dining facility on the way. This particular dining facility was a real treat. We didn't have to wait in the long lines and we could watch TV; the simple pleasures of life.

"Ate Up Like a Football Bat"

Hundreds of soldiers passed through the TMC each day, following the same protocol and decorum as with their units—standing at parade rest, sitting silently, and responding with sycophantic courtesy to any personnel in the clinic.

For many soldiers, sick call was preferable to training with the battery because of the slight perks, the greatest of which was some time and distance away from the drill sergeants. It must have seemed to our drill sergeants that Fourth Platoon was engaged in full-blown abuse of the system—a malingering epidemic. Each morning at "first call," when one of our leaders gave a formal account to the first sergeant, it was no minor embarrassment to have to report that seven or eight or nine soldiers a day were at sick call.

As it turned out, I didn't have pinkeye, but the doctor prescribed me some eye drops to get rid of the irritation, and loads of medication to deal with the respiratory infection once and for all. Doctors at Basic gave out medication more liberally than candy—it was nearly impossible to get the latter. With my bag full of treats, I caught a van back to my battery area where a drill sergeant picked me up on his way out to where everyone else was training. A lesson learned was cleanliness. Though the connection between cleanliness and health was apparent, seeing all our sick soldiers helped engrain the lesson into my mind.

There was also a connection between cleanliness and safety when it came to our weapons, as DS Jones' earlier demonstration was meant to imply. All the time spent getting to know our rifles was well worth it. Before we would ever fire a shot we would clean those rifles inside and out a dozen times. The rifle first had to be taken apart, which was a fairly simple process. *Forrest Gump's* impressive performance against the clock notwithstanding, we were never timed.

In fact, speed was a vice, as illustrated by an experience with SGT Stevenson. Cleaning was an activity that was assigned when there was nothing else planned. The less prepared our cadre was, the cleaner our weapons got. Banished to the drill pad one afternoon, we were tasked with cleaning our weapons. In the buttstock of every training M16 A2 is a compartment for a cleaning kit, which included small brushes, wired bristles, and a tiny bottle of CLP (Cleaner, Lubrication, Preservative) oil. Judging by my empty bottle, the kits were rarely inventoried, so we were just left alone to do pretty much whatever we could figure out with the equipment.

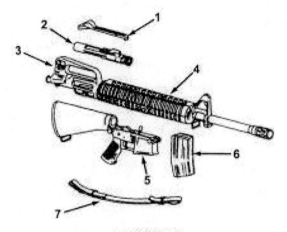

M16A2/A3

1-Charging Handle Assembly
2-Bolt and Bolt Carrier Assembly
3-Detachable Carrying Handle
4- Upper Receiver and Barrel Assembly
5- Lower Receiver and Buttstock Assembly
6- Cartridge Magazine
7- Small Arms Sling

So on this fine day I, along with each of my platoon mates, had set up a nice little cleaning area in front of me as I sat in formation on the drill pad. I had done what I thought was a

"Ate Up Like a Football Bat"

fairly thorough job cleaning my rifle, and in good time. As I was contemplating reassembling it, I noticed SGT Stevenson out of the corner of my eye. He held his sinister gaze. Knowing that he had me targeted for something, I moved ever more slowly, hoping that he would give up or become distracted before I got my rifle put back together. Sensing what I was up to, he called me by name, "Stowell, what are you doing?"

"I guarantee that rifle ain't clean," he cut into my feeble attempt at a reply. Like the famous Supreme Court definition of pornography, he would know clean when he saw it, but would refuse to give us a clear standard of when to stop. The lesson was not lost on me, though, so for the next hour I sat rubbing parts of my dissembled rifle stupidly to appear as if I was hard at work. In BCT, the bottom line was never productivity, but merely activity.

"I hate privates. When you are done with Basic, you will feel the same way. – DS Jefferson."

Surely, all 54 privates in Wolfpack read the inscription etched on the wall of stall #3 in our barracks latrine many times over. The message, whether written by the man himself or ascribed to him by some anonymous vandal, only amplified his reputation as a mean son-of-a-bitch.

The rumors about DS Jefferson started to spread almost upon our arrival. The fact that Fourth Platoon was short one drill sergeant compared to the other platoons, all with three, was apparent. Jackson and Robertson certainly took liberties portraying Jefferson, our platoon drill sergeant, as cruel. One of their favorite motivators was to remind us of DS Jefferson's imminent return.

"Privates, you think we've been tough on you, you don't even know. Drill Sergeant Jefferson doesn't fuck around. I'm telling you privates, he's not the one you want."

My first encounter with Jefferson was the morning of his

long-anticipated return date. Usually I was safe from visitors to our bay, since my bunk was next to the rear (read, "privates'") entrance. Jefferson was an unconventional NCO in a lot of ways, and on this morning he didn't disappoint, arriving at 0430 through the rear entrance. I don't know if I was dumbstruck simply by the fact that he came in this way (it was highly unusual) or by his dominating stature and countenance. He should have been a football player (Lawrence Taylor comes to mind).

While making my bunk I caught his eye, and instinctively did the safest thing I knew at the time—I went to parade rest, and stood there silently. Likewise, he must have been caught off guard by my reaction. No doubt he was thinking, "who is this idiot and why is he standing at parade rest staring at me?" The moment, though only a few seconds, was uncomfortably long; then, he simply moved to the front leaving me unharmed.

He went into the office and we continued our morning routine, apprehensive. A few minutes later he called us into classroom formation; I'm sure we had never moved faster.

"Without hesitation, state your name, where you're from, and why you joined the Army."

The private closest to him followed his instructions. Then a confused silence descended over the platoon. Who was next? The Army taught us to count off smartly in neat rows. We didn't understand how to operate in this crazy, haphazard classroom formation. The quiet was broken by Jefferson:

"Front-leaning rest position, MOVE!" We scrambled and followed the cadence.

"I said without hesitation!" We all realized our collective mistake, yet our fear of the new drill sergeant kept us frozen and unable to speak. Nevertheless, a few privates continued on with the order.

"Private Troth. Mississippi. I joined the Army for my dad."

"Private Walker. Missouri. I joined the Army to make my

73 | "Ate Up Like a Football Bat"

Father proud."

"Private…

"Stop! You're all going to say the same thing anyway," interrupted the drill sergeant.

I wasn't going to say the same thing; I joined for entirely different reasons, but Jefferson didn't care. He obviously never intended for the entire platoon to share information that would make us seem anything more than raw material in his soldier factory. That was never the point. What all the drill sergeants regularly tried to do, was to give us instructions to see how quickly and precisely we would respond. Jefferson just upped the ante by increasing the pressure. Nobody could apply pressure better than he.

His arrival came mere days before we completed our CLS training. On our second Saturday on this side of the tracks, we took our final examination, which came in two parts. The first segment assessed our understanding of the functions of the Combat Life Saver, including the steps for the nine-line medevac request. The second component was a performance assessment on initiating a saline lock for an intravenous drip. Testing was an all-day affair, mostly spent waiting in lines. Somehow I got stuck in a group that had to wait the longest. It's natural to want to find the most efficient route through any circuit, but futile in any Army one. Whatever time is saved finding paths of less resistance is lost waiting for the rest of the group to catch up. Moreover, our NCOs displayed a compulsive desire to try to manage any movement of troops, when usually the randomness of the crowd would otherwise find the smoothest configuration. The free market versus a command economy was Basic Training. Everything was centrally-planned, and all power was held by those managers that allocated resources. No trust whatever was afforded to the individual to make a wise decision, and something as important as getting people in the right lines was too risky to leave to the collective judgment.

At any rate, I was orphaned by our platoon, so while I waited for my test, most of the other soldiers in Wolfpack were getting better acquainted with our new bully-in-chief. Jefferson decided to assert himself early by declaring that our heads had entirely too much hair on them. He had marched the rest of our platoon to the barbershop. The last thing I wanted in the entire world was to piss this guy off by showing up conspicuously as the only one without a cleanly-shaven head, so I scrambled around trying to figure out if I should go alone to get my haircut.

I resolved to take the risk, so I set off toward the barber. I spotted DS Jefferson standing with our platoon which was poised silently in formation (it was easy to be silent with big, bad, Jefferson glaring at you). I approached him hesitantly.

"I came to get a haircut," I announced.

He glowered at me. Jefferson was like a crooked insurance company, who turned away every applicant the first time around. His response algorithm had him ignore or belittle whoever was asking a question on the first attempt. I was summarily rejected, but pressed the issue.

"Should I get in line?"

"That's a stupid question."

Twice foiled, I didn't know what my next step was. This man was going to scrutinize my every word.

"Did they get haircuts?" I nodded to the platoon formation.

"Why are you asking me stupid questions?" He motioned toward someone standing at parade rest, "Take off your cover." The soldier revealed a white, freshly-shaved scalp. "How did you get that rank, asking all those dumb-ass questions?" he spat at me.

Whether my questions were dumb or not, I learned quickly. No more questions. I went to get my haircut without another word.

Because of my detour to the barber, I was one of the last

soldiers called in to demonstrate my ability to prepare the casualty for the lock, and "stick" him. Drill sergeants thought they were finished, and when I was presented to DS Lanka, he was annoyed that he would have to supervise one more trainee. He had been sitting all day long watching others go through needle after needle to successfully introduce intravenous solution via the arms of nervous privates. At any rate, he didn't want to be with me, and he didn't attempt to hide his displeasure at my appearance. I didn't help my case when I slid my chair back and knocked over his Diet Pepsi; he admitted as much.

"That's one way to piss off the drill sergeant."

This wasn't going to be my best test. My battle-buddy and I, PFC Yeidder, sat down, removed our ACU tops and got ready to do the very serious work of a Combat Life Saver. I was Yiedder's guinea pig as he proceeded with near perfection to sterilize the site on my arm, apply the small tourniquet, find a good vein, and puncture it with an 18-guage needle.

The needles had an indicator to verify that a vein had been struck. A small chamber would "flash" with blood when the pressure of the vessel forced blood through the needle. No flash, no vein, and the needle couldn't be reused. Thus, finding and prepping the right vein was an imperative both in terms of time and patient cooperation.

The steps were fairly simple—they were in our yellow book, which I had studied more than anyone in the platoon. But Lanka hovered over me, spitefully examining my every move. If I put my glove on before I wiped the skin with alcohol, I had done it wrong. After I had tied the tourniquet to enlarge the vein, he commenced nagging me to take it off before my patient lost his fingers due to lack of blood. My task became to please the drill instead of to initiate the saline lock.

My anxiety heightened as I tried to remember the steps and correct myself against his edgy remarks. Every time he made a critical comment, like about how the angle of the needle was incorrect, I had to rethink it, which did no good because the way I had done it was the way I studied it. I knew of no alternative.

By the time I placed the needle between my fingers, my hand was shaking. My battle-buddy couldn't have felt too confident, but he encouraged me respectfully. He knew Lanka was a dick, but Yiedder was also surprised and probably somewhat disappointed that I didn't rise above the level of his insanity. Nevertheless, I stuck him perfectly in a big bulbous vein. But when I tried to insert the catheter, I pulled the needle out too quickly and it bent. It must not have felt too soothing in my buddy's arm, but he was stoic and patient, more than I can say for Lanka, who was fuming. I went to his other arm to start over, but by now I was so uneasy that I missed the vein completely. Blood entered the flash chamber, though, and Lanka passed me grudgingly.

It wasn't my greatest day. Earlier, DS Robertson had called me over and stood on a chair so he could bitch me out from on high.

"Why on earth did you keep my platoon up all night moving furniture around? Who told you to wax the floor?"

There were no good answers to these questions. A few days before DS Jackson had given us the unambiguous order to clean and wax our disgusting floors by this very day. The previous evening he had given me the equipment and supplies necessary to get the job done and watched as we began moving the wall lockers toward one side of the barracks to make way for the broom and wax mops before he left for the night. The plan was to move the furniture before lights out and have the fireguards do the floors in shifts. In the middle of the night we could move the furniture to the waxed side and complete the job.

Robertson was livid because several privates were falling asleep during the testing. Now, given the verbal reprimand I was receiving, there were several things that I desperately wanted to point out to DS Robertson. First, Jackson had unmistakably sanctioned the floor waxing, having aided and abetted our effort, after lights out, to begin the task. If he didn't want us to wax, then it was nothing short of entrapment. Second, we had moved all the furniture we were going to move by the time DS Jackson left, not in the middle of the night, as charged. Yes, the furniture was heavy, but with 54 privates it took about 20 minutes. Third, Robertson himself ordered that six of us at a time stay on fireguard for some trivial embarrassment our platoon had caused him. Whether we waxed or not, nearly the entire platoon was up, following his orders, not mine. Fourth, sleeping in a classroom was nothing new. Members of our platoon and the battery regularly fell asleep during classes. Fifth, DS Jones from Second Platoon, who was on CQ that night, interrupted our effort just after 2300 and issued a cease and desist order. He told our soldiers that it was forbidden to work after lights out. The ironic thing was then, that I got chastised and we hadn't even accomplished what I was accused of orchestrating!

These were the bizarre rules of Basic Training.

After the two embarrassing episodes during CLS testing, my confidence was at a new low. It seemed I was as ate up as anyone. I had been placed in a position of some responsibility in the platoon, but was earning only contempt for my efforts to get things done. DS Jackson never once stood up to defend my floor waxing initiative. I was also deeply humiliated by the Lanka affair. Thirty one years old, smarter and more accomplished than any of these haughty drill sergeants, and I was acting like a scared little kid when confronted by them. The Army was supposed to make me more manly. Something was going wrong.

The next day we marched—loaded up with heavy rucksacks and our new battle rattle—to the CLS range ten minutes from the Starship. We formed up as platoons in a swampy mess just behind the bleachers that we sat on a week and a half before for our initiation festivities. The smell of fetid water and sweat saturated the air.

Helmets and eye protection were the two rules inviolable at the range. "Wearing" the helmet meant keeping the chin strap fastened tightly. There would be no John Waynes here, as the saying went. But after one road march, the fabric chin strap, marinated in perspiration, stank and rubbed and chafed—acne and rash were soon to follow. The helmet pads took on the characteristics of a football jockstrap that had seen more than its share of action and less than its share of washing. Any opportunity to remove it from one's head was a welcomed one. Not surprisingly, the NCOs saw fit that we wore the helmets nearly at all times.

We split into several groups at the CLS range, one group for a block of instruction on nutrition (Those of us who were able to fight off the sleep learned that the others' inability to stay awake was due to the heavy foods we were all consuming each morning). At other stations we practiced responding to casualties and transporting them in a variety of improvised carriers. One involved using two sticks and a general issue blanket to make a nifty little stretcher able to hold the heaviest of privates relying only on the friction of the wool fibers. DS Rodriguez led that particular drill, and assigned me to be the casualty.

"Stowell, show off your acting skills and fall over dead when I say 'bang' you fall over like dead."

As much a thespian as Rodriguez was a wordsmith, I decided to show them what a specialist was made of and infuse our range activities with a jolt of enthusiasm. On cue, I ran across the grassy area and at vocal indication of enemy fire I flipped as if hit by several rounds. The world spun around me and I hit the ground hard, totally disoriented. My comrades placed me safely in the gurney, and I was taken back to our mock base camp 15 meters away with only a splitting headache from my fall.

For those times when you had to evacuate a wounded soldier

"Ate Up Like a Football Bat"

and you didn't have sticks or blankets lying around, there was the fireman carry and the shoulder drag, which we practiced in the dirty ditches. We also evaluated make-believe casualties using the assessment procedures we learned from the slideshows, first checking for responsiveness, then for respiration. If the casualty was breathing, then we could continue to assess for bleeding, broken bones, shock, burns, and head and neck injuries; if not, he was a goner.

The idea was that the range would add a dose of realism to the drills we saw and read about in the classroom. We worked under the heat of the sun and the pressure of a highly-scripted scenario, all under the watchful eye of a mentoring drill sergeant. Well, watchful, at least.

Jefferson had arrived from his medical leave amid many reports that Fourth Platoon was all jacked up. His remedy was straight forward, and followed a bit of logic: "we fucked up when we were in the bay," so he wasn't going to allow us in the bay. Beginning his first day with us, DS Jefferson found ways to keep us outside. Sometimes he just locked us out, forcing us to sit for hours on end on the bleachers. What was painfully dampening to my battle buddies' spirits, was refreshingly uplifting to mine. I loved our alone time on the bleachers. Other times he took even that away, leading us in "training" like the time we practiced shooting stances on the lawn. After an hour or so, he ordered his two House Mice up to our dayroom to sort through some old uniforms. We dismissed ourselves about an hour before the platoon finished; those poor souls arrived late that night, exhausted and chastened, and we passed out the ragged ACUs for use in "combatives."

A couple of days later the entire battery was bused to a gymnasium to learn Army-style hand-to-hand fighting techniques based on Brazilian Jujitsu. I wasn't much interested, but feigned concentration on the instruction. During the lecture all 200 of us were gathered around the lone speaker, facing center and barely able to hear. DS Robertson called me over to talk with him and Jefferson.

Jefferson interrogated me about everything from training to my marriage, and seemed interested in why a 30-year old would sign up for something as dreadful as Army BCT. From a series of quick-fire questions, he learned of my wife, my MOS, my unit, my hobbies, and my civilian profession. Robertson interrupted with a question of his own, which I answered. Jefferson cut back in, "So are you going to answer my question?"

"What was the question?" I politely asked.

"Don't make me repeat it. I hate repeating myself."

In those few moments, I thought harder than I've ever thought before, not wanting to disappoint this man. My mind's gears cranked away as I coaxed the hamster to run the wheel faster.

He turned to his colleague: "I asked a question, didn't I Rob?" Robertson seemed a little caught off guard, but blurted out a "yes," with the sound and look of a soldier who understood his own place in the pecking order. To this day I remain convinced that Drill Sergeant Jefferson did not ask a question. Nevertheless, I humbly submitted that he had taught me to pay "attention to detail."

The combatives training was soon forgotten, but I always did pay that attention to every word the drill sergeants spoke to me. "Attention to Detail" is an article of faith in the Army. In week one, it is illustrated colorfully by drill sergeants greeting soldiers with, "Hello Private US Army!" to those who inverted their nametapes and the US Army tapes. Once soldiers mastered the art of getting dressed properly, attention to detail must be applied to such things as having rucksack straps rolled up tight, tucking in laces on all shoes displayed on wall lockers, and making sure both buttons are snapped on one's canteen pouch, even if one button is broken.

"Ate Up Like a Football Bat"

Of course, it is blasphemous to say that anything is trivial. Just as a teacher can use looming report cards, college admission, or job market cruelties as a stick to get his students on the move, so can drill sergeants use the certainty of a combat tour to force trainees to think twice about letting small stuff slide.

What was more important—the big picture, or the individual strokes? I had struggled with the question in my classroom, trying to figure out if students needed a broad exposure to unifying concepts, or the practical experience of dealing with the details of individual problems, recognizing patterns and anomalies in information. While the modern U.S. military seems to want soldiers who understand the big picture and can make critical decisions accordingly, the Attention to Detail model still rules at BCT. Soldiers familiar with little more than their immediate realm of action are more easily controlled, and control was the name of the game here at Sill.

One of DS Jefferson's good friends was DS Jones, of Second Platoon, with whom he had much in common. For one, they both hated Fourth Platoon. Jones' reason for despising us was that we weren't his; from our perspective he molly-coddled his own soldiers in direct proportion to doing everything he could to make our lives more difficult.

A case in point was the laundry room, which we shared with Second Platoon. There was some elaborate schedule set up in an attempt to maximize fairness that was much too complicated to ever work at a place like Basic Training. The main problem was that neither privates nor their drill sergeants could remember the schedule, so that every day became a dispute. More than once we would appear, arms very much full of soiled clothing, only to discover that the other platoon was merrily washing theirs.

In fact, it probably was our turn. Second Platoon had a reputation of having lots of time on their hands, while the opposite was true of us. As part of the Army program of turning us into fearsome fighters, we were not afforded the opportunity of washing our clothes.

It was the height of irony: 50 plus young men, many of whom had left the nest for the first time, were in a forced-grow-up camp, and were prevented by their adult supervisors from cleaning their clothes! We were systematically denied the god-given right to wear laundered garments.

Some privates were reusing their underwear at alarming rates, and there were a few of us who donned ACUs five or six times before finally judging them unwearable, a pretty loose standard at BCT. The situation got so bad that I began washing clothes in the shower. My platoon-mates watched me quizzically as I scrubbed through several pairs of undergarments and socks in the warm water while I rinsed the Cheer suds off my clothing and body.

Our drills dismissed our pleas for leniency, explaining that we hadn't earned the privilege. To be sure, there were occasions that we would just go to the laundry room without asking for consent. That was risky business, though, as a cycle of laundry would take over an hour and a half. We were likely to be called up for some punitive exercises while our wet clothes sat in the washer, begging to be dried mechanically. Chances were that, while our clothes occupied valuable washers (there were usually only four functioning machines), Second Platoon would descend on the laundry room and, finding our clean wet clothes in the way, simply remove them. (There was a strange legal loophole that precluded us from seeking damages for laundry removed if it was there under illicit circumstances.)

DS Jones would facilitate their removal. On more than one occasion he came storming into our bay, scolding us violently about laundry room etiquette: "get your fucking clothes out of the laundry room or I'll have my privates throw them out!"

Reason dictated to us that common thievery would be the

result of unidentified clothes lying around in the vicinity of 100 young men required to wear the exact same outfits. When our clothes went missing under such a regime, we chalked it up to experience. I rarely left my clothes unattended, and if I did I asked a trusted mate to keep an eye on them. I never lost a single article of clothing. The same couldn't be said for everyone else in my platoon. Some privates had chronic clothing loss syndrome, and were desperately hanging on to a few coveted items. Nevertheless, everyone realized that lost or stolen clothing was at least bad luck, at most negligent. What it never was was Second Platoon's problem. Whatever our clothing troubles—and they were plenty— they were kept within the platoon.

Second Platoon had a different tactic. At least once a week we would get a lecture from Jones about theft and how we were in constant communal violation of the Army Values whenever one of his privates lost a piece of clothing. On one occasion, he was either so fed up with us or his own privates (we would pay, either way) that he told Jefferson we were thieves, knowing that Jefferson would come up with some elaborate method for setting us straight.

We were on the bleachers when our platoon drill sergeant popped the question. "Who has the private's clothes?"

Well, I didn't, I thought to myself. Looking around I discovered that everyone else in my platoon had similar thoughts. Perhaps someone knew who had PVT Green's clothes, but nobody said peep. Jefferson had a way—he told us that if PVT Green didn't have all his clothes back in 20 minutes, he would conduct a search of the entire bay and promised to send anyone who had clothes with that name on it to jail. PVT Green's clothes showed up.

While many in Wolfpack felt justified in blaming all of our misfortunes on the drill sergeants, we could have easily pinned them on a few select soldiers. One of the biggest thorns in our platoon's proverbial side was Hamblin, the most offending narcoleptic in our CLS classes. Aside from a tragically low level of common sense and ability, he fell asleep during nearly every class, meeting, or formation. Hamblin was able to sleep while standing at attention. Perhaps because he was always unconscious when we were given critical information and instructions, he always seemed to be a step behind. A step behind at Basic Training will get you run over or thrown from the path.

DS Robertson singled Hamblin out almost immediately, and loved to torment him for falling asleep. During classes, whether in an auditorium or in the barracks, Hamblin would get caught and ordered to the front-leaning rest. Remarkably, no matter how obviously he was sleeping, he would always vehemently defend his honor and wakefulness. Though he might literally snore, head hunched down, he insisted that he was just reading or thinking. He was certainly not the brightest bulb, but he wouldn't admit it readily.

Hamblin was a perpetual mess. His wall locker was a disaster area of the first magnitude. He was frequently unkempt, wearing mismatched uniforms and an unshaven face. He also insisted in starting quarrels within the platoon. It was generally agreed that he was the main reason our platoon appeared to be ate up. Lowest on the pecking order, he would absorb all the shock of our destitution.

Platoon life was full of ups and downs. By Week Three, Fourth Platoon had more of the latter, but we were very aware of our predicament. Knowing that the drill sergeants saw us as incorrigible, incompetent fools motivated us to square ourselves.

We would soon find out that there were more drastic remedies for our disorders.

"Shovel it Down, You Can Taste it Later"

WEEK 3

ARMY FOOD AT BCT was, surprisingly, fantastic. Those who are skeptical have never visited the dining facilities at Fort Sill. It was no coincidence that the Army didn't make it. In fact, commanders at Fort Sill seemed very proud of their realization that the Army made lousy food; When LTC Pastore briefed us in Week One, he boasted about the foodservice contract and how it had come a long way in terms of nutrition and appeal since he was in Basic.

Then and now, Army food is chow. Chow is much more than just Army food, though. Chow is a noun and a verb; it is a thing and a place. It would be perfectly grammatical at BCT to say, "let's go chow some chow at chow." It summarized the whole dining experience.

One theory as to why we all liked the food so much was that we had to wait so long for it. This meant, of course, lines.

The rituals of the chow line were some of the first that we learned. Back at 95th, for example, the fourth rank was invariably ushered into the chow hall first. Naturally, when formation was called, there was a mad scramble for the fourth rank. Those brave privates who got stuck in the first three would do their best to cut in the moving file later. It was never a matter of getting food first—there was always plenty of it. The carrot was getting out of line and maximizing the time away from the drills. Logic in a normal universe would dictate that the first in the chow hall would be the first out, and that everyone would get equal time. In the parallel Army world, however, it only mattered that we were all out by the same given time. A few extra minutes to sit at a table and enjoy food—the reward for getting into the hall first—were precious.

On this side of the tracks, the routine was roughly the same in principle. Drill sergeants would drive our column formation to one of two entrances and park us in front of the doors. The entrance to the dining facility—D-Fac, to us—was in the breezeway of the starship, with an inlet about 30 feet long and 15 feet wide. Two full platoons could easily fit inside the inlet, and often our entire battery would squeeze between its walls.

There we stood, often behind several other elements, for several minutes per meal, just waiting. We were in formation, so neither talking nor moving was tolerated. Two columns on either side of the inlet, pressed up tight against the wall, unnaturally close to one another, we left a center channel as a stage for our drill sergeants to pace back and forth, performing their feats of discipline, wisdom, and humor. Whether we were there as a battery or platoon, the drill sergeants would take the opportunity to train or belittle us; to them they were one and the same thing.

"Get smart!' drill sergeants would say, a cue for everyone to retrieve their *Smartbooks* and read something. They never told us what to read, and trainees would often sneak letters between their pages. Sometimes we were rewarded for studiousness, getting ushered to the front of the line for answering questions from our *Soldiers' Guide*.

Dozens of batteries ate from the same D-Fac. The breezeway full of traffic, congested with other columns, like semi trucks jockeying for position to make a turn into the fuel point or head out into the open air. Soldiers in twos, threes, and fours were the taxis and motocycles, scurrying about as quickly as they could. It was a NYC intersection, and our drill sergeant was the traffic cop.

"Permission to pass the formation, drill sergeant?" stray privates from other batteries would timidly ask before they continued on their merry way. Sometimes they got consent, other times drills would just ignore them. Usually, they were scolded.

"Give the greeting of the day and *move the fuck out*!"

Formations waiting for chow were unbearable. The breezeway is aptly named, but once inside the small inlet that led to the main doors of the D-Fac, there was no movement of air, and 200 bodies had the tendency to raise the temperature. We resolutely stood, sweating inside the cove, a virtual brick oven of privates. Facing us was a glass wall and double doors. Passing through the double doors we were officially indoors, and customarily removed our headgear. But the line-waiting continued. Like a blockbuster Disneyland ride, just when you thought you had arrived, there was another set of switchbacks mocking your disappointment.

Inside, we formed a regular, old-fashioned, civilian line that snaked toward the actual door to the D-Fac. The wall opposite the entrance was all glass with curtains spilling from ceiling to floor—mostly unnoteworthy, except for the occasional rat that scurried up the curtain, daring the hundreds of soldiers to continue their advance. The sight of vermin just yards away from where we were about to eat didn't seem to faze anybody, least of all the drill sergeants. Bad for morale to mention it, I suppose.

If one soldier from a platoon was admitted into the antechamber, then the entire platoon was crammed in; drill sergeants prided themselves in their ability to stuff unconscionable numbers of privates into small spaces. As we mastered the Army credo, "hurry up and wait" we did so "nuts to butts." The term was not hyperbole, either; we were expected to stand so that we made physical contact with the soldier ahead, and were monitored closely for compliance. To make it clear, Robertson instructed us to stand close enough "to taste the guy's neck in front of you."

Basic trainers are obsessed with making efficient use of space, as long as it was at the trainees expense. Back in Reception, we were taught to "snake," a complicated tactical procedure whereby a single file line "zig-zags." Back and forth the line of soldiers moved so that gobs of people could proceed in an orderly fashion.

The chow line implied its own set of customs and courtesies. For instance, if a drill sergeant entered the antechamber while we were in line, the first person to notice would sound off, "Make *way* for the drill ser-*geant*!" in an iambic beat. Immediately, the rest of the soldiers in line would likewise follow, smashing themselves up against the steel stanchions. Privates are the untouchables of the U.S. Army, and no self-respecting drill sergeant would dare graze one while winding his way through the line into the D-Fac, unless he was trying to knock one aside purposely. On cue, even the most undisciplined groups would part like the Red Sea for a drill sergeant.

Some platoons, who were more proud of their drill sergeants than we, got very creative with their signals to part the crowd. Second platoon was the best example; they had rehearsed and perfected an elaborate hip-hop-style incantation that almost always wrung a smile from their faces.

We tried our hand at such a sound off. Inspired by Robertson, who insisted on us shouting, "Infantry-*man* coming *through*," we decided on bellowing, "The King is in the house! Boom! Boom! The King is in the house!" every time DS Jackson needed way made. Jackson wasn't impressed.

Aside from the expectation to make a path one drill sergeant wide whenever one entered the antechamber, trainees were required to act like Buckingham Palace Guards. On the other hand, drill sergeants would regularly see what they could do to rattle us. During our first week, while we were still going to the D-Fac as a battery, I was confronted several times by DS Martinez, who knew that I had an M.A. and was a teacher. "What was your major again, Stowell?" he asked one afternoon as I prepared to enter for lunch.

"History, drill sergeant."

"History, huh? Let's see how good your history is. When was the Army born?"

My scholarly mind turned on in a fit of excitement. I had, indeed been a history major in college three years before, with an emphasis in early United States history. I had also taught World History for one year in East Oakland (before switching exclusively to math, my minor.) One strategy I learned from studying history was to infer historical facts from what I already knew. In all the books I read, several of them about the American Revolution, never had I come across the Army's birthday. But I was a smart guy, I had a master's degree for crying out loud, and I wasn't going to let this opportunity to impress an NCO pass. This was what I did best, and I was going to enjoy it.

Though I had no idea when the Army's birthday was, I knew it had to have been created in response to the British military buildup in the colonies during the 1770s. The Americans had declared their independence from Great Britain in the summer of 1776, but that was the culmination of several skirmishes that had devolved into an undeclared war against the crown starting with the Battle of Lexington-Concord the previous spring.

All this went through my mind in a matter of about two seconds before I triumphantly declared, "Drill Sergeant, the Army was born in 1775, drill sergeant."

"What day?"

How could anybody possibly know the exact day the United

"Shovel it Down, You Can Taste it Later"

States Army was created? Turns out that each soldier who goes through BCT is expected to memorize every obscure written fact that passed before his eyes.

"It's in your *Smartbook*, soldier," Martinez noted with a hint of annoyance.

I guessed May, incorrectly. Martinez guided me to the right answer—14 June. "Resolved, that a General be appointed to command all the continental forces, raised, or to be raised, for the defense of American liberty." The resolution, adopted by the Second Continental Congress, established the Army as we know it today. It was right there in my *Smartbook* all along.

"When is Flag Day?" was the next query. I surrendered without a fight. In an embarrassing episode I learned that Flag Day is the exact same day as the Army's Birthday, coincidenatlly. Martinez couldn't let that one go unpunished, so I had to stand at parade rest and take his criticisms about how poor my history knowledge was. Within earshot was DS Rodriguez, who loved to pick on trainees at high volume.

"Your history sucks!" he shouted about half a dozen times.

My only response was, "Yes, drill sergeant."

Emboldened to continue his harangue against me, he began talking about me to his colleagues. "He thinks his history is good, but it's only... *mediocre!*"

The absurdity of his insult was matched by the vigor with which he pronounced it. He seemed prouder of using the word "mediocre" than he was upset for me not measuring up. His zeal in slurring me continued for days that stretched into weeks; every time Rodriguez saw me he would remind me that my history sucked. One such time, DS Jones from Second Platoon overheard. Always a showboat, Jones wanted a piece of the action. "So you're a history major? Let's see what kind of history you know. Who invented the stoplight?"

"I'm gonna have to guess, but I'll say Garrett Morgan

(remembering the only 'famous black inventor' name that came to mind from many years past in school), drill sergeant."

"You might be right." He betrayed his own ignorance. "Who invented the refrigerator?"

"I don't know, drill sergeant."

"Who invented the hanger?"

I repeated my previous answer.

"Who invented the elevator? The door knob? The hinge?" Each of his inquiries was followed by an admission that my knowledge fell far short of Army standards. "Do you know why you don't know? Because that's *black* history, something they don't teach in this country."

I'm not sure who invented the suitcase, the electrical outlet, the plastic bottle cap, or the staple, either, because *A Survey of Ordinary Objects and Their Inventors* was not offered when I studied at Cal State Hayward, nor was such a survey in my *Smartbook*. My urge to give a smartass answer was easily kept in check by my fear of being singled-out and embarrassed. The *doorknob*? Seriously?

Jones must have read a list of black inventors who have been shortchanged by history's esteem, because as it turns out, a patent was filed for an improved door knob, as is cited by several articles on the topic, by one Osbourn Dorsey in 1878. He was an American of African descent. His legacy ran deep and proud in the chow lines at Fort Sill in the summer of 2007.

We had time to ponder such matters of great import as the line snaked through the antechamber back and forth, each soldier inching along heel to toe, breathing in the damp hot air from his battle-buddy's sweaty neck, eyes drilling a hole in the back of his head until he arrived face to face with the drill sergeant standing before the final doorway between him and food. Drill sergeants had to report the number of soldiers eating to the cashier, and then usher us in.

"Shovel it Down, You Can Taste it Later"

"Ten," he would announce, by way of invitation, upon which the first soldier in line would sound off with "one-zero, drill sergeant!" and step past the counter, apply a dollop of hand sanitizer, and took his hard-earned place in the cafeteria main line. Each proceeding soldier would count down in proper military fashion: "...zero three, drill sergeant; zero-two, drill sergeant; zero-one, drill sergeant;" until the drill sergeant saw fit to admit another group of five, ten or fifteen soldiers into the Army Buffet.

Often times the wait at that last checkpoint was excruciating, not because of wait time but because several drill sergeants might be gathered there to harass. It was at a moment like this that I had my quizzical encounters with Martinez and Jones.

Nevertheless, I looked forward to every meal, every day. They were the rest stops on a long, hot, uncomfortable drive on the bumpy Basic Training Highway. At 0400 each morning, the barracks light went on signaling the start of our day. It was excruciating to have to go from fast asleep to fully alert in a matter of seconds, but the thought of chow made it slightly less painful.

Breakfast in the chow hall was All-American. Nearly every morning one had a choice among eggs, sausage, bacon, waffles, pancakes, an entire array of fruits, yogurts, breakfast pastries, cereals, and a variety of milks and juices. It was a veritable smorgasbord of breakfast bounty, one for which I would cheerfully go out to PT each morning knowing that I was that much closer to a feast.

Though eating chow was enjoyable, and waiting for it was easy, it was also risky. During Week Two, we were standing in line waiting to be counted in to the D-Fac one evening, properly snaked and standing heel to toe, while DS Eppinghaus was near the counter laughing it up with Robertson. From the day I took my place among the class of beings to stand on two legs, I had taken my ability to rest for granted. The chow lines cured me of that. Concealed by rows of rigidly upright soldiers, it was tempting to sneak a lean on the brick wall, just enough to displace a few pounds from the painfully tired soles of one's feet. Such were the ways of our silent resistance.

On this particular afternoon, Zaccardi did what every other private has done in chow line. He leaned for a moment against the wall. Eppinghaus caught him out of the corner of his eye and did his sergeant's duty and chastised him:

"What the hell are you doing private? Do you think you're back on the block?"

Assuming the drill sergeant's inquiry was in the spirit of his joking with his colleague just moments before, Zaccardi, with a slight grin and the kind of chuckle one makes to acknowledge another's good faith attempt at humor, Zaccardi answered appropriately, "No, drill sergeant." Laughing, in any form, however, was a definite no-no, and Eppinghaus b-lined to him like a Tomahawk missile.

Eppinghaus had the hilarious habit of punctuating important points in a one-to-one conversation ("conversation" used very loosely, of course) with a private by making a karate chop motion with his hand. The chops came dangerously close to the recipient's face, testing his ability to stand still and look forward. Since every point Eppinghaus made to a private was, is his mind, of utter significance, the entire message was delivered with a series of elaborate blows. It looked like the drill sergeant was trying to stab him.

On this particular day, these particular karate chops were amusing to Zaccardi, who probably didn't exhibit enough sobriety to convince Eppinghaus that he took him seriously. Thus ensued a drama that would embroil us for weeks.

The drill sergeant notified the private of his intent to issue him an Article 15. If privates weren't paying attention before—a drill sergeant up in a private's face had become rather routine—the mention of an Article 15 piqued everyone's interest. Sure as eggs is eggs, Eppinghaus paid a visit to our platoon barracks, to formally present Zaccardi with the charges from the Uniform Code of Military Justice, Article 81 paragraph 3: disrespectful deportment toward non-commissioned officer. He was called out and forced to sign the accompanying paperwork. Stalin and his show trials had nothing on the leadership at Foxtrot 1/40.

At this point, the barracks lawyers began offering up their advice. For my part, I urged Zaccardi to fight the charges, on obvious grounds. He never stood a chance, though. Zaccardi was intimidated in front of the Battery Commander, the First Sergeant, and Eppinghaus himself into admitting guilt. He was given two weeks extra duty.

As delectable as the D-Fac food was to everyone, it wasn't always feasible to get there. Basic Combat Training often took place far from the battery area. Our first of such training opportunities came a week before. Orders to pack our rucksacks signaled a march to the range, this time to Treadwell Tower in the morning. After a hearty breakfast, we loaded up our equipment that had been placed in neat piles, dress-right dress on the lawn, with rifles leaning against our helmets, muzzles to the left, dust cover up.

Gathering it up and putting it on we marched in two long files straddling the roadway that led to the southeast. We were hundreds of extras in a stereotypical Vietnam War movie, straggling along as if we had been looking for Charlie for days, eager to pull the trigger on the slightest movement in the brush.

We had all anticipated the day trip anxiously. Executing the course at Treadwell hinted of a promise to be freed of the repetitive tedium that was beginning to plague us at the barracks. Endless cleaning, studying, interrupted by physical punishment for crimes undefined, and seemingly unending subjection to NCOs' best attempts at personally hurtful humor in an attempt to toughen us were wearing thin on us. Perhaps once we began engaging in truly arduous physical tasks, even the grumpiest of drill sergeants would slough off their crusty veneer under the eroding necessities of leadership.

While on a road march we were taught to carry our rifles at "the low ready," which meant muzzles pointing slightly downward to the outside of the formation, one hand on the grip and the other hand on the magazine weld. Each weapon came issued with a strap that we hung around the neck, yet it was useless since it was forbidden to lower the rifle enough to rest its weight on the strap. Very quickly one's arms wearied of carrying an M-16 at such a position. But the heat got to us quicker than the muscular demands of the march. Fortunately, Treadwell Tower was less than two miles from our barracks, so the trip ended up being more of a rehearsal for much longer marches to come.

There was a sizeable field in front of the tower complex where we grounded our gear. At length we were herded to the bleachers where we were subjected to that time-honored military tradition, from which not even a trip away from the classrooms, barracks, or drill pads could save us—the briefing. A qualified, highly-trained, expert NCO had to explain to us the rules of behavior, as read from a clipboard. This was the range: the place where combat skills were taught and learned. Sure, we had already been to the CLS range, but that was practically the backyard of the Starship, and it was really just a field used for all sorts of stuff. The Treadwell Tower range was different. It was farther away, for one. But it was dedicated, hallowed, consecrated to the training of soldiers and nothing else. This was the place where Army commercials were made.

Safety, of course, was paramount. Whenever so many young men find themselves in such settings, be it a shooting range or a ropes tower, the risks skyrocket higher than the tower we were about to ascend. Our leadership took every precaution to minimize them.

At this range, the task was to climb ropes, netting, and ladders to the top of the 40-foot tower, and then rappel down, so the risk of injury was significant, especially if measured by the length and depth of the briefing. The obligatory presentation also served as an overview of the ropes course. We moved as a semi-organized mass from one station to the next, as range cadre explained how we would perform each stage of the course. Stage one: climb a small tower to a platform to cross three different rope bridges that got progressively more difficult in sequence. Of course there were safety nets below, and part of our briefing was learning how to fall. There was even a correct way to fail.

Moving around the tower, we crowded in a holding pen to see a demonstration of what to do on the second platform. Then at the next briefing station we discovered that we would be tying our own harnesses before the climb to the top of the tower for the finale: rappelling down from its apex.

Latrines and water supplies were pointed out as part of our briefing. Adequate hydration was preached like salvation to a zealous congregation. On Treadwell Tower day, the temperature was rising to an uncomfortably dangerous degree, and the Oklahoma humidity—perhaps less than alarming to many from the southeast and central United States, but a new and utterly unpleasant phenomenon to me—was wringing the sweat right out of us. Hydration was of the utmost importance.

Fittingly educated on all aspects of the course, we split into teams to begin. I was in line to start at the very beginning, while the other half went to the Swiss seat station. In line, we were temporarily freed from drill sergeants' oppression. It is difficult to overstate the relief that just a few moments of their absence bestowed. Standing in line, we bragged and bantered, listening to the rock music blaring over the horns. It was fun and relaxing, and a much needed repose from the rigid routines of the previous days.

Lines were still lines, and we waited in them interminably, especially at the range. But it was much easier to do so while talking and laughing with the other soldiers. Many would shout encouragement to their platoon mates and friends as they struggled up the commando bridge. Oohs and aahs were heard as a soldier fell from the rope, landing with a thud on the air mat below.

The course itself was also enjoyable, yet tough. Every stage was a physical challenge, and many tried my courage. The course's moniker derived from then 1LT Jack Treadwell, who was awarded the Congressional Medal of Honor for heroism during the Second World War. On March 18, 1944, while in command of Company F, 180th Infantry Division, Treadwell singlehandedly captured four pillboxes during a seeming stalemate and led his company to break the previously-impenetrable Siegfried Line. The breach sped the retreat and eventual defeat of the German Army.

Treadwell grew up 20 miles outside of Lawton, Oklahoma, and has found his final earthly resting place at the Fort Sill Post Cemetery. On the range house at Treadwell is a mural dedicated to the man whose name it bore, and the Army Value, "Personal Courage." I read about him that day at the cadre's invitation, and was reminded of why I had enlisted. Building Personal Courage was the purpose of putting all trainees through the tower course as a requirement for graduation, and I reflected on its meaning.

It was one of the Army Values that we were supposed to study and live each day. Personal Courage meant "facing fear, danger, or adversity." If nothing else in my life had been adverse, this certainly was. I was miserable and lonely, but I knew it was where I needed to be. The courage that I needed just to be there was highlighted against the backdrop of a growing despondency the weeks before I shipped. The gloom remained, and I was compelled to muster all my courage simply to keep my head up. Fittingly,

"Shovel it Down, You Can Taste it Later"

then, I relished the Personal Courage ropes course at Treadwell Tower.

The first climb was more difficult than expected, rungs on the ladder further apart than was naturally easy to climb. Upon my arrival at the top, the supervising drill sergeant was yelling at me to go, never minding that I had to adjust my goggles in order to see just where I was going. For some reason, the Army has institutionalized the belief that soldiers won't learn unless someone yells at them. I suppose the rationale is to provide a stressful atmosphere so they will develop a reliance on doctrine in the face of danger or adversity, back to the Personal Courage value. Whatever its supposed benefits, it was annoying. Yet I was beginning to have fun, and at the other side I waited with several other privates on all fours. DS Williams was in charge at this stage—an affable man who was strict without being sinister, and who smiled at least as often as he scowled. He motivated me with his genuine mentorship and encouragement. While we crawled along, tired and excited, someone inadvertently knocked over his mug of ice cold refreshment. Bracing for a barrage of insults and reprimands, I was surprised by his tolerant temperament. He sarcastically joked about how someone must have done it on purpose, and lightened everyone's mood with a joke. Two rope bridges and an exit fall to the mat later, and I was off to tie a Swiss seat.

Distinguished by its simplicity (seven steps get your from a single 15-foot piece of nylon rope to fully functional harness), it is better known for its distinct discomfort to the male groin area. Part of the joy of tying a Swiss seat was binding one's junk between two strands of a thick nylon rope. NCOs were on hand to ensure that the harness was tight enough to restrict any unnecessary movement. In fact, we squatted low and pulled the ends of the cords taut between our legs. Fifty sets of testicles bulged between the V in the front of the rope seat. A yank from the back of the harness and a slap on the ass by cadre was the go ahead signal that we were ready for a test.

I moved on to the test tower where I learned that I was a knucklehead because I held out my left hand instead of my right. There were worse things to be, I supposed. After a swing across an imaginary pit, the culminating obstacle stared at me from 40 feet above. On the drill sergeant's command, I ran across foam matting to the base of the tall tower. The climb was about five times as lengthy as the one to the rope bridge platform, and I was tired and overwhelmed at the end. Like a veritable concierge, DS Robertson welcomed me at the end of the ladder and directed me up a set of stairs. He used the opportunity to engage me in a discussion about the misfortune I had of being a member of Wolfpack. I certainly wasn't immune from Army programming, hastily agreeing with every word my drill sergeant said and turning my back on my battle buddies, simultaneously missing an opportunity to tell him how ate up *he* was. I was at the climactic point of the Personal Courage course, and the lesson that had embedded itself deepest was to avoid risk. My chosen response got me out of there, though, and I moved on up to the pinnacle of Treadwell, crawling toward the rappelling edge.

I had rappelled many times before—rock climbing with friends in the granite canyons to the east of my hometown of Salt Lake City was a habitual pastime in my formative years. Nevertheless, I never rappelled with an Army drill sergeant inches from my face, just waiting for hesitation or a wrong move. It was confirmed that I was a knucklehead by the drill sergeant in my lane when I didn't crawl far enough toward the wall. Other than that, I did well enough for the NCO to not yell. In fact, he made some polite conversation, which was something new to me at Basic. DS Jones chimed in that I was "old and married," a bit of an oddity in Foxtrot. I descended fluidly, satisfied that most of the drill sergeants had my best interests at heart.

By noon most of us had finished the entire course, our stomachs grumbling and our skin beading sweat. Life on the range at Army Basic Training usually meant two things: hunger and heat. The solution for the former was the Meal Ready to Eat, or MRE. We were ecstatic to break into our first MREs. The novelty of meal in a bag generated an enthusiasm that tantalized our taste buds. The time it took to break into the cardboard box and open the individual hermetically-sealed pouches, then to heat the entrée only intensified our cravings.

My very first MRE was Menu 9: beef stew. Each package includes a magnesium heating pouch that, when contacted with water, reaches temperatures beyond 200 degrees in an instant. One only has to place the entrée and sides dish pouches next to the searing plastic envelope. The meals are loaded with 1200 calories among its main dish, two sides, crackers or bread, cold beverage, hot beverage, dessert, and for the lucky ones—candy.

"Like kids in a candy store" takes on new meaning for soldiers who discover an MRE with the sweet stuff. Whether it was the M&Ms, Skittles, or Tootsie Rolls, privates went to great lengths to get their hands on it. At first sight, market values were established and immediately spiraled out of control. Candy sold on the black market—in blatant violation of regulations—for upwards of $40. It wasn't uncommon for soldiers to sneak foodstuffs from MREs, or even from the D-Fac for that matter, back to the barracks for resale.

Whether it was from a package or a buffet line, there were always plenty of sweets. Lunch and dinner at the D-Fac offered—besides a wide variety of entrées, soups and salads—cakes, pies, and soft-serve ice cream as part of its usual fare. The only things that were off limits were coffee and soda. We could eat like kings. We just had to do it quickly.

"Shovel it down, you can taste it later!"

"Shovel it Down, You Can Taste it Later"

Drill sergeants would sometimes eat in their reserve section, taking turns to patrol ours. Talking had no place in the D-Fac; eating was a task, and we weren't on task unless we inhaled our food. The general rule was that when the last soldier to enter the chow hall finished eating, everyone from the platoon had to pick up his tray. Of course, any drill sergeant could order us out at any time.

Sometimes it paid to get out quickly. Waiting for the entire platoon after eating meant standing in formation, but without a drill sergeant present. That's where the gossip spread, rumors floating around the chow hall fairly like contagions. The mill had begun grinding out substantial rumors, and it was in a post-meal formation that we first heard about 1SG Gulliksen's foreboding discovery: a box of donuts. Apparently they were discovered in Third Platoon's laundry room, after some first-rate detective work. We knew we were in for it.

Nothing was said for the next few hours, but on our way back from dinner, something seemed different. Ominous. Maybe privates were murmuring, or maybe the drill sergeants were quieter than usual, but there was a foreboding that settled on the entire battery.

Upon our arrival, we were instructed to sit in the bleachers. First Sergeant gave us some speech about trust, responsibility, and discipline, all of *his* favorite values. Then he dramatically threw the loot on the ground as a climax to his monologue.

"We've got contraband!"

Sounds of disgust and amazement poured out from the four corners of the battery. Gulliksen walked around seeking looks of approval from his cadre, and getting them in spades. This was their moment, and they were relishing it. I could barely see the box lying there in the middle of the concrete pad that led straight through the battery and up the stairs. Some of the soldiers in our platoon began to murmur, and it quickly became evident that those weren't donuts at all.

I was the last one to assume a box of cigarettes, but I had never smoked. Many privates no doubt recognized the container immediately, and weren't surprised. I shouldn't have been; dozens in Fourth Platoon made public their taste for tobacco, smoke or otherwise, and their plan to immediately indulge once they were out of Basic. I could never understand why anyone would resume the habit after a pretty effective nine-week quitting program. Yet so many in our battery would have probably lit up right then and there given the opportunity.

Our overlords finally had the goods on us, and began to prepare for a justifiable crackdown. Never mind the obvious facts that, first, we were all too new to have the gumption to buy an *entire carton* of cigarettes, let alone smoke them, and second, there was never any evidence that tobacco was smoked in or near our battery. Non-smoker though I may have been, I could have recognized the smell of tobacco as well as anyone. And as efficiently as that mill was operating by Week Three, someone in our platoon would have heard about smoking in the boys' room.

Two theories of the origination of that carton emerged immediately: some AIT soldiers planted it in our laundry room as a random act of violence; or, more likely, the cadre simply said they found it. At any rate, the NCOs' purpose was served, and they had license to begin their reign of terror.

One platoon at a time went toes to line while the NCOs conducted a full search of their barracks. I was pretty excited to see it firsthand, knowing that I had absolutely nothing to hide. As we waited on the bleachers, the sergeants eagerly went upstairs to perform the shakedown, platoons in tow. Fourth Platoon was, as was customary, last, offering us plenty of time to contemplate our fate. Our framing of the situation was defined by that pack of cigarettes that had been thrown onto the ground—anything

"Shovel it Down, You Can Taste it Later"

short of that and we would come off looking like model citizens, I figured. Besides, I didn't have a single item that was illegal, and I hadn't seen much of anything in the barracks that led me to believe anyone else had, either.

We made conversation about what might happen, to the sounds of furniture being tossed around on the floors above us. One by one, the platoons moved upstairs. Worry was painted on the faces as the next platoon made its way up. The passing time and the thuds overhead coaxed a laundry list of worse case scenarios from Wolfpack. At length, we were ordered upstairs.

"Toes on line!" We knew that there would be no opportunity to hide or toss anything at this point. Whatever one had hidden in the dark of his locker, it was going to see the light of day. I was confident that it would be rather painless for me.

My confidence was shattered almost immediately. Though I had nothing to hide, and therefore nothing to fear, I nevertheless found myself on the losing end of the cadre's bludgeon. They were out for blood, and to send a message: the inmates would not be running this asylum.

Almost every soldier had something, as it turned out: cookies, crackers, gum, sugar, salt, and after-MRE chiclets. Tiny half-ounce bottles of Tabasco sauce were the hottest items, so to speak. Small players in the local underground market, but in the aggregate the engine of the black economy.

The items were revealed as soldiers opened lockers under the cadre's orders. I opened mine for SGT Williams, whom I expected would realize that I had nothing of interest. He was a rookie free agent giving it his all to show the scouts he was indeed a good find. All my possessions were dumped. Each neatly folded, rolled, or otherwise stowed item was torn apart and a thorough search was made. Here I thought he would take it easy and limit his search to obvious delinquents. If he thought he was going to find something of interest, he was as disappointed as I.

Not the first sergeant. He operated under the assumption, nay, the certainty, that everyone had something contraband. He strode along authoritatively, informing us what idiots we were for concealing such illegal items and promising to find them. As he passed by my locker, he seized on my hygiene bag—a conservative American Tourister toiletry pouch that contained extra soap, deodorant and razors. Claiming it was a civilian bag, he threw it in a trash heap emphatically. As soon as he rounded the corner I scurried it away safely back in my own heap of belongings strewn-about on the floor.

Gulliksen then fixated upon a clue. With a Holmesian determination, he followed a trail of dust that led behind my locker. Just a day or two before, the pipes in the latrine backed up cruelly, such that each morning all eight sinks became a cauldron of morning stew—toothpaste spit, razor rubble, and other byproducts of the pre-dawn routines of 50-plus soldiers—each sink's sewage bubbling up into the other, incidentally costing us precious time and resulting in tardiness and its accompanying punishments. Our cries of complaint became sufficient to warrant a plumber's visit. The professional had to knock a hole in the cinder block wall to access the drain pipes. Said hole still existed, veiled by my wall locker. It was no disguise for our wily first sergeant; he immediately asked for help to move the impediment and demanded a flashlight, which I sycophantically supplied.

Other NCOs, meanwhile, were busy going through other lockers. While most had only small items of contraband, one private had more to worry about. His locker was an unadulterated snack shack.

"Cakes and pies!" bellowed DS Robertson triumphantly.

Apparently, this young man from South Carolina would regularly sneak cellophane-wrapped desserts from the chow hall. "Fattie cakes," they were called, and drill sergeants tolerated them only so they could bludgeon us with their inevitable effects.

"Shovel it Down, You Can Taste it Later"

Though what they had collected so far was enough to make a point, the cadre was intent on striking something more incriminating. After all, there was the hype they started with the cigarettes. Though illicit, Tabasco and sugar were hardly controlled substances. Far from finding any alcohol, tobacco, or other drugs, they set their minds on another type of contraband. Rumors had flown about since day one that PV2 Fattie Cake had a cell phone. I heard the rumors myself that someone was making calls from a mobile, but gave them nothing beyond the first thought. I assumed they were true, but didn't care. I had made the mistake of thinking that I could sail through Boot Camp by minding my own business. On this night I would learn that that was a mistake.

As childish as it now seems, drill sergeants are experts in the tactics of intimidation and power dynamics. Here I was, a 30-year-old man, more educated than every NCO on the floor (six in all) and I was scared in a very real way. It wasn't the dread that comes with doing something for the first time, nor was it the trepidation one feels when he is unsure of something. The fear that swept over me was a new kind of fear, not acute, but total. It was terror: an exhausting fear, that the drill sergeants achieve by making us feel isolated and small. It would have been indescribable but for stories I had read. The world of *1984* was coming to life right in front of me. Emmanuel Goldstein was the private who refused to submit himself completely to the drills, and we were forced to hate him. We shouted responses to their demands as if our volume conveyed our disgust with anyone who would not fall in line.

Drill sergeants yelled and they yelled. And as silly as it seems, it was a very effective form of psychological control. It didn't seem to matter what they yelled, either. Some drill sergeants cursed, others ridiculed. Others, especially the First Sergeant, railed on about how inadequate and disappointing we were. The theme was always the same, though: we were not men worthy of being called soldiers.

We just wanted the yelling to stop. Privates became anxious to cooperate. Too tired to continue to resist, privates began to surrender their minds and souls to Big Brother. I got my chance when DS Robertson approached me and asked what the hell was going on in his Bay.

"I know you know what's happening Stowell," he said, eyes piercing me as I stood at attention. I told him that I didn't know anything about the cell phone, but that a certain private Sanchez had confided in me that he had used the payphone on several occasions during the night, according to what Sanchez had confided in me some days prior. I didn't feel guilty about giving up Sanchez. First of all, this was not "us against them." At least not for me—yet. At that point I felt no allegiance to the other recruits. I was a man among boys, and had more in common with the NCOs running the raid than with any other soldier. But I never loved Big Brother.

Secondly, it really pissed me off that we were in this mess because of the behavior of the teenagers with whom I was forced to train and live. Their misbehavior deserved to be exposed for the sake of the rest of us who wanted to get through Basic as peacefully as possible. A third reason I was remorseless was because I valued our drill sergeants' trust more than the other privates'. Two weeks previously, I was teaching high school students. Now I was forced to endure mental and emotional abuse—the likes of which would get any teacher fired—alongside boys who still hadn't graduated.

Our battery executive officer seemed to perceive that I occupied a unique position in the platoon. 1LT Henley was a tall and attractive African-American woman who commanded a level of esteem among the privates that the male officers could never attain. She was as elegant as a soldier ever could be, and as the only female of any rank within a very wide radius, we always gave her as much respect as we could muster. Speaking about me in the third person, and standing only feet away, she noted incorrectly that I was prior service, and that I must know something. After she asked me point-blank about the cell phone, I stood at attention and responded in way that would make DS Eppinghaus proud, "No ma'am, I don't know anything about the cell phone. Believe me, if I knew anything I would give it up." She was unconvinced. She walked away repeating what she had said about me before.

I sought out DS Robertson to notify him of some information that may be useful. I told him that I had seen some privates looking in the ceiling vents one night. It was true that a few soldiers had taken an interest in the grates that covered the air duct openings, and I sincerely hoped that they had hidden the cell phone up there so that the shakedown would mercifully end. They tore apart ceiling tiles and removed the vent covers, but came up empty handed. The failure only steeled their resolve.

The drama continued for over an hour. Our NCOs' determination increased every moment that passed by without a major discovery. False leads and dead ends drove them into a frenzied state of agitation—the yelling got louder, the insults and threats became more malevolent, and their overall temperament more violent. Furniture was hurled through the air alarmingly, and more belongings were scattered about.

By this time, they had questioned anyone who may have had knowledge of the cell phone. They had searched the ceilings, bathrooms, and light fixtures. They continued to throw furniture about; one had to presume for fun more than anything else. Any normally-wired person would have bored of it by this time, but our Training NCO was a different sort of animal.

SGT Stevenson was a dick by nearly every private's assessment. Best known for blowing his stack when PVT Rogers spilled a couple of drops from a leaky canteen onto his paperwork during Week One, he was out to revamp his reputation. During the raid, Stevenson caught his second wind as I was getting exhausted from merely watching the spectacle. He tossed a couple of beds and tipped a few lockers before he revealed something that got everyone's attention. "Stevo," as his peers referred to him, acted as if he had just found the Holy Grail. The look on his face was as that of a man possessed. If soldiers could face down battlefield enemies with as much ferocity, our national security would be sure.

"*Ohhh!*" he exclaimed as he held up some generic-looking power cord. With the same gusto that he showed upon its discovery, he threw the device on the floor, and stomped on it with all his might, his facing glowing with an intense look of concentration and delight. It was his best effort impress his peers, but what he displayed in zest and energy, he lacked in simple investigative how-to. He and the other NCOs stood over the closest thing they had to evidence—a pile of destroyed electronic gadgetry.

Finding the power cord only inflamed the passions of the cadre even further. They tore through the lockers that had been previously untouched with a ferocity that exceeded their previous efforts. It seemed proof enough that we were indeed hiding something, and deserved every bit of abuse they could dole out.

DS Martinez surpassed all the others in his quest to humiliate us. During the search for the elusive cell phone (which did, in point of fact, exist), Martinez took great satisfaction in launching threats of sanctions against us. Effectively labeling every single one of us as co-conspirators in the cell phone crime, he warned that we would all lose a rank.

"Blanket demotions!" he shouted over and over, as he walked up and down the aisles ripping off soldiers' chest rank insignia and stomping it with his boot on the floor with much pleasure.

When he came upon me, his eyes widened with the delight that apparently accompanied the weight of demoting a specialist.

"You better hope they find that phone, Stowell" he said emphatically, "You have more to lose than anyone." He tore my insignia off and threw it on to the floor as hard as one could toss an inch-and-a-half piece of fabric. As soon as he had his back turned, I scooped up my rank and proudly put it back on my uniform. Had he made his point? No! A second time he passed me by, repeating his performance—ripping off my insignia and casting it on the ground with a reiteration of his threat.

As absurd as they were, Martinez's threats had the desired effect on some of the privates. Many were so worried about losing hard-earned rank and the pay that went with it, and understandably so. I would have been furious if I left Basic Training a private having arrived an E-4. I was one of two specialists in the entire battery, the only one in our platoon. When anyone charged that I didn't do anything to earn the rank (as the Battery First Sergeant once did) my response was, "I went to six and a half years of college." I earned that rank just as anyone else earned theirs. The modest increase in pay seemed like a small nod in light of the sacrifice I had made to get there.

Before the contraband raid, I had always thought of Martinez as one of the most reasonable drill sergeants, but his little act sent me the message that none of the drill sergeants are reasonable. From that moment on I avoided giving NCOs the benefit of any doubt. For all intents and purposes they were irrational, illogical, schizophrenic megalomaniacs hell-bent on proving to the privates the mettle that had earned them a spot in the drill sergeants corps.

Eventually the NCOs tired of the game. It was past 2300 hours and they wanted sleep at least as much as we did. Our Bay lay in ruins—dozens of lockers tipped and emptied, bunks flipped, gear and personal belongings strewn everywhere, looking as if ordinance had exploded inside. Our concerned drill sergeants left us with an order: have this place in order by 0400 the next morning, and, by the way, conduct fireguard in full battle rattle.

"I feel like a Jew," said Zaccardi, regard the *Gestapo*-like treatment we had just been subjected to.

The comment wasn't meant to be a joke, and it gave me a brand new desire to resist arrogant police tactics. Screw cleaning up, we decided. What could they do to us that would be worse than this? My bed was more inviting than the mess that surrounded me, and I surrendered to the promise of rest. I hopped up and took refuge in my sanctuary in the middle of this communal hell.

Jackson arrived to a modestly cleaner mess the next morning—he was more angry than the night before.

"Y'all trying to piss off the drill sergeant?!" he exclaimed. "Front-leaning rest position, MOVE!"

We knew it would be a long week. Surely, the events of the night before were part of a plan to shock us into a recommitment to discipline and respect. For me it had backfired.

In recollecting his WWII heroics, COL Treadwell said, "...in war there occasionally arises a peculiar situation in which one man alone can accomplish more than a company. I had a hunch this might be one of those times."

I seconded his hunch. We did our PT and marched off to chow like any other day.

"Front-Leaning Rest Position, MOVE!"

WEEK 4

SLIDING MY MEAL tray down the buffet line, I helped myself to a triple layer chocolate cake, its innards moist and smooth. Some privates topped even the luscious chocolate icing on the cake, going à la mode. The desserts were always tasty, and their goodness helped me forget the torment. Our drill sergeants allowed this obvious lack of discipline to infest our ranks, knowing they could more than compensate for the caloric intake by burning them off in their own unrelenting way.

Every morning, except on Sundays, we would form up on the drill pad wearing our "PTs," a handsome array of heather gray Army tee, shorts that bared enough thigh to have last been stylish sometime in the mid 1970s, white crew-length socks, and our running shoes. Of course, our two-quarts were still part of our uniform, and we carried with us a PT mat, rolled up, held in our left hand.

Formation was at 0515, but like everything else at BCT, it was advertised as 15 minutes later than they actually wanted us there. So dutifully, each day long before dawn, we stood in the darkness and humidity as bleary-eyed offerings to the mosquitoes circling about the drill pad lights.

Oklahoma bugs seemed bigger and more plentiful than anything I was used to in the San Francisco Bay Area. Cockroaches were bulbous and red, moths often came in the bird-sized variety, and there were other critters that I didn't recognize. The mosquitoes were the worst, though, not because of their size but their number and tenacity. My first morning outside in shorts was a rude awakening: a dozen monster bites. Even with liberal amounts of deet the critters would manage to find some skin, usually by biting through socks and tee shirts. Though the Army issued us repellant, the smart soldier bought a more functional brand at first opportunity.

Our morning PT formation was our "first call," during which drill sergeants would report to the first sergeant, accounting for every soldier in their respective platoons. It began on the first sergeant's command.

"Fall IN!"

"I am an American Soldier!

I am a warrior and a member of a team!

I serve the people of the United States and live the Army Values!

I will always place the mission first!

I will never accept defeat!

I will never quit!

I will never leave a fallen comrade!

I am disciplined, physically and mentally tough; trained and proficient in my warrior tasks and drills!

I always maintain my arms, my equipment, and myself!

I am an expert, and I am a professional!

I stand ready to deploy, engage, and destroy the enemies of the United States of America in close combat!

I am a guardian of freedom and the American way of life!

I am an American Soldier!

It was the Soldier's Creed, which every private was charged to memorize. We said it in unison at the tops of our lungs every morning. A stirring statement, one could derive a life philosophy in nearly every line. In fact, it was the Soldier's Creed and the moxy with which it was recited that motivated so many of us. I was proud to say that I was an American Soldier, and humbled to have been given the opportunity to train in order to deploy, engage, and destroy the enemies of the United States of America in close combat. As a broadcast journalist to be, I had little chance of ever facing the enemy up close, but to always stand ready to do so was a monumental responsibility, one for which I was in awe.

Not a month earlier I was standing in a high school classroom in the Bay Area, teaching math to at-risk teens. I had done an abrupt ideological about face, going from such an anti-military mindset to one that took a statement declaring our alacrity to destroy our country's enemies as a given. Needless to say, it was a culture shock—one that I thought I was ready for.

Getting up so early for an exercise routine was a shock, too. The Army thrives on shocks, though; distressing situations provide opportunities to rely on military principles of teamwork and obedience. Just as combat requires exact obedience of its would-be victors, so does survival in Basic Combat Training. I decided that if I was to actively grow from the experience, then I would have to find my emotional and mental footing. Those were the trials most demanding—a soldier is refined by fire, not chiseled like some sculpture.

The physical tasks were demanding, too. "Pain is weakness leaving the body." They didn't tell me what crying meant. Combat requires that every soldier be prepared to endure physical trials unimaginable to most people. And they wanted to push us to the limits from day one. The physical training program was the first piece.

117 | "Front-Leaning Rest Position, MOVE!"

Each morning after first call we would march out by platoon to the adjacent field and begin our physical training. In the dark of the early morning we lumbered along sleepily, the upper-cased black ARMY displayed across our shirts reflecting in the street lamps. One-hundred fifty yards later our battery was amassed on the field. The drill sergeants maneuvered the four platoons into a pinwheel formation around a wooden platform, on top of which another cadre member stood.

"Extend to the left, MARCH!"

"From front to rear, COUNT OFF!"

"Even numbers to the left, UNCOVER!"

Although clumsy and slow at first, within days entire platoons would react automatically to the commands. A giant accordion of soldiers would open up laterally, turn heads and count off in unison, and stagger themselves depending on their number. We could have been performers in a Michael Jackson tribute.

The cornerstone of the PT program was Conditioning Drill 1 (CD1)—a set of exercises designed to target every muscle group in the body. But soldiers can only do CD1 when they are properly arrayed. Not particularly rigorous, CD1 is another opportunity to practice discipline and uniform responses to simple commands. By discipline I am referring to such time-honored practices as not flinching when a mosquito lands *anywhere* on your body.

"Let 'em get some of that!" DS Robertson would holler. Doubly a reminder to apply sufficient insect repellant, and a discipline drill, mosquitoes seemed to serve the beckon call of our drill sergeants.

"The Bend and Reach!"

"*The Bend and Reach*!" We echoed the command to prove adequate motivation.

"Starting position, MOVE!"

Nearly every command in the Army has two parts: the preparatory command and the command of execution. Upon hearing "Starting position" a soldier knows what he will do, and that a verb is soon to follow—"MOVE!" The execution command is the cue for everyone to go to the starting position in this case. It's almost elegant in its design.

Ask twenty privates fresh from Basic to recite or lead CD1, and nineteen would go dumb trying to remember the phraseology, order, and voice-inflection rules of commands. Yet all twenty could follow the routine to exactitude. We were a pack of Pavlov's dogs; our reward was simply to not get yelled at.

"The Rear Lunge!"

The Rear Lunge!

"Starting position, move!"… "One – two – three."

"*ONE!*" We bellowed back. The CD1 repetitions were all done in four counts, the last of which was called out by the soldiers in tow. The instructor would inflect his voice on the three counts prior to the last repetition, which put us back in the starting position. Naturally, we remained in said position until given a new command: "Position of attention, MOVE!" With a jarring urgency, the formation would snap back to attention.

"The Highjumper!"

"*The Highjumper!*" We rolled through the exercises obediently. DS Robertson was the essence of duty as he led us through the drill. "You won't do these retarded exercises in a regular unit," he offered candidly. Anything that DS Robertson disliked was "retarded," be it a drill, regulation, or person. Retarded as they were, we followed the exercises to a "T." That phrase had military meaning, as well, according to Robertson. "T" stood for "trained." A soldier did something "to a T," only if he was properly trained. If it was not "to a T," then he needed retraining, which usually meant "correction through physical exercise." But that was in the bay, and in the mornings we were outside on the PT field, doing the bare minimum.

Besides, it was always the drill instructors leading PT, and they never made a mistake. Not anything major that couldn't be corrected by a simple, "as you were," the great eraser. It is the polite military way of saying, "my mistake," or "sorry about that, I screwed up." A perfect example was when DS Jackson would call us to the position of attention before putting us in the starting position, which is an egregious breech of protocol. It would happen like this:

"One, two three"

"*Halt!*"

"Position of attention, MOVE!"

We delayed a response. At that point our minds attempted to tell our muscles to obey the command and put our bodies at the position of attention, but our muscles only knew of one thing to do after our mouths shouted out "halt," namely, to go to the "starting position." These were the types of ethical dilemmas in which we would find ourselves at Basic. Luckily, DS Jackson would come to his senses before half of the platoon decided that the position of attention was less uncomfortable than the starting position and say those magic words, "as you were," which would put us into a forgivable limbo until the command loop would reset and we would get an order that everyone's brains and muscles could agree on.

"As you were" was a phrase that only NCOs could use, not because it violated any rule for a private to pronounce it, but because its use was a subtle art form, and before anyone below a sergeant's rank ever mastered the art, NCOs would unleash a tirade upon him for being so maladroit as to get himself into a situation that necessitated the phrase. So we followed along dumbly as the drill sergeants imposed order, in nearly perfect fashion, each morning. Most of the time, they got it "to a T."

The arrangement of the exercises was one thing that was flawless. After the first three exercises followed: 4) The Rower, 5) The Squat Bender, 6) The Windmill, 7) The Forward Lunge, 8) The

Prone Row, 9) The Bent-leg Body Twist, and 10) The Push-up. I never heard a drill sergeant lead them out of order. How? "Be Right Here Real Soon, We Found Panties Behind Popeye's." Angry drill sergeants devised the cleverest mnemonics.

The Squat Bender

Starting Position   Count 1   Count 2   Count 3   Count 4

If CD1 was the foundation of PT, then the runs were the buttresses. Twice weekly we grouped ourselves into ability groups to go for multi-mile runs round the post. I would almost spoil the ending to say now that these were known as AGRs. Ability Group Runs were three- to five-mile-runs at a pace designed to push a soldier to better times in the final test, the AGRs were led by drill sergeants, partly there to set the pace and partly there to guard formation.

Off the PT field we'd march after a session of CD1, rolling along to a common cadence:

"One…two… three…four…left…left…left…left; Yo left pick it up yo left—*Drive on!*—Yo left pick it up yo left—*Drive on!*—Yo le-eeeyeft, right yo left—*Drill sergeant get busy one time!*—Yo le-eeeyeft, right yo left—*Pump, pump, pump, pump it up!*

"Double time!" the drill sergeant squawked. And the privates repeated, at which point the drill would begin his double-time cadence and get us running.

There are three "times" at which we march. "Quick time" is the normal pace to get from point A to point B. According to the manual it is executed by walking 120 steps per minute. The "double-time" is 180 steps per minute. A "mark time" is a quick-time march in place.

"Left, left, left, right le-eft—*Left, left, left, right le-eft*—Left, left, keep it in ste-ep—*Left, left, keep it in ste-ep*—We love to double time—*We love to double time*—We do it all the time—*we do it all the time...*

We ran for about half a mile like that, while NCOs measured our motivation in decibels. We never sounded off quite good enough for the drill sergeants—to me, singing cadence while running was like serenading a girl: cute in the movies, but in reality corny and awkward.

After the motivational warm-up phase, we opened it up to a workout pace, and the cadence ceased, but we were still expected to maintain ranks. It was all so dogmatic. Routines and traditions were blindly adhered to without the slightest thought as to whether they were in anyone's interests. We couldn't stretch before a run, we couldn't drink water during PT, and one had to kneel on his right knee—not his left—afterward, until every private was back in platoon formation.

What may have been detrimental to soldiers' short-term health was yet another opportunity to ingrain discipline. "Running is as much mental as it is physical," one drill sergeant said. He was absolutely right. On many runs, I wanted to fall out so badly, but the mere thought of attracting that kind of attention to myself was more painful than the run. I thus exercised my physical strength and my mental powers during AGRs.

I also ran with the thought of my wife, so they had emotional value, as well. As I ran, I would take in the beautiful Oklahoma sunrises and think about how proud I was making Esther. During any form of exercise, I would remind myself that the Army was sculpting my body for her. I prayed, meditated, and thought about all the bad things happening to me, trying to keep an eye on all the good that would come of it. For nine weeks during the cool June and July mornings, I would let out cupfuls of sweat and stress in the humid air. For me the AGRS purged my mind, body and soul, of the negative.

It was also a pretty straightforward way to get fit, and I relished it in that sense. But I understood my body and what it could handle. Having come from a family of runners—my father was a championship track coach for years, and my siblings had gone to college on track scholarships—I believed I knew more than the NCOs who parroted anything they heard about fitness. I put myself in B-group, knowing that I would advance to A-group (the fastest) quickly. After my first experience with A-group I decided I was a B-man, and there I stayed.

Falling out of an AGR was a cardinal sin. With eight or nine drill sergeants taking charge of three ability groups, there were at least three NCOs in each formation. Usually we had a training NCO or cadet (an officer in training,) plus the BC (battery commander), and perhaps even our battalion commander or command sergeant major (CSM.) We were always under watch during the run, like a chain gang serving a hard labor sentence. To break the imaginary chains that held us together was asking for a world of hurt.

They had us believe that all these leaders were there with us, running in their distinctive vests, to motivate us. If so, the line between motivating and reprimanding is very thin in the Army, yet everybody wanted in on the act. Anybody could hoot and holler meanly under the guise of motivation. Others tried to motivate more sincerely. During one run, PVT Joe Sanders was next to me in formation when the drill sergeant leading the pack halted the entire group. Most kept running in place, but I wanted to walk.

"Keep running," Sanders encouraged.

Only nothing this 19-year old had to say was going to encourage my 31 year-old ass after two and a half miles at 0630. I took full advantage of the no talking rule at times like these. Sanders was persistent though, and oblivious to the fact that I was amazingly able to keep perfect pace with everyone just by standing there. I wanted to stand there, but Sanders wanted me to push myself. At the very least, he wanted the NCOs to hear him wanting me to push myself.

"Come on Stowell, keep running," he continued.

"No!" Ignoring him didn't work; an abrupt and honest answer did. Once the group got going again I managed to keep pace just fine. Sanders sucked wind worse than I, so I guess I should have been encouraging him. But then there was that no talking rule.

Initially I had been excited to run. It's one of those things that civilians take for granted—as I had. Running, whether in around beautiful Lake Merritt in Oakland, or the mountain trails of Utah, was supposed to give release. The freedom and exhilaration that the wind and scenery provide are salutary. Running in the Army wasn't quite so therapeutic. In stark contrast to the independence that going on a jog is supposed to afford, we were told to make a column formation of three ranks. Why we ran in three files instead of four, I never knew. The column was quite long, some 80+ in B-group, usually led by DS Jackson. We were marched out onto the road; moonlight still bright in the dark morning sky.

Drill sergeants surely learn how to manage large formations in their training, but they certainly aren't taught the first thing about fluid dynamics. With so many soldiers packed together, accidents were bound to happen. I was scared to death running so tightly, with privates nipping at my heels, soldiers to my left and right. Not a few fights broke out right there in the AGRs: privates running too slow or cutting someone off. Runners were known to get tripped or shoved, and many an inter-platoon feud was initiated by a nudge, budge, or shunt, whether accidental or intentional.

Nevertheless, AGRs got us fit. Over the course of my short Army career up to that point, I lost somewhere around 25 pounds, and I was never particularly overweight. According to published weight standards, I was 20 pounds under the maximum when I enlisted. By the time I shipped I had lost about five pounds (stress could have been the main cause for that) and during BCT I went from 188 to 168. One drill sergeant seemed chronically concerned about my weight. "Stowell," he would ask regularly, "How much weight have you lost?"

I am built on a wire frame, so fat deposits on me are like ballasts on a canoe. Thirty years had blessed me with love handles and a stomach that made my wife cringe; my portlier features were exaggerated by my bird chest and skinny extremities. I was also beginning to boast some fat under my chin that, if not treated soon, would have evolved into a full-blown neck roll. Within weeks it was disappearing; first from my face, then the sides, and finally my stomach. My face, in particular, began to look almost gaunt, chin fat all but gone, my features were more chiseled.

My appearance made quite an impression on me. It was a universal ritual inside the barracks to examine oneself in front of the mirror, before and after showers. My vanity demanded it of me too, and daily, I had more with which to be pleased, as I saw the fat melt away and my upper body muscles show more definition. How proud my wife would be (though the gains would be temporarily offset by the hideous farmer tan we all had in common.)

CD1 and the AGR were important parts of the regimen, but I attribute my weight loss to several things. Regular sleep patterns, regular and proportioned meals, high levels of activity throughout the day, and lots of water all played important parts in my thinning out. But grueling physical exercise was the most prominent feature in the plan.

The morning routine with the battery was only a fraction of our total workout. We averaged around two hours of PT daily—the hour to hour and a half as a battery, followed by anywhere from 20 minutes to two hours as a platoon in the evening. The evening PT was usually billed as "correction through physical exercise," and often bordered on abusive.

Abuse took two forms: physical and mental. Physically, the PT sessions were very trying for me. I was 11 years older than the average private in our battery, and recovery time seemed to correspond with age. I was a full-time athlete in high school, and a recreational athlete since, and I always considered myself able to handle any reasonable amount of physical activity. Drill sergeants were eager to prove otherwise, and they relished the opportunity to break us. Creative and punishing workouts were devised and both Jackson and Robertson vied for the reputation of giving the toughest, engaging in a showmanship that broke the mind, spirit and body. What they failed to achieve in intensity they made up for in duration.

It would begin with someone screwing up, which was only a matter of the drill sergeants choosing which screw-up to punish.

"Front-leaning rest position, MOVE!"

Our offenses were often very petty; for example, not sounding off loud enough. "You want me to motivate you? You have to motivate me!" (Who asked to be motivated?) Another typical cause for a drill sergeants' indignation was movement while standing at attention.

The workout might begin, though not necessarily, with a justification. They might list our offenses for the day, rail on about how they got up every morning and gave 110%, and needed for us to do the same, tell us that they had better things to do than to work us to a dripping sweat, and cap it by criticizing our incapacity to learn simple lessons. "You are some dumbass privates, but you're gonna be sexy privates." I supposed there was some consolation that we would ultimately see benefits from such an education.

Our nightly corrections had its advantages over that done in the field from our perspective, as well, at least for me and the dozen or so privates stationed in the back of the barracks. The other saps were in direct view of the drill sergeants. Safely in the rear, and behind one of only a few double bunks in the entire bay, I could slack off on at least two thirds of the exercises.

Sure, drill sergeants had ways of monitoring; roaming the way I would circulate my classroom to prevent problems from flaring among my students. Drill sergeants had a giveaway Achilles heel, though: their need to hear themselves say the cleverest, most insulting things to privates as loudly as they possibly could. Their vanity was a warning trump to their approach. Me and my geographically-blessed loafer platoon-mates would feign effort, fatigue, and pain in direct proportion to drill sergeant's volume. As he turned his back or headed up the other aisle, we could safely rest, face down on the floor that was mopped of our sweat that very morning. I got very well-acquainted with those few tiles to the side of my bunk. Countless hours were passed staring straight down, wondering when the ordeal would end, and imagining the rapture I would experience when I finally got to see my wife again. A quick glance to the right would tell me where my subjugator was, and reveal how many other privates were taking unauthorized breaks.

Perhaps our shortsightedness prolonged our torment. It doesn't seem a stretch to think that drill sergeant knew we were slacking, but it was a natural physiological response to the pain I was in, and I'm sure my companions shared. To not admit as much would be to understate the agony I frequently felt.

Though we were warned that PT would be the rule rather than

the exception, I still resented it. As a professional educator, I had acquired an unwavering belief in clearly communicating objectives to learners. In our situation, we were given lessons under false pretenses. In hindsight, I appreciate the physical trials I had to endure, growing stronger and fitter. But I also like to remind myself how hard it was, how badly it hurt, and how it was sold to me by snake oil salesmen marketing an entirely different package.

Sometimes I couldn't hide. On one occasion, three NCOs patrolled the barracks during a PT session, so that I had no opportunity to rest. We had been going full steam for over an hour straight, doing the same exercises in CD1, with a few of the drill sergeants' personal favorites sprinkled in: legs-lifts, for one. I put forth maximum effort, to the point that whatever stomach muscles I had were completely useless. For all I tried, I could not keep my legs the obligatory six inches off the ground, and the pain that shot through my abdomen was intense. I felt like I was on a medieval rack, the sting reaching up to my chest. By this point, the hard tile floor had worn any padding on my backside raw, so that the pain was attacking me all over. Nearly in tears, I could barely respond when SGT Williams said, "What's the matter. Stowell?"

I formulated my response, "these are killing me," and I really meant it.

"No," he replied. "Bullets are killing soldiers in Iraq."

Poor choice of words on my part, I had to concede. But my mind was in that moment, and my body was in pain. He didn't empathize. Nearly all of our NCOs had been in combat and had undoubtedly experienced pain far worse than what I was at the moment. Though not much of a salve, his words at least provided me perspective—perspective that was lacking in all the others' attempts to motivate us.

The go-to motivational strategy was to argue their belief that we weren't able to do it. I agreed in at least one respect, that I was unable to *want* to do it. It is difficult to muster any enthusiasm for a man who constantly belittled me and my peers, though at times I agreed with their conclusions. I have no doubt that NCOs wanted us to excel, but they could have made some feeble attempt to convince us. The irony of reverse psychology is that when you tell teenagers that they suck a bazillion times, they actually start to suck. That irony was lost on the NCOs of Foxtrot.

Basic Combat Training as an institution was a quasi-religion. There are the clergy (NCOs,) scriptures (Army Field Manuals,) rites of worship (D&C and PT) hymns (The Army Song,) and sacred spaces. The spaces that were inviolable at BCT were the kill zone and the drill pad.

One morning, due to rain, we conducted CD1 on the drill pad. As we extended to the left and spaced ourselves out for the exercises, DS Jefferson's eye caught something very disturbing.

"Who spit on my drill pad?" The tone in his voice and the look in his eye indicated that this was a matter not of mere saliva, but of desecrating a holy place.

We didn't hear the end of the spit on the drill pad until PVT Satterwhite confessed, realizing it was safer to hope for the mercy of a benevolent god than test his omniscient wrath.

While drill sergeants were very good at indoctrinating privates with the official religion, some had a harder time respecting soldiers' actual faith. DS Robertson made no bones about his disdain for traditional worship.

"This church thing's starting to really irk me," he told us during the drive to our LDS service. "All you need is a quiet corner and your Bible to practice religion." We all knew the impossibility of finding such a place in the barracks, but kept our thoughts to ourselves.

PVT Asa Sanders was a regular target of Robertson's disdain. Sanders would regularly get mail from fellow parishioners back

129 | "Front-Leaning Rest Position, MOVE!"

home, and the drill sergeants never let him live it down. Sanders was very proud of his piety, and the drill sergeants thought they were utterly clever when they said things like, "Sanders, the Lord wants you to do [insert Army task here]." One time, Sanders couldn't master a command in our Drill and Ceremony routine. To Robertson's way of thinking, conventional methods of motivating Sanders apparently weren't working, when he had a revelation that might as well have come from Heaven itself. He thought he'd instill the fear of God in Sanders.

"Satan worshipper!" he bellowed, frustrated that the young private wasn't doing as ordered.

Sanders, wrought with a new conviction, mended his ways.

Usually, drill sergeants tried to stay out of our religious lives. We were forbidden from attending services on the first and last Sundays of BCT, but other than that we were free to worship to our conscience's delight. So on the second Sunday in Foxtrot, I was glad to take advantage of my—proud to say—Army-long three-hour service. Having learned my lesson during Reception about leaving my worship opportunity in the hands of an NCO, I tried to ever-so-delicately remind DS Robertson about our early service, which I was pretty sure commenced at 0830. He assured me that we would not be late.

We slept in until 0530 on Sundays, and spent an hour and a half on barracks maintenance. Breakfast chow lasted until about 0745, depending on the lines, so it was easily 0800 by the time we marched back to our barracks.

"If a private needed to know anything, an NCO would tell him." It was the Army's promise that went unfulfilled at Reception. Desperate for some old-time religion, I took matters into my own hands and recorded the meeting schedules for all worship services that were posted on a bulletin board outside the D-Fac. Nobody paid much attention to the bulletin boards—it was just too much work in the face of the requirement to stand at attention or parade rest on the way in to chow, and run a near-sprint back to formation on the way out.

Robertson was confident that our service didn't start until after 0900, just enough time to dust us off a little bit. Armed with my newly-acquired information, I rustled Tapp and the several other LDS churchgoers and told our drill sergeant, unequivocally, that our service was at 0830, only minutes away. He demanded the makeshift schedule that I had documented so he could anticipate other soldiers' service times. This was crazy—didn't the drill sergeants have a schedule? (Every week thereafter he looked to me as an expert on service times, having forgotten—or perhaps, not—that I had surrendered the information to him.)

Frustrated by our needs, he nevertheless knew the consequences of denying us an opportunity to worship how and where we desired, and grudgingly drove us to the auditorium. I carried with me my journal, scriptures, and some letter-writing materials. Upon sighting the stamps, DS Robertson suspiciously asked what the hell they were for. His style of worship didn't involve any writing. At that time, my style included pouring out my soul to my wife, and he wasn't Mormon, so what the hell could he say about it?

I cried every time I went to church. The first time was the most emotional—it was so closely connected to my churchgoing back home. The LDS experience is remarkably consistent the world over. Our meetings are organized and conducted with a reverent, comforting sameness that makes it easy to feel at home in any congregation. In my previous life as a civilian, I was a member of the Oakland 9th Branch. As an Army trainee I belonged to the Fort Sill Serviceman's Group. The only significant differences between the two were the uniform attire of parishioners and the conspicuous lack of females in the latter.

There were some women who volunteered to help make the servicemen's worship experience more full and rewarding. A

"Front-Leaning Rest Position, MOVE!"

sister greeted me, recorded some contact information, took my picture, and gave me a set of military scriptures. All were much appreciated. She also emailed my wife with the offer of relaying any messages that Esther wanted delivered to me; she sent my family members the photo as proof of life, and though I had brought scriptures from home, the set she furnished were better suited for life in training.

If nothing else came from my time spent at BCT, I became more reliant on God, more grateful for my health, prosperity, and family, and more aware of how I lived. Spiritual lessons complemented everything else I was learning.

Each Sunday we marched ourselves back to the barracks where our compatriots were usually waxing. Sunday was a day to clean, both barracks and personal effects. Loads of time were spent in the laundry room, mostly inefficiently. It was a great place to take a nap or write letters while waiting for a washing machine to become available.

Inevitably the cry would echo throughout the battery, "drill sergeant wants everybody upstairs!"

"Front-leaning rest position, MOVE!"

Privates asleep, going downstairs out of uniform, writing letters, or disturbing the drill sergeant. Sundays' semi idle time was a petri-dish whose culture spawned reasons galore for drill sergeants to smoke us. Correction through physical exercise was effective only to the extent that it was consistent, and we consistently seemed to be off-task on the day of rest.

Ostensibly, one of the reasons for the copious amounts of such correction was to prepare us for the looming APFT, or Army Physical Fitness Test. The first one was administered during our second week of training on the rough side of the tracks. Though they worked us to the bone in preparation for the assessment, they wanted us to do well, presumably for bragging rights among cadre. The night before the test, DS Jackson ordered us go to bed at 1930, before the sun had even set. I could certainly use more APFTs.

Drill sergeants were demanding; that they had the right to expect top performance was never disputed. Every single drill sergeant who demonstrated or led exercises excelled at them. Even the older gentlemen could knock out 40 push-ups without even looking like they were making an effort. Nevertheless, when test time came around, they wore their ACUs and campaign hats, a not-so-subtle message that they weren't there to coach us.

It was still well before dawn when we lined up for CD1 as a warm up, clad in a slightly different uniform. Each soldier was branded with a mesh tank marked by platoon color and a unique number. SPC Stowell became "Blue 21." We were divided into several groups, each assigned to a single drill sergeant, who acted as scorer. Their difficulty counting and organizing us was still as pronounced as ever, as they continually adjusted each group, sending privates to new lines.

"You are about to take the army physical fitness test, a test that will measure your muscular endurance and cardio-respiratory fitness," echoed the drill sergeant's voice through a megaphone. "The results of this test will give you and your commanders an indication of your state of fitness and will act as a guide in determining your physical training needs. Listen closely to the test instructions, and do the best you can on each of the events." Drill sergeants demonstrated proper army pushups according to standard, accompanied by the manual's set of official instructions:

"On the command 'go,' begin the push-up by bending your elbows and lowering your entire body as a single unit until your upper arms are at least parallel to the ground. Then, return to the starting position by raising your entire body until your arms are fully extended. Your body must remain rigid in a generally straight line and move as a unit while performing each repetition."

133 | "Front-Leaning Rest Position, MOVE!"

Throughout the reading, a pair of drill sergeants demonstrated, one doing a textbook pushup, Vanna White in a campaign hat pointing out the features of his exemplary form.

"At the end of each repetition, the scorer will state the number of repetitions you have completed correctly. If you fail to keep your body generally straight, to lower your whole body until your upper arms are at least parallel to the ground, or to extend your arms completely, that repetition will not count, and the scorer will repeat the number of the last correctly…

…blah, blah, blah. These instructions were to be taken very seriously, yet no one really paid much attention. After all, they were just push-ups. Following a similar routine for sit-ups, we were herded into our respective lines, where we waited, scorecards in hand, backs to the scorers. The drills sat on milk crates as we prepared to push.

One by one we were called forward. A dozen at a time, privates would begin on the word of the NCO in charge, and start pushing. On this early June morning, the vast majority of us were nowhere near to being in adequate Army shape, and our drill sergeants let us know out loud. Though we were not supposed to be watching, we couldn't help but sneak peaks at whatever was causing the NCOs to scream things like, "Come on, puffy! Push harder!" Or, "You're pathetic, an embarrassment to this battery!"

Many privates were angry at what they saw as unfair scoring, having knocked out 60 or 70 pushups, only to have 40 of them count. I had the opposite problem. While every one of my pushups counted, I probably gave too much effort on each one, so embarrassed was I to risk ridicule for not having done it properly, that I was exhausted of strength and energy long before the two minutes were up. That, and I was plain weak.

I finished one push away from a passing score. Soldiers of my age group needed 30 pushups to earn 50 points on a quasi-percentile scale. Most privates, aged 17 – 21, needed 35 successful pushups to earn the passing score. NCOs blathered on like grumpy old men indignant about the luxuries that we had taken for granted. They complained that the Army had relaxed its standards in the few years since they had attended BCT. A maximum score of 300 was earned by topping out on each event—around 75 pushups and sit ups, and a two-mile time close to 13:00. Yet we, as BCT soldiers, were only required to score a 50 on the scale, undoubtedly too easy for the tastes of our heroic drill sergeants. After recording my score, DS Eppinghaus flipped my card away repugnantly.

The first test was relatively unimportant, though, as we would be given two more administrations as a battery. Even a passing score this time wasn't good enough to meet the requirement of BCT. No, this was a "diagnostic" APFT, which is shorthand for "the test to give drill sergeants unbridled and undisputed license to work us harder than ever before." Nothing short of a perfect 300 would satisfy; DS Jackson said he would settle for 50 pushups and sit ups, something he must have known to be a near impossibility.

After repeating our routine to earn a sit up score, each group that had scored with the same drill sergeant was separated into two running teams, A and B. Then, a change of plans. We were to run according to our number, even and odd. No, wait, there's got to be a better way to do this. In classic military fashion, what should have been a simple task required an alteration at every link in the chain of command. Every additional pay grade gave wisdom unquestionable by those of lower rank, and incomparable to mere common sense. It must have been 1SG Gulliksen, then, who finally came up with the idea to run us according to platoon.

The run course was the road that circumscribed the Starship; we ran slightly less than three full laps. True to the manner in which we trained, we were allowed no time for warm up or stretching, and the first two-hundred meters was a mad dash;

"Front-Leaning Rest Position, MOVE!"

an explosion of testosterone spilled on the track. Many of the eager soldiers could scarcely conceptualize two miles or imagine how the second one would feel after sprinting the first. I saw the backs of dozens of soldiers who zoomed past me in the early part of the run, only to overtake them later as I ran at my deliberate pace. During my teaching days I was also a varsity track and field coach. I ran smarter than I ran hard, and maintained an even tempo throughout, shouting "Jumpman 21!' to let DS Eppinghaus know I had completed my first lap at around 4:30. Other soldiers shouted various slogans and waved their arms about to gain the attention of the cadre in charge of recording their time. I wondered if the shouting was a logistical necessity, or simply another way to exercise total control over the privates and get a few laughs in, as well. On my third shout I stepped across the line at a respectable 14:40.

Now with hard data to prove that we were soft, the battery leadership was ready to load us with additional PT tasks; we were quickly introduced to new workout routines. One morning during Week Four we headed to the parking lot after our stretching and conditioning drills where the drill sergeants did their absolute best at lining us up for our next exercise.

Despite their efforts, the laws of fluid dynamics remained poised against them. With no clear markers on the blacktop, still wet from overnight rains, NCOs attempted to stand us, shoulder to shoulder, between two orange cones. A flimsy ribbon of soldiers 200-strong waved a couple of hundred feet along the parking lot, bowing here and bending there. One drill sergeant yelled for the middle of the line to back up, while the ends would follow suit, moving the entire group out of place. Another obsessive NCO moved the cone to better fit the ersatz line. Their frustration corresponded to their lack of understanding of the concepts, "parallel" and "perpendicular." They knew, as we all did, what a straight line should look like. They were altogether clueless, however, about how to connect two distinct points in a plane with 20 NCOs acting as independent gravitational points, toward which handfuls of privates were more than eager to move, not because it made any sense, but because the trainees were powerless to straighten the line themselves. Others would begin bickering and arguing about the position of their neighbors, which only served to bolster the drill sergeants' sincere belief that we were all mentally deficient.

It was just a line, but it was emblematic of the relationships and outcomes of the Basic Training in Foxtrot Battery. Drill sergeants expected that we perform perfectly on demand. They didn't seem to realize that ordering around 200+ young men implied all sorts of organizational considerations, and that results could be explained, at least in part, by the conditions and setting in which we were thrust. Needless to say, there was no thought whatever giving to systems thinking. Their problem-solving efforts usually amounted to no more than pathetic lamentations: "It's not that hard!" As frustrating as it was for the NCOs, it was at least as frustrating for me. I took the view of learning leadership skills as well as warrior tasks, so I did my best to maintain a keen, objective habit of observation, and with the simplest things, like forming a straight line, I observed ineptitude on the part of those in charge.

We never did get it quite straight, and it was such a monumental effort that we almost forgot there was purpose to getting us thus aligned. We were taught "Military Movements," a fancy term for "running." We ran with high knees, we ran sideways, and then we ran fast. TRADOC had formulated what is quite possibly the most natural thing for young men to do.

On the cue, "The verticals!" ("*The verticals!*") the first rank stepped up to the imaginary (and imaginarily straight) line.

"Go!" the entire battery rejoined "*Falcons!*" as the soldiers burst off their mark.

"Front-Leaning Rest Position, MOVE!"

We trod along with high knees, and again the infatuation with straight lines came into play. Some soldiers were going too fast, others too slow, and the line just didn't look good enough. Drill sergeants would frustratingly tell us to speed up, or slow down, as the case demanded, and every private adjusted his speed accordingly, giving the line an undulating feel. It never occurred to the DS X that an order to speed up in the middle might influence a few privates towards extremities to do likewise, triggering calls by DS Y and Z to slow down.

Our sideways running began with the bark, "The laterals," on which we would face the instructor, sound off with "*Falcons*!" and move sideways amidst painful cries that we weren't in unison.

It was on the third of the Military Movements that drill sergeants actually may have had fun. The Shuttle Sprint was a chance for guys to run as fast as they could to the opposite side (designated by two cones,) and then again to the other side. Drill sergeants had reputations to uphold, and as the leaders of the exercise, they were obliged to run in line with the rest of us. The first sergeant even ran.

I may have been the wisest person there, comfortable to admit to myself that I wasn't the fleetest of foot. Some of the NCOs weren't as secure, and came quite close to pulling a hammy trying to show up the trainees. Our PT regimen was rounded out with a pull up routine, which we did once a week on a set of bars near our PT field.

Nothing seems more elemental to the Basic Training experience as physical fitness training, and nothing was. Whether punishment or prescription, the opportunities to become fit were greater than I had ever experienced in my life. It was often hellish, and always exhausting.

More tiring training lay ahead of us far away from the relative comfort of our PT field and the Starship.

WEEK 5

"We Are Heading to The Range"

I LAY ON a hot concrete slab, perfectly still. My uniform at that moment included full body armor, helmet, knee and elbow pads, though I had foregone the goggles that were obstructing my view. Ahead of me was a field that would soon be populated by plastic silhouettes, appearing, then disappearing seconds later. My rifle was trained on the spot where the first target was likely to appear.

The NCOs seemed relieved to have the Combat Life Saver course behind us. Partly, no doubt, it was because they weren't experts in CLS themselves. Mostly, however, fulfilling the new CLS requirement meant that they could begin training us for the mother of all Initial Entry Training components: Basic Rifle Marksmanship, which had begun in earnest at the beginning of week four.

The grueling two-week regimen called BRM was a drill sergeant's chance to prove his mettle to lowly privates. I knew the feeling well as a teacher—it was always exciting to get my hands dirty with the challenging tasks that I'd assign my students in my classroom back home. Though the guys in the brown rounds would scoff at the comparison, showing off on a complicated math problem may have

"We're Heading to The Range"

fulfilled the same spirit of adventure for me as firing the weapons that define American soldiers did for them.

For DS Robertson especially, it was an opportunity to shame us with his awesome infantryman skills. He, and many other drill sergeants, already liked to demonstrate how highspeed they were by toting their deluxe rucksacks, designer boots, and slick shades on the way to the range. Superiorly outfitted, they were ready to outperform us in shooting.

Basic Rifle Marksmanship sets the minimum standard by which all U.S Army soldiers need to shoot in order to lay claim to any aptitude for warfighting. I was not in the Army to fight, *per se*, so I didn't feel guilty for my inability to hit a target, yet I became easily frustrated when I didn't succeed as quickly as others. It sure wasn't for lack of practice.

Previously, we had rehearsed our shooting stances in the open space near our barracks. Wearing the same gear we had on the firing line, we would kneel and aim our weapons at some imaginary distant target. On our second Saturday at BCT, we had performed the mock fires on our drill pad in various shooting stances. It was a bit relaxing, as we were occupying time that was scheduled for another range, the plan having been altered due to inclement weather. The entire battery formed lines running through different drills, the purpose of which was to become rifle marksmen. Many sins are forgiven if mastery of an M16 is attained. I thought I had a leg up with a portion of common sense exceeding that of most other soldiers. I was woefully surprised that effective aiming and firing of a rifle took much more than intellect.

The mind had something to do with it, though. The keys to good marksmanship were in our *Smartbooks*, which, if memorized and applied, helped the soldier immensely. Four components were involved: Steady position, Aiming, Breath Control, and Trigger Squeeze; simply keeping the principles in mind would better one's shooting. There were also drills that helped us master each element—

posing in the various shooting stances for minutes at a time, for instance.

So on the day that the drill pad was our range, we spent hours perfecting the keys to marksmanship soporifically. The waiting gave me time to think and reflect.

I had often thought that Basic Training was harder for me as compared to my younger peers for several reasons. The teenagers came from a world that talked down to them. Most of them hadn't ever been in positions of authority, so taking orders from NCOs was second-nature. They were also unaccustomed to thinking beyond the moment, so the thought of many long weeks ahead made little impression on them. I, on the other hand, came from a world in which I was the authority, in which people, including subordinates, respected all, and in which adults solved problems through thoughtful, civil discourse. That world had shattered on 31 May, and I was staring at the pieces during these dull moments.

I attempted to share my misgivings with DS Jackson, who made himself available during our marksmanship training.

"What's that you wanted to talk to me about, Stowell?"

I stammered along trying to explain how dutiful I intended to be, but how difficult it was to live among teenagers. Then, I told him what had been weighing heavily upon me for the last 24 hours.

"I already missed my wife's birthday, and tomorrow is our first anniversary. We've never really been apart since we've been married..."

"—and now you're in here." Jackson empathized and shared his experience being away from his wife during a deployment to the Balkans in the late 90s. "Tell you what," he said. "Tomorrow when you get phone calls, I'll have you keep time. You be the last one to the phones and you can talk however long you want."

Often, it was during training outdoors that gave NCOs an opportunity to commiserate with the trainees; the trainers were

"We're Heading to The Range"

probably as miserable as we were, for different reasons. I for one, missed home intensely, and felt apprehensive about the unknown, upcoming events. NCOs, on the other hand, knew exactly what was ahead, knowing that it would be long and dreadful.

Before we go delve into BRM completely, one particularly dreadful range awaited us. The East Gas Chamber (E-Gas) was the stuff of legends, and we had to pass into immortality where we went during Week Two. Passage through the gas chamber has been a BCT requirement since as early as 1943, when troops heading overseas got doses of tear gas at a training complex at Camp Blanding, Florida[1]. As then, our objective was to learn how to prepare for and respond to certain chemical attacks, best accomplished by sucking in large volumes of poisonous gas. Painful, personal experience would teach us the consequences of being ill-prepared.

Several classes preceded our outing: cadre with expertise in Nuclear, Biological, and Chemical (NBC) warfare taught [us] the steps to a chemical attack, how to don the protective (pro-) mask, and when to administer an atropine and pralidoxime chloride antidote. It was as easy as stabbing oneself with a four-inch needle in the thigh.

A road march was planned for our transportation to the gas chamber range, but some heavy rains rendered the 5K route impassable by foot, so we hopped on some buses. Once there, the immediate order was to dress in our NBC protective gear, *sans* mask. In small groups we rehearsed the drills as we pressed through the Oklahoma forest in a single file, our protective masks, or "pro-masks," at our hips.

"*Gas! Gas! Gas!*" I heard the shouts before I saw the smoke, and instantly reached my right hand across my body to pull the face protection out of the hip pack on my left. Donning the mask was more complicated than it appeared to be, especially in a

---

[1] Camp Blanding, a National Guard training center in East Florida, was used as an active duty training facility during World War II.

panic. As dutiful flight attendants instruct passengers to put on air masks before helping others, so we got into the pro-masks before passing the word onto others. The muffled sounds eeked through my rubber face.

"Gas! Gas! Gas!"

The time requirement is nine seconds, but with a mere few days practice, I was probably nowhere close to that. At the E-Gas range, I "died" according to our NCOs' diagnosis. They made me finish the other small drills quickly anyway. Disrobing revealed how intense my body heat was inside the NBC gear. I, and all my clothing, was completely soaked with sweat. My leather boots were saturated, appearing as if I had just emerged from a swimming pool. It was a fantastic relief to let the hot air swim over my wet skin.

A battery formation, a briefing, and an hour in the hot sun, and we made our way to the chamber. Two dozen or so at a time we filed into the building, which we discovered was divided into two parts. Now in the antechamber, we walked around the empty room under the direction of DS Jackson, who was wearing a full complement of NBC gear.

The fog in the air obscured my vision only slightly, but the power of the teargas was disproportionate to its pall. Additional wisps of the white haze seeped in through a heaving curtain, the only barrier between us and the other side of the chamber.

Almost immediately the gas began pricking at my neck; I worried. Was it supposed to feel like this? Pricking became stabbing—unbearable, all I could do was tighten my neck and hunch my shoulders, though I knew it wouldn't relieve the pain.

At that moment, DS Jackson ordered us to remove our masks. We knew it was coming, and I assumed it would hurt, but I was wholly unprepared for the absolute pain that I experienced. One breath of the chlorobenzalmalononitrile sent me into a violent convulsion, and after stating my name and rank as directed, I

"We're Heading to The Range"

replaced my mask as quickly as I could, trusting in its protective attributes more than ever. My inability to breathe for a moment either made me forget about the pain on my exposed skin, or some physiological reaction caused my nerves to retreat. Regardless, I was shocked just in time to advance to the actual gas chamber.

I was amazed at how heavy the fumes were, several times the density of those in the antechamber. Several of the cadre were in the room: one female sergeant stoked the container that heated the chlorobenzalmalononitrile, or CS[2]—which is in solid form up to temperatures of 200°F. Hot clouds of the sublimating stuff billowed from the center of the chamber; again we moved clockwise around the room until we lined its perimeter. Situated, we were told to lift our masks and inhale deeply. Noxious fumes filled the void between the plastic face gear and my face. I forgot for a moment what it was to breathe. As I struggled for air, DS Robertson shouted at others to take manly breaths.

"Come on Zaccardi, you better breathe it in!"

The poor guy had already filled his lungs with the vapors, but Robertson hadn't seen it. Meanwhile, another private vomited inside his mask. My eyes watered and my nose ran. I lost sensation and control of my mouth, yet my lungs were wrenched, still reacting wildly to force the gas out. The result was coughing and spitting uncontrollably. Sharp twisting pangs in my sides told me that this stuff was not healthy.

After several seconds of terror, my awareness restored with the pro-mask back in place. Then the order came: we removed our masks completely and did our best to execute the procedure outlined in our brief. The idea was that the soldier nearest the

---

[2] CS is the active ingredient in tear gas, named for two Americans, Ben Corson and Roger Staughton, who discovered it in 1928.

door would lead a train of privates quickly outside. When it came time to execute, panic ruled over self-control and many privates didn't remember at all what to do. Each second worsened the situation, the immense pain in my mouth and lungs combined with the razor-sharp nicks on the skin to drive me mad. In my helplessness I opened my eyes, inviting the gas to burn away at my pupils.

Eventually we made the move out the door where fresh air awaited. Drill sergeants were on the other side to lead us around the side of the building and taunt us. A cameraman captured the scores of privates drooling, crying, and dripping mucus down their faces. We flapped our arms like idiot ducks; drill sergeants told us that doing so would disperse the harmful gas more quickly.

Many said they wanted another run at it—they were lying. I can understand how emboldened they must have felt to successfully pass through the course. For them, their manhood was affirmed by denying that some obviously hurtful experience had no affect on them, or by professing a willingness to subject themselves to repeat it. For my part, I professed honesty. Though proud in a bizarre, masochistic way, I would deny any common sense that I might otherwise lay claim to if I ever agreed to go through the gas chamber again.

Treadwell, CLS, and E-Gas all out of the way, Foxtrot Battery was prepared to focus on the core of warrior training. Having practiced our marksmanship elements at the battery; positioning, aiming, breathing, and trigger squeeze; it was time to see if our practice resulted in accuracy. The Engagement Skills Trainer (EST) gave us the chance.

The object of the exercises at the EST was to first practice zeroing, a process we had rehearsed earlier with our real weapons on the drill pad. At the EST, we assumed the prone position in front of giant screens featuring digital images of earthen ramparts

"We're Heading to The Range"

behind the standard silhouette cardboard targets.

The size and clarity of the projected image was in direct contrast to the obscurity of what we were supposed to do. I just didn't see the big picture of BRM, EST, or the task at hand. To zero, one had to aim at the center mass of the roughly human silhouette. Three strikes within a certain radius would indicate steady position and aim. "Three shots" were the instructions we got, so I gave it three shots.

"Lane 11," the civilian in charge called to me, "you fired three rounds within about two seconds."

Wasn't that the point? I quickly figured out that, no, that was not the point. Instead, I was to fire, relax, reset, and fire again at the same point, but it was never explained to me, and the incident exposed me as a firearm illiterate. My ignorance gave me an opportunity to learn quickly, and on the next iteration, when a new set of privates replaced those who had already accomplished the task, I zeroed the fake weapon on the fake target. I exited the building without fanfare.

It had begun to rain, and lunch chow would be served—another MRE. We were issued our plastic pouches and began to eat. No matter how bad the situation (we were forced to sit in formation on the concrete slab that was fast accumulating muddy water) we stoically kept our bearing. It would have been exceptionally uncomfortable to sit cross-legged without having to worry about the creeping tide attacking our foodstuffs. To ease the awkwardness, we sat back-to-back in such a way that we could lean rearward propping up a battle buddy.

This was too much for Jefferson, who ordered us to refrain. Having offered no explanation as to why we had to sit upright facing the same direction, he left me to conclude that he simply did not want us to be comfortable. This wasn't story-time on the rug in kindergarten. Some of the popular contempt was infecting my attitude toward our platoon drill sergeant.

The last week of June marked our Duty Week. DS Jackson made the announcement curtly Sunday night as if we had grown up with the custom. Jackson arbitrarily decided it should rotate among the squads within our platoon, starting with the third. That was my squad, and the extra duty would divert my energies away from the tasks that I was already assigned. Perhaps he wanted to stretch me further as a test of leadership. It was also a possibility that those tasks were meaningless, a trite gesture more than an indispensable post. More likely, he forgot. At any rate, I was buckling under the pressure and responsibility—losing sleep, losing my composure with other privates, and neglecting some of my self-assigned duties, like writing in my journal and to my wife.

The upside of all this new activity was that time passed more swiftly. By the end of June we were nearly half way through our training, though nobody had any confirmed completion date. I had already written to Esther asking her to pass news my way—she being privy to all sorts of information to which I was not. In fact, the NCOs of Foxtrot made a point to keep us in the dark about most things pertaining to the outside world.

Our Duty Week coincided with our first live shooting range, to which we went on Saturday, 30 June. Third Squad met up with DS Jackson early in the morning, and we loaded the "Duece and Half[3]." The ride was a welcome relief from road marches—the standard method of transportation to any range. Yet someone had to set up the battery equipment before everyone arrived on site, and I was happy enough to do it, especially given that we got a 25-minute nap in the back of that truck.

By motor vehicle, the shooting range was so far because of the water level in the creek beds. A mile away from our barracks

---

[3] a two and a half-ton truck manufactured by AM General, the maker of the High Mobility Multipurpose Wheeled Vehicle (HMMWV), or Humvee.

147 | "We're Heading to The Range"

ran East Cache Creek, whose banks were overwhelmed with rushing muddy water from the month's consistent rainfall. Over it spanned an old railroad trestle, used as a foot bridge, about thirty yards long. Since no vehicles of any sort could pass over it there was a concrete water crossing for the convoys that ran parallel to the bridge. A couple feet of water flowed over it during all of June and the first part of July, so all motorized traffic had to follow a circuitous route that used public roads. Sometimes such water crossings had no alternative bridge for a foot crossing; we relished the opportunities to arrive at ranges, like E-Gas, on buses which also followed lengthy routes.

The firing range was a field enclosed by two parallel ramparts. On one side were the firing platforms, to which led steps up the 15 foot embankment. On top of the embankment, spaced about 10 meters apart were the firing positions. Each lane had an opposite target frame fifty meters away on the facing embankment. We had to haul sandbags to the firing platforms in each lane for soldiers to use in the prone supported firing position. We also had to make sure water coolers were adequately filled, shade tents were erected, and hundreds of magazines properly loaded with the 5.56 mm ball rounds. Jackson charged me with the last task, since it required strict accounting of inventory.

Each magazine was to be loaded with 18 rounds, and we had to make sure that we knew how many rounds were being unpacked, loaded, and fired. I managed a small crew to systematically load new cartridges, unload spent ones, and replace the ammo canisters at each lane between firings. I was the Henry Ford of Foxtrot.

For the duty platoon, the range was a lot of work; for everyone else it meant standing in line. Each firing iteration took 15 minutes. The soldier fired three rounds in an attempt to zero like he had at the EST. Then he and a drill sergeant would march to the far end of the lane and examine the shot placements on the target. Depending on where the rounds hit, adjustments would be made to the rifle sights and the soldier would repeat the process until he had hit three rounds center mass on the silhouette.

With 25 lanes in operation, and 20 soldiers finishing each hour, the prospect of a ten-hour day loomed over us. The weather made it feel longer, with heat intensified by our full battle rattle and mud boots. Warrior tasks, leadership, organization and logistics, and personnel management was on full display at our ammo shack. While I led the ammo detail, privates ran to the lanes to pick up empty magazines and replace them with full ones. This had to be done quickly, before soldiers came back to the platforms to shoot again.

Time was of the essence, but all the immutable laws of the universe were suspended to accommodate Army rank. In the early afternoon, our battalion commander paid a visit, stopping in at the ammo shack to chat with us. I found LTC Pastore to be very genuine and approachable. He asked about life in the barracks and how we like Basic. Conditioned to the interrogation in the style of a drill sergeant, nobody spoke up at first for fear of recrimination. But Pastore lived up to the reputation he established during Week One as congenial. The mood began to thaw, and privates opened up. Commissioned officers were minor celebrities at BCT. Our soldiers began babbling sycophantically, seeking approval.

The tower cut in: "Stand up, walk toward your targets."

I interrupted the toady prattle and ordered the privates assigned to the lanes to move out. LTC Pastore looked at me with a mixture of confusion and disdain and asked "What are you doing, hero?"

Not knowing if he was flattering mocking, I explained that I was in charge of the ammunition detail, fearing what I knew about DS Jackson more than what I didn't know about Pastore. I immediately changed my position.

"We're Heading to The Range"

"Maybe you shouldn't tell them to move out while their battalion commander is talking to them. It's not real courteous, is it?"

"No sir." It's not. I am a knucklehead. And I learned more from your quiet yet firm correction than from a thousand of the drill sergeants' heartless reprimands.

MREs were our lunch on the range, but if we were still out by dinner time, we were in for one of my favorite treats—the Hot A. Meals of the heated variety are a hallmark of the preeminence of humans in the biological order, our conditions at Basic notwithstanding. Whichever platoon was on Duty Week set up the food—brought in from the D-Fac in insulated containers.

On dinner break we lined up in a snake just like at the chow hall and filled our Styrofoam plates with wonderful cafeteria food. The only complaint I ever heard of the Hot A was that it wasn't enough, but the delectability of it more than compensated.

"Stowell," interrupted DS Robertson as I began to dig in. "Make sure all the trash gets into bags around here."

I couldn't escape from responsibility. But I had to return to the ammo detail and zero my own weapon, so I delegated the task to PFC Vadney, who was always ready to help. Though not official, I was acting like a platoon guide, something that seemed more and more like an excuse for the drill sergeants to shift responsibility, work, and stress to junior enlistees. But the stress at this point was still, more or less, equally shared. After a full day of zeroing, we packed up the deuce and a half and headed back to the battery. Thinking that we had worked hard enough to make our drill sergeants proud, Jackson quickly dispelled the misunderstanding.

"Y'all embarrassed us in front of the whole battery!"

Jackson's displeasure was apparent, if its cause a little obscured. He let it be known that we were unworthy of any of his respect for two good reasons. First was our generally lackluster performance on the range. Many of us still hadn't successfully zeroed our rifles, and several privates looked like it was their first time on a shooting range. It probably was, but it was nonetheless an unforgivable betrayal of the preparation we were offered by the sergeants. The second reason was that we had more than one heat casualty. Our NCOs could tolerate inferior performance in our shooting drills, but could not suffer interruptions to training because privates couldn't lift their canteen to their lips. Eighty-seven degrees in complete body armor feels more like 187, and the feeling should have been a cue to everyone to drink water in abundance.

"Finish your canteens," he commanded, as we sat in classroom formation in our bay.

No problem. I knew well that water was the nectar of the wellness gods, and took every opportunity to drink more of it. According to the Army, one quart per hour was required to replace the water lost to sweat and evaporation during hard work and a high heat cat. It was fairly easy to polish off the half empty one-quart canteen that we had been carrying on our pistol belts. Within a minute, there was no water left, proven by the inverted containers hanging over our heads, only a few drops falling to our nearly-bare scalps.

The flip side to the doctrine was that no circumstance necessitated drinking more than one quart in an hour, and doing so put one at risk of water intoxication. DS Jackson didn't let some Army doctrinaire and his risk assessments get in the way of his wily punishment. He had a point to make, after all.

"Go refill 'em. You got two minutes."

We rushed to the latrine, where the six sinks were barely deep enough to accommodate our canteens. When the hard plastic vessels were topped off, we hurried back to classroom formation to show that we complied.

"Drink it all."

"We're Heading to The Range"

Could I believe this? I had faithfully drunk my required amount all day long. So far I had not come near any heat casualty myself. I was forced, with my 53 compatriots, to chug down another quart.

In his diatribe, DS Jackson screamed, "I have only one loyal private," without making eye contact with anyone. He repeated the directive; the third quart went down more painfully than the second, and some privates were unable to do so without vomiting. Doubtless this was more dangerous activity than not drinking water at the range, but someone's anger, already kindled, had to be doused, and copious amounts of water were the only way to do it. We would learn hydration discipline if it took ten quarts each.

"Refill 'em." Three quarts we drank, in the space of about 12 minutes. After we were released to take our bloated selves to bed, one private asked me if I felt guilty. Jackson had succeeded in welling feelings of remorse from many in our platoon, but I didn't feel any such guilt. I knew I was doing my absolute best, assuming that I was the "one loyal private" of whom Jackson spoke. Yet, even his recognition of my effort was no consolation. I had arrived at a point mentally, spiritually, and emotionally that I was doing everything for myself. I had broken free of the need to please.

Almost all of our waking hours over the next week were spent on range or en route thereto. We had Sunday off, but on Monday we headed to a different zeroing range to allow the quarter of the battery that hadn't zeroed on Saturday to do so. This range was quite the same as the previous one, and we got to work immediately.

I was one of the unfortunate souls who hadn't mastered his rifle, yet I approached the task with confidence. Following orders from the control tower, and with another private laid beside me as a coach, I fired off three rounds on command. Then we marched en masse toward the paper target 50 yards away to stand in mud while a drill sergeant approved, or offered advice to correct our grouping.

My first group was unsuccessful, but I had three shots tight, just off center mass. I simply had to adjust my sight post to get the shot group where it was supposed to be. On my next attempt I overcorrected, and made the necessary adjustments. On the third try I fired two shots center mass and one errant. This would be an easy fix.

Another try, another wayward round.

We had begun at 0900, and by midday the sun was beating down fiercely. Five, six, and seven attempts were made with similar results. Just as it seemed I was on the brink of zeroing, some tiny error in my aim would disqualify the group. I had to successfully group on consecutive tries in order to complete the task, and I was consistently hitting only five of six shots accurately.

By my ninth attempt, I think I reached that point of frustration that one of my students must have felt for not being able to solve a math problem that everyone else in the class appeared to have grasped easily. This wasn't sniper school, it was *Basic* Rifle Marksmanship. The analogy works if the student was a ninth-grader and the problem on a fourth-grade level.

The black steel of my M16 burned my hands every time I picked it up to aim. DS Rodriguez empathetically suggested that I take a break and relax for a bit. I was anxious, but I did take a couple off iterations offs. By 1400 I had resumed and made three tight shots at center mass of the human silhouette on the target. I was confident about my chances, and Rodriguez encouraged me. "Two more shots right there and you're done."

On the next iteration I hit those two shots, and waited proudly for Rodriguez to send me off with a "Go." The gods conspired against me—DS Lanka appeared and, having no idea of the assurances Rodriguez had made, sent me back to the firing line. I

153 | "We're Heading to The Range"

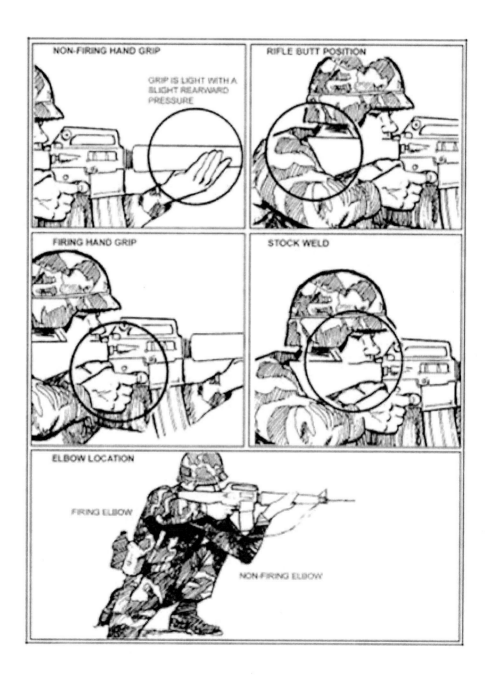

was out of place to tell him what progress I had made.

Utterly defeated, I renewed my futile attempts to zero. Several tries later I was given a "go," simply for firing so many shots. My target was riddled with bullet holes, but I was socially-promoted, as it were. The teachers just got tired of dealing with me. By then it was dinner time, and Hot As hit the spot left void by seven hours in the hot sun with no lunch.

From the zeroing range we marched a mile to the FOB. At the mock "Forward Operations Base," we experienced what life is like during an active deployment to a combat zone. That is, a combat zone thirty years ago, say, in Vietnam.

It seemed everything at Fort Sill was built with jungle warfare in mind, and only recently (and hastily) adapted to a desert operations. So it was with the FOB, where dozens of green tents formed rows along the edge of a dense, deciduous forest.

Living at the FOB had a list of advantages. One was that we were afforded more time to relax and connect with one another. The second was that there was no cleaning involved. It was a short list.

Among the drawbacks to staying at the FOB were having to operate in insufficient light, an absence of decent restroom facilities, uncomfortable bedding, and lack of showers. Tapp and I improvised by undressing completely, save our flip flops, and pouring canteen water over our soiled body parts under cover of darkness. The cool water was jarringly refreshing, and with a little soap we were fresher and cleaner than any other soldier in the battery. Another trick that I employed to compensate for the Spartan hygiene accommodations was the fungal powder issued to us on day one. A little of that in places where the sun didn't shine—who needed a shower?

Fireguard was still a requirement at the FOB, and I had to delegate authority to a soldier in each of our three tents to ensure it was handled. DS Jackson had given me a walkie-talkie so that he could keep tabs. The communication was one way—I could never understand a single word that man said over the radio.

FOB life did not exempt us from the daily PT routine, made all the worse given our austere environment. At wake up, we shaved, brushed teeth, and dressed in our "combatives" uniform. I led the platoon in a march to an open field of weeds and brush to lay down our PT mats—the same ones many of us were sleeping on only minutes before. PT at the FOB was awful. The insects were infinitely more abundant, and the grass many times wetter. We bore the routine with a soldierly stoicism, and ate an MRE before packing up and stepping off to the next range.

Such was life during the heady days of Week Five. Having zeroed, we worked our way toward the ultimate goal of qualifying on pop-up targets with more Engagement Skills Training, followed by a trip to a live range.

The live range gave us the opportunity to see the targets pop up in sequence—at 50, 100, 150, 250 and 300 yards. Forty silhouettes would spring up one at a time every few seconds. A computer display indicated the number of hits. After exiting the secure section of the range, which was enclosed in a chain-link fence, we had to go through a "shakedown."

I "shotgunned" my rifle according to protocol, removing parts in such a way that the buttstock pointed downward against my chest, and the barrel of the rifle was bent backward over my shoulder, exposed for a drill sergeant to look through it. The sooty removed parts in my left hand were proof that I held an unloaded weapon.

"Drill sergeant. No brass, no ammo, drill sergeant! Wolfpack for life, drill sergeant; Wolfpack for life! Woop-woop!"

I shouted the phrase just like everyone else as the drill sergeant frisked me and rummaged through my belongings, which were ample, looking for loose brass. It was one part safety precaution and two parts opportunity for NCOs to rough us up.

On the range one afternoon, I roughed myself up. A little too eager to get things done, I was loading a steel rifle rack into the back of a truck, when the rack got caught on a lip in the bed liner. I pushed it in with all my might, not having removed my right index finger quickly enough, and all 70 pounds plus the force of my thrust collided with my poor digit. At the risk of sounding melodramatic, I couldn't believe that so much pain could be packed into such a tiny extremity. Within hours, my blackened finger began to swell. That night I couldn't sleep for the pain. It wasn't until a chronically-ill private shared some of his freely-acquired pain medication that I was able to get some shut-eye.

After more outings to EST and another practice range, we were as prepared as we could have hoped for our official qualification on Friday, 7 July. I liked my chances due to my high score relative to other privates in the platoon.

The scenario was this: a private would enter the range with an unloaded weapon, which a drill sergeant lubricated and cleared. Moving to an available lane, the private would wait his turn, seated below the platform. On command, a line of soldiers approached their respective platforms in unison, fully equipped; magazines loaded with 20 rounds apiece had been laid out ahead of time by a detail. Facing the targets, the privates assumed the prone position awaiting instructions from the control tower.

"Pick up your first 20-round magazine."

"Lock and load."

"Fire when ready."

Targets appeared and the rounds from 30-some-odd lanes split the air with endless cracks. Besides adequate skills, the task required some strategic planning. We discovered, with some innuendo from DS Jackson, that it was easy to recover the loose unspent rounds from previous iterations and load them into our magazines, which had capacity for 30 rounds, all before the voice from the tower told us to fire. Employing this stratagem to its

157 | "We're Heading to The Range"

extreme, one could pilfer all the rounds from a full magazine—stored in the ammo can near the platform—and load ten rounds into each magazine. It was possible, as I proved, to fire off 60 rounds, instead of the prescribed 40, during a single heat. "You ain't cheating you ain't trying," Jackson would say.

On my first iteration I scored 22—one shy of the requirement to pass. I was devastated. On each of my three subsequent attempts I cheated more and performed worse. After the fourth failure I formed up with the others who had yet to qualify.

By then we were about 35 who hadn't hit the requisite 23 targets, and DS Orozco took it upon himself to remind us of our incompetence: "You're not going to graduate! If you had just done as drill sergeant said...but no! You wanna do your own thing! We told you exactly what to do! Some of you will say that you're just not skilled at shooting...bullshit! All you had to do was what we told you. We gave you time to practice, but it's your own fault. You're a bunch of sad, sorry privates who can't follow instructions. We'll just have to recycle you!"

Jefferson asked me if I had qualified yet. Though not embarrassed, I also didn't want to disappoint. "You know you can't be APG, Stowell, if you don't qualify."

Yeah, I knew. I took a break and regrouped on the bleachers where everyone waited, pondering my task. Marksmanship was a holy sacrament in this insane cult, and I was an apostate until I could hit the targets 23 times.

I cried.

I thought about my wife.

I contemplated my injured finger, now barely small enough to fit in the trigger guard.

After three more unsuccessful attempts, I was among the poorest marksmen in the Army. If soldiering had everything to do with aim, our enemies had nothing to fear from me. For my pride, and for America's wartime success, I turned to God, reading a passage from my Mormon scripture:

> "And if men come unto me I will show unto them their weakness. I give unto men weakness that they may be humble; and my grace is sufficient for all men that humble themselves before me; for if they humble themselves before me, and have faith in me, then will I make weak things become strong unto them.

Weakness, in my case, was terrible aim. But the verse gave me some insight: faith could be a valuable tactical tool. I had no facility with weapons, and all that I was required to do had to be taken on faith—faith in those who had instructed me. DS Orozco was correct, in at least one respect. I just had to do what the drill sergeants had taught me. Forget trying to outsmart the system. Forget the cheating and the extra rounds. I was sufficiently humbled (humiliated, more appropriately), and it was time to just do it without thought or reliance on my own wits.

My first order of business was to abandon the goggles that the Army insisted I wear. They were the ones that fogged up at the first drop of sweat. I foreswore any extra rounds lying on the ground, and I fired at the targets as they appeared. Though my finger had been throbbing in agony during the previous iterations, I blocked the pain. I was sure and true, the clarity of my task was absolute.

The moments before DS Martinez announced to our line our scores seemed more of a formality to me. I exceeded the minimum passing score easily, and the nightmarish ordeal was over.

It was such a relief to have earned a marksman's rating that first day. We had several soldiers in our platoon, two dozen or so in the battery, who hadn't. They spent the next day on a similar range. Meanwhile we went EST to begin the next exercise.

One private, the ever-sleepy Hamblin, never did meet the minimum 23 shots to pass; this despite the claims from drill sergeants that they laid in nearby lanes firing at the pop-ups in his behalf. Sounded like an indictment against their own marksman skills, but he was the one who hadn't fulfilled the requirement. More insults and condemnation were heaped upon him.

The range was our home for many more days and nights in the weeks to come, for Advanced Rifle Marksmanship, conditioning, additional weapons training, land navigation, urban warfare, and grenades. Ironically, the more time I spent in the field, and on the range, the more I regarded our barracks as home.

A comfortable night's sleep was a rare thing, as the range made painfully aware. After nearly three weeks training on ranges, the only thing we had to look forward to were many weeks more.

One particularly memorable range was conveniently located some five kilometers away, but we were able to find a 10-kilometer route. A road march of that length was exhausting. As per usual, we stepped off early in the morning to avoid midday's oppressive heat. The humidity, however, seemed to compensate, and ten minutes in to it, I seemed to be soaking with sweat.

Long marches necessitated breaks for rest and water, and drill sergeants justified the brief breaks by calling an ambush. At the signal we dropped to the prone position and aimed our rifles to the perimeter of our formation, which would often be strung out a mile or more. Thus the respites, which often became power naps, also gave the laggers time to catch up and reform.

It was a fact of the foot-march that some soldiers couldn't keep up. The rule of thumb was to keep five meters' distance between you and the soldier to your front, but again the laws of fluid dynamics were against us, and the giant slinky undulated down the road. With my long legs, I always did pretty well to keep in line, but some just couldn't manage, and more capable or motivated privates behind them would pass them by. Eventually, a group of lame and tired soldiers accumulated in the back, some of them totally unable to continue. They were invariably scooped up by a troop transport and deposited safely at our destination.

The grenade range was bicameral. On one side of the road the range cadre gave us the classes about the four types of grenades: M18 and M83 smoke grenades, for signal and concealment; ABC M7A2 CS (Teargas) Grenades for riot control; AN-M14 TH Incendiary Grenades for destroying equipment and starting fires; and the M67 Fragmentation Grenades to kill. On the other side of the road we used the weaponry. In practice lanes, we heaved empty grenades and detonators. Drill sergeants heaved the "lookers" onto the ground. We were instructed to toss, then immediately drop behind a wall in a kneeling position to avoid flying shrapnel. The NCOs were more than happy to assist anyone who showed any reluctance to descend.

Marching up to the back side of a hefty hill, we went to throw on the live range. It was exhilarating to hear and feel the quaking of the ground when the grenades exploded. While one soldier at a time assumed his position at the lane, the rest of us waited in a bunker, where earth and rust rained down after each explosion.

On my turn, I walked around a side of the hill that provided natural protection to the soldiers in wait. It was a gloomy day, and the smell of gunpowder and dirt lingered from so many explosions before me. Just as I had carried two glasses of beverage clasped tightly against my chest for every meal, I held the grenades next to my body armor and deliberately stepped into place surrounded by three shoulder-high concrete walls. An NCO inspected my every move.

Following his commands I gave him one of the grenades, and held the other in my right hand.

"Remove the safety clip."

At that moment, a live explosive device, capable of killing and mutilating both soldiers in the pit, was in my hand. It was nerve-racking and exhilarating.

"Prepare to throw."

In a word, awesome.

"Throw."

I hurled the device and crouched down. The earth shook around me, shrapnel flew in all directions. As I stood up after the detonation, dust, dirt, and smoke were still settling. In the distance I saw the wounds in the soil, the ground gutted from so much ordnance. I repeated the procedure for the second grenade with as much pleasure as the first. As much death, destruction, mayhem, and misery as they cause, the weapons of Army Basic Training were a delight. Throwing grenades was no exception.

Our life on the ranges of Fort Sill had their good moments.

"A Master's Degree in Moronism"

WEEK 6

THE LAST SOLDIERS in the battery trickled out of the chow hall, while the rest of us found our weapons. We carried our M16s almost everywhere—except to the D-Fac. While we ate, two soldiers from each platoon had to stay outside and guard the weapons left behind in neatly stacked teepees. I had found mine, and held it in an unauthorized position while I adjusted my headgear. It just so happens that the length of an M16 from buttstock to muzzle is such that, if I were to place it end down on the ground, the tip of the barrel would fit snugly in my crotch.

DS Eppinghaus traipsed toward me. "Specialist, do you like to fuck?!" He said it loud enough for the entire battery to hear.

Several synapses fired. I knew he was talking to me, the only specialist around, but what the hell kind of a question was that? I realized just in time, and gave the only good answer.

"Yes, drill sergeant!" I quickly removed the rifle from the offending situation, having taken his hint.

It wasn't enough. Once wound up, Eppinghaus had to play it out.

163 | "A Master's Degree in Moronism"

"Do you like to beat guts? Do you like bumpin' uglies? Making love? Having sex?" I wasn't sure if he wanted responses to all of his questions, and at this point I was more than a little annoyed that he was using my penis's potential to make a point, namely: "don't point your weapon at your dick!"

I never knew I was such an idiot. I was probably the best-educated man in the entire battalion, as measured in degrees. Mine was an M.A. The only other one I ever heard mentioned was that of LTC Pastore, a self-reference. Most everyone else in our unit was either pre-collegiate, with the rare four-year degree sprinkled in among a couple of trainees and a few drill sergeants.

I was under no illusions that my master's degree would spare me any of the mental distress or physical toil, but I had hoped that it would make known my sincerest desire to serve for duty's sake. DS Jackson had sought out the services of my intellect early on when he had designated me as House Mouse; my duties were significant, but not intellectually challenging. For example, during our weekly bedding turn-in I had to ensure that the proper number of soiled sheets was turned in, and that the correct amount of clean linen was passed back out to the privates. Somehow, I could never get it right, though, sheets were like the missing sock in a dryer.

Jackson clearly trusted me, though, and I him. My relationship with DS Robertson, on the other hand was more complicated. The youngest of the drill sergeants in Foxtrot, Robertson struck me from the beginning as a straightforward soldier concerned above all else with propriety and decorum. He was obsessed with neatness and order, always cleanly shaven and perfectly primped. He demanded the same elegance and precision from his troops.

"Did you shave this morning, private?" He asked of at least one of us daily, usually PVT Volpe, who always answered in the affirmative. Though Volpe put razor to cheek faithfully, he never removed enough whiskers to keep the drill sergeant off his case.

Volpe even had a hard time convincing the rest of us, as many of us would lean in for a closer look at what was gaining so much attention from DS Robertson. "Do you know how to shave?" was the collective rhetorical question.

I got asked the question the day after we had spent the night at the FOB, but knew that, in the Army, ninth-tenths of being correct is confidence.

"Yes, I did, drill sergeant," I replied.

"Oh yeah? What did you shave with, Stowell?"

"Canteen water and a razor blade—no mirror, and in the dark, drill sergeant," as confident as could be.

My answer exemplified my manner toward him. Robertson wanted us to think he was cool. He had the fact that he *was* cool working in his favor, and the younger soldiers in our platoon were awed, so Robertson got along just fine. The rebel in me approached him differently. I was not in awe, though I did recognize his discipline and humorous way of teaching us. I rendered him his due respect on a different level. He could tell that I wasn't as impressed with his ribald frat-boy persona. Once, when he was briefing me in the office, he sneezed. The result was no less than five inches of snot hanging from his nose. With a look of pride (that he could blow such a string of mucus), and embarrassment (that the string was not longer) he asked, rhetorically, "Is that gross?" Without waiting for an answer, he rationalized, "I *am* human. Superhuman, maybe, but…"

He could tell by my response that I wasn't amused. After that, he didn't try to win me over with tales of alpha-male heroism on the latest X-Box war games. Instead, he addressed me as more of a peer, or as close to a peer as a drill sergeant and a trainee could possibly be. One afternoon, as I stood in line for the barber, eyes straight ahead, he asked me, "What is your MOS again, Stowell?"

"46 Romeo, drill sergeant," referring to my broadcast journalist job contract.

"What the fuck? Why didn't you do something cool, like infantry?"

"My wife wouldn't have let me join if I chose a job like that."

"Your wife's got you by the fucking balls."

"And I'm quite comfortable, drill sergeant."

I then dared to ask him how his wife liked being married to an infantryman. His response betrayed his apathy about how his marriage figured in to his career. Then, when I asked him how he liked his Army MOS, he replied, "11 Bravo[1] is cool normally, but this," he said, referring to his current assignment, "this shit's for the fucking birds."

His calling as a drill sergeant was bittersweet. He likes the status and prestige of wearing the drill sergeant's medallion on his chest, which all drill sergeants, active or not, wear as part of their uniform. He hated, however, dealing with privates. I think in some respect I was the anti-private—not so green, not so immature, not so frightened, and not so eager-to-please.

Robertson also had a sophomoric sense of humor, one that I admired, for it was reminiscent of how I dealt with my high school students, only with infinitely more cuss words. He frequently referenced my civilian career in jesting admiration.

"Were you teaching in 2001?" he asked, gauging how our timelines fit reminiscently. I wasn't, by the way.

"You know, I oughta kick your ass, just because you're a teacher. I would love to have kicked my high school math teacher's ass."

He belittled my college experience as much as my profession. In formation at the chow hall, he bellowed a command that required no response. I gave a hearty one anyway.

---

[1] Every MOS in the Army has an alpha-numeric designator. 11B (bravo, using the Army's phonetic alphabet, is the infantryman. Thirteen series (13-F, 13-B...) is artillery, and 46 series is public affairs.

"Aren't you supposed to have a master's degree, Stowell?"

"Yes, drill sergeant!" I said hesitatingly, knowing it would only invite an insult.

Pause.

"Yeah, a masters degree in *moronism*!"

That was his position, not having developed much of an appreciation of intellectual achievements. I lived up to the billing quite well, too, managing to act the moron more than my share, and not just in front of Robertson.

My accession to the position of platoon guide seemed a foregone conclusion. Since the beginning it seemed that I would eventually hold that title and bear that responsibility, by both Jackson and Robertson in the early part of June, then by Jefferson when he arrived.

DS Jackson had put me in charge of just about everything in the platoon, from fireguard to linens, and everything in between, including mail. Acting as courier for outbound letters seemed an uninteresting task, but it drew the envy of everyone. Privates were to deliver their mail to me by 0500 every morning, so that I could take them to the US Mail box some 200 meters away from our starship. It was a welcomed routine that got me out of the barracks, if only for a few moments.

The phone call that we were awarded at the beginning of Week Two was under my supervision, and I discovered quickly the obligations that come with such responsibilities. Privates took opportunities trying to get extra phone calls and extra minutes. I sympathized with the yearning to talk to family after weeks of living among perfect strangers. The stimulation of so many motivated men and boys, operating on high levels of testosterone (sometimes acting to compensate for a lack thereof) was contrasted by the monotony that was an inevitable byproduct of the narrow demographic of Basic trainees. After

167 | "A Master's Degree in Moronism"

all, despite representing many regions of the country, myriad religious backgrounds, infinite family circumstances, and just as many reasons for joining the Army, the reality was that we embodied a relatively narrow slice of American life. Moreover, all the relationships were roughly the same; that is to say, we had intense peer relationships, and not much else. The drill sergeant-trainee relationship was shallow and lopsided. All this is to say that the desire to talk to family and friends, to cultivate the rich relationships that we had spent a lifetime to develop, was indescribable against the monotony and sometimes misery of BCT. When I was in charge I mercifully gave them their precious extra minutes.

Because he had placed faith in me, I did not want to disappoint DS Jackson. I didn't hope to please him for its own sake. Rather, I genuinely respected the man. I was also determined to get through Basic as painlessly as possible, and I had a natural inclination to follow rules and expectations diligently —if it happened to be in full view of the drill sergeants, so it was.

Another duty I had was that of janitor—the man with the keys. The most important key to our platoon was to our "day room," a venerable treasure trove of goodies, principle among which was highly-coveted toilet paper. At the beginning of Basic we were instructed on the proper management of the prized commodity: keep track of your own roll. When you need a new one, you must exchange the old tube.

As bearer of the key, I was master of the TP. I strictly enforced the empty tube turn-in policy, to many privates' chagrin.

"Please," they would beg me.

"Go find an empty roll, and I'll give you a new one." They were easy enough to find—soldiers who were fresh out of mom's house where toilet paper was free, were often careless.

There were also MREs and powdered Gatorade in the day

room. We didn't care much about the former, since we ate them all the time on the range. The latter was quite a temptation, but the threat of a serious consequence kept it safe. I made a habit, however, of keeping a foil pouch of the thirst aid in my locker and rucksack, for official reasons. Robertson had asked me how many ounces were in a gallon. I feigned a knowledgeable answer, mumbling some quick calculation to add to the air of authority. He wanted to know so that he could fill his Bubba Keg with yummy Gatorade.

"This is your task now, Stowell. Every morning, before we step off, you need to make sure that my Bubba Keg is full of Gatorade," he insisted. "Not too sweet, and not too watered down. I don't care how you do it…do your mathematical measurement or whatever, but it better taste perfect."

I ripped open the first pouch and headily dumped half of the powder into the ice water that nearly filled his container. He looked at me with deep concern.

"How do you know that's right?"

"It'll taste wonderfully," I assured him.

He never complained.

On the evening of 2 July, Robertson addressed the platoon and confirmed a rumor that had been going around for several days. There was to be an Independence Day concert, the details of which were expounded upon no more than to say it would be $20. Apparently, our brigade command wanted all privates to participate in the Fourth of July celebration.

"Now, I know you don't want to go to this concert. Nobody from the other platoons is going, and you don't want to go. So let me ask you a question," he asked with nerve. "Who wants to go to the concert?"

At least 20 privates raised their hands. Robertson hadn't made himself clear.

"A Master's Degree in Moronism"

"I don't think you understand," He might as well have waved his hand acknowledging his Jedi powers. "*You don't want to go.* This concert is a waste of time. You do not want to go, I know it. Now, who really wants to go?"

Again the 20 – 25 privates.

It was at least half the platoon that ended up going. The rest of us "loyal privates" were rewarded with extra cleaning, a little down time, and a short call home.

It was Jefferson who was in charge on the Fourth. After nearly three weeks with us, he still managed to keep himself elusive. Nobody really got to know him, not even I, despite the hours I would spend with him as House Rat (he would never dignify Snider or me as a "mouse"). The job had many benefits under Jackson's reign, mostly grief with Jefferson. Snider and I would report when called, usually without the right answers. On one occasion, we sat at his feet on the office floor, presumably to organize paperwork. Robertson and his superior sat at their respective chairs watching the one and only Rachel Ray.

"Drill sergeant's a fucking chef," Jefferson declared.

It sounded amusing to me, so I let out a complimentary chuckle.

"That's not supposed to be funny!" he proclaimed angrily. "I can't tell you a goddamned thing!" He feigned disappointment that we acted the swine not worthy of the pearls he cast before us. We'd just as soon he remain quite anyway, so that we wouldn't have to walk on verbal eggshells every time we had to formulate a response.

During our BRM training week, all the other platoons had platoon guides (PG), assistant platoon guides (APG), and squad leaders. Earlier in the week, DS Jackson asked me who would make for effective squad leaders, to which I gave my opinion. It was on the morning of 5 July that he finally handed the reins of responsibility over to me officially.

My tenure began in the chow line, when Jackson announced somewhat matter-of-factly that I was PG, and Slater was APG. The four squad leaders were named, Zaccardi was among them as I had recommended. We were "leadership," which meant that we would be getting smoked on behalf of the entire platoon. We wouldn't last very long anyway in the revolving door that Robertson, Jackson, and Jefferson spun with malicious delight.

My appointment to the office of Platoon Guide, ended up being no more than a nomination. That very day, Jackson called us over to relay us an instruction. Jefferson was there with him and gave us a quizzical look. He matched the look with a question to his colleague.

"Who's this?"

"This is the PG and APG," replied DS Jackson.

"No, fuck that. Sanchez is PG, and you APG," he said nodding toward me. Slater was out.

Jefferson had been impressed with Sanchez ever since he stood up to the drill sergeant the week before. Our platoon drill sergeant was angry with us after a member of Second Platoon turned in Sanchez' weapon. Following protocol, Sanchez had left it with all the other weapons, in our laundry room during a meal. When he couldn't find it in the stack, he reported it to me. I reported it to DS Jackson. Our best guess was that our battle buddies in the other platoon were trying to screw us over. It worked. DS Jones appeared in our bay one night and presented the firearm to Jefferson. Very calmly, Jefferson asked Sanchez why he had left it in the stairwell, where Jones said his soldiers had found it.

"I left it in the laundry room with the other weapons, drill sergeant," said the 4-foot-11, 18-year-old, one-time delinquent, Sanchez.

Jones' stood while his credibility was challenged by a trainee.

"A Master's Degree in Moronism"

"No, you left it in the stairwell," came Jefferson to his defense. "Now why did you do that?"

Sanchez, planted firmly in the position of parade rest, stood his ground. "I didn't, drill sergeant. I put it in the laundry room."

Forgetting that all parties could be telling the truth, Jefferson was nevertheless losing his patience. Here this private dared to give his own side of the story rather than the drill sergeant's. We were all frozen, waiting to see what would happen.

"You're a fucking liar, private. You left your weapon in the stairwell." Jefferson said, teeth now clenched and brow furrowed in a mounting rage.

"No I didn't drill sergeant." Sanchez' boldness had crossed all limits previously established. He was clearly out of his place.

Jefferson almost lost it. In a moment of self control, he stepped into his office. Jones stepped up. "He's giving you the right answer, private. All you have to do is say that you left it in the stairwell. He's *telling* you what to say."

Our platoon drill sergeant returned, expected an easy resolution. A final time he asked Sanchez, "Where did you leave your weapon?"

Not having particularly endeared himself to his platoon mates up until that point, Sanchez stood on the threshold of hero status. Could he maintain his poise? I wondered, as I'm sure everyone did, whether this little soldier could muster the bravery to continue to believe himself.

"I left it in the laundry room, drill ser—"

"You little son of a..." Jefferson leapt up like a puma and darted toward his prey. Wolfpack split in two, making ample way for the beast, whom nobody wanted to get near. He bounded over two beds and swooped down upon on his kill. In an instant, Sanchez's collar was in the grip of the huge NCO, who carried him the length of the bay and into the latrine. Sounds of yelling snuck through the door, and we all feared for our comrade. Whatever happened in that bathroom was never mentioned.

PVT Sanchez became a legend that day. Jefferson always referred to him as a "fucking liar," but after the assault he respected him.

It really helped. We moved to the relaxed position more uniformly in a sharper manner, enthusiastically belting "*Snap*!" every time.

Thus began my tenure as assistant platoon guide—serving under Baby Joey Sanchez. I was quite thankful to have been relieved of PG duty. I wrote to my wife on 5 July that "it was a good move and has already taken some pressure off me." Now it was Sanchez's turn to be a dick.

He was given the PG patch to wear on his left shoulder hook and loop tape—a sergeant first class insignia with three pointed stripes, called "chevrons" and two "rockers" underneath. I wore the staff sergeant rank, with only one rocker, and squad leaders got the sergeant's insignia, which comprised just the three chevrons.

Though I was still genuinely intimidated by DS Jefferson, I knew when I had to communicate with him as part of my duties. I was still the Keymaster, and anytime he needed access to the day room, I was on scene. He had me run errands to retrieve new supplies and take inventory of them. He assigned me to lock up the garbage cans each morning, in addition to locking up and turning out the lights.

One morning Jefferson saw me on the drill pad for first call.

"Why weren't you the last one out? Come see me after PT for you counseling statement."

The question was a body blow. It had been several days since we were even in the barracks, and in my determination to be ready for the day's events I hurried out, neglecting my responsibility. Without saying a word, I ran full speed back up the rear stairs and ushered everyone out, locking the door behind me.

"A Master's Degree in Moronism"

The pressures of these mundane duties, when the margin for error was zero, were high. After shouting at me one day in his office for some minor offense, he ordered me on an errand to the CQ. I ran outside with all deliberate speed, pausing on the steps to put on my boots. The hiatus gave my mind and emotions time to gather themselves. I broke down. Could I continue like this? In retrospect, I suppose he was simply trying to teach me a lesson. I wouldn't go so far as to say that he knew what the exact lesson was, but he figured if he could turn up the heat to maximum on me, it would serve in the long run.

Another example was when we were having our platoon photo taken. My master's degree had qualified me to assemble the letters on the sandwich board identifying our unit. Though we were only yards away from our drill pad, I naturally carried my rifle slung over my back.

As I turned to remove the case of letters from the back of the photographer's van, my skyward muzzle came dangerously close to my drill sergeant's face. He made clear that he could have me arrested for assault.

"That's a weapon, right? And you almost hit me with it, right?

Were it not for his beneficence I might have been in the brig that afternoon.

Within a week, Sanchez was fired for not remembering how to salute an officer while under arms. His successor was fired for a different misdemeanor, as was his successor's successor. Fat Walker even got a shot at it, but lasted less than a day. Finally, Slater was promoted. The office of squad leader also became a farce—untenable positions of musical chairs. Drill sergeants could contrive just about any justification for firing a leader within the platoon, and they did. For some reason, I was always spared.

As I directed the cleaning of the day room one afternoon, I overheard Jefferson ask Robertson, "How come Stowell been APG so long?" as if to say that two weeks was much too long for any private's sense of humility.

"Smart," was the reply. I was definitely appreciative of the remark, but a little unsure about how my intelligence kept the APG chevrons on my shoulder. I can only surmise that all of our NCOs wanted to send the message that they were most definitely in charge, and that trainee leadership was insignificant and therefore interchangeable. On the other hand, they hedged their bets by leaving me in the mix, to ensure that some order was maintained, relieving themselves of unnecessary headaches.

As leaders, much of the responsibility for motivating and disciplining the platoon fell to us. On the range, we had to keep soldiers awake and alert. In formation, we had to keep privates quite and still. Everywhere we went, we needed to make sure that everyone was accounted for at all times. The motivational speeches fell to us, and "leadership" took on a frustratingly mean tone. In class formations or on the bleachers, each student leader did his soldier best to get top performance out of the privates. With drill sergeants as our only examples, the favorite tools were shame and condescension.

On 12 July we marched several kilometers to SPOT-C, another weapons range. Standing in line for 30 minutes at a time earned one a chance to engage in reflexive fire. On my turn I walked toward the target, rifle at the ready. A drill sergeant gave a command and—"Bang! Bang!" Three imaginary rounds sliced the air toward our targets. After the dry line, we fired reflexively with blank rounds. Tat! Tat! Tat! Then it was to the live line, where, you guessed it, we shot 5.56 rounds at targets while we crept toward them deliberately.

The temperature exceeded 90 degrees again, meals and rest time felt amazing. Rest, was, however, relative. We still had to set up our own shelter for the night. Not surprisingly, Wolfpack was crowded out of the best real estate for our 20-man tents. We erected it and arranged our cots neatly atop the uneven ground.

"A Master's Degree in Moronism"

After the horizon had completely obscured us, we formed back up for the final phase of the mission—to fire reflexively relying on night vision scopes and lasers. With only two files moving, the entire battery waited in pitch blackness, slowly inching toward the fire line. I suggested to a battle buddy that we just head back to the tent, that nobody would ever know we didn't complete the task. By midnight, that idea was sounding ever more appealing.

At length we arrived at the head of the queue, and we had to grope for the sweaty helmets that had been equipped with the night vision (and worn by 100 other privates). Shooting was exhilarating, though. The Night Optical Device made everything glow eerily green in the luminescent monocular, and the infrared laser sight appeared a bright green light that pointed the direction of the muzzle. On the command, "Fire!" dazzling green tracer rounds burst toward the targets.

After the drill and the shakedown, (No brass, no ammo, drill sergeant!) we looked forward to a long night's sleep, but DS Robertson gave me strict instructions to have everyone up by 0400. We organized the fireguard and caught forty winks. At the appointed hour, I led by example and got my happy ass out into the wilderness to conduct my morning rituals. I was ready to go, but our NCOs didn't stir.

I told our tent mates to pack up first, and then they could stand by in the sleeping position. As soon as we reclined, thunder rolled. It made me feel cozy to lie in my sleeping bag, teeth freshly cleaned, knowing that I was ready to go in a moment's notice.

Raindrops began to peck at the tent. The pits and pats made me more tired and comfortable. A drizzle gave way to a torrent, and we were soon in a full-fledged monsoon, sheltered by our canvas home. A full inch and a half fell within two hours, and shortly after 0600 hours, Jefferson's voice called out, "Let's go, Wolfpack! Emergency trans will be here in 15 minutes!"

We emerged from our tent to see the devastation: genuine

rivers flowed through our encampment. Army gear was washing away in the currents before our eyes. Most tents stood in feet of water. It turned out that our location, which we had thought a curse the night before, was the only one not deluged.

The rains were still hammering the area, and soldiers were scrambling to the buses. I can only imagine how chaotic the same scene would have looked if the players were under weapon fire instead of water. Discipline and order were imperative under all circumstances, as I realized then.

Discipline usually meant cleanliness. If the barracks weren't spotless, leadership was pushing. "I'm going to make you into a leader," DS Robertson said to me as I lay in the front-leaning rest at the head of the platoon. I spent nearly every waking hour inspecting and encouraging our platoon members to pull their weight. When a drill sergeant saw that something was wrong—and there always was—I and the other trainee leaders were doing punishing physical exercises. Discipline underpinned leadership.

Leadership had its benefits. It entitled us to call out the cadence, which was fun, and to supervise while waiting in line, which was infinitely less boring than to stand at parade rest. While I was in charge of the platoon element, I usually interacted with soldiers, quizzing them or telling them stories.

I convinced myself that part of my opportunity was to become a better teacher. In my civilian role, I had seen other teachers act as autocratic task-masters who relied on strictness and intimidation in their classrooms. Mine, however, is a style that challenges more conservative practices. By observing my NCOs, I could learn something about leading and teaching, even if they relied on outdated philosophies. Technology, popular culture, and the affluence have greatly affected the generation that I taught, and that was there with me at BCT.

It had also occurred to me that too much may be made of the

177 | "A Master's Degree in Moronism"

generation gap that exists between most of our drill sergeants and their trainees. Armies have been around for a long time, and their training methods are time-tested. Perhaps they serve to bridge the gap between generations, and differences should be ignored for a time. It is certainly not without value to learn in new ways, even if those ways run against the natural grain of the soldiers. What other choice was there?

I was learning a lot myself. Despite my constant introspection and observation, not all the NCOs appreciated my mind. While at the zeroing range, I passed by two NCOs and overheard something quite extraordinary. Drill sergeant Orozco, who was standing near the first sergeant, asked his superior how I could have gotten to be a specialist.

"College, probably," was the correct reply.

"It's bullshit," retorted Orozco. "Nobody ought to be able to earn past E3 without graduating Basic."

What was *bullshit* was this guy's assumption that a college degree wasn't as challenging as anything the Army had thrown his way, or that it wasn't valuable to the Army's mission. I regret not having said so to his face. This was the same drill sergeant who challenged me in front of the entire battery some time later, during our class on land navigation. We were learning how to read terrain maps and follow azimuths[2] to navigate large areas armed with only a compass, protractor, and coordinates. During a break, Orozco was sufficiently peeved about something, and erupted in a typical display of drill sergeant disgust. To me, he sounded fairly like Miss Othmar. I vaguely understood that he wanted us to raise our hands if we wanted to be here. I thought it was more or less rhetorical, and at any rate, did not want to fuel his egocentric rant, so I kept my hand comfortably on the table. He seized on my

---

[2] An azimuth is a directional line measured as an angle clockwise from north. In map reading, one would find north using a compass, and measure the angle of deviation to the destination using a protractor. With the proper starting point and angle, a line could be drawn on the map and followed to the destination.

inaction and directed the next question directly to me.

"You don't want to be here, private?"

"Not really, drill sergeant."

"Why?"

"I'd—"

"Stand up!"

I stood properly at parade rest. "I'd rather be with my family." It seemed like an answer that nobody could find fault with; though the question was most certainly loaded.

"Why did you sign the dotted line?"

The man had the attention of the entire battery, and the promissory approbation of the drill sergeant cadre, yet the best he could come up with was, "*Why did you sign on the dotted line?*" Had he never heard of such a thing as duty? I thought it was more admirable that I was there even though I'd have rather been *anyplace else*. I knew full well that *he* did not want to be there, so to denigrate me for exhibiting a bit of candor was at best disingenuous.

I approached DS Jackson about the incident later, in his office. As I began to explain that I had answered the way I did—which was honestly—because I thought I was training to be a soldier, not a babysitter. I often felt like the latter.

"Relax," he told me as I got emotional about the subject. "Everyone on the battery knows who the good soldiers are. Don't worry about it."

He seemed to be letting me know that sometimes the other drill sergeants didn't know what the hell they were talking about.

My explanation to DS Robertson was a bit more to the point.

"Because I don't want to be here, drill sergeant," I told him in the middle of a drill.

"Why don't you want to be here?"

"Because I hate living with 53 privates." I missed my wife, and I missed my students. There was so much about Basic Training that was like a cheap imitation of my real life, and I longed for the genuine article. Fourth Platoon was *like* my family, but it *wasn't*. It was simply the closest thing I had, and it was proving disappointingly inadequate.

"OK," he conceded the point." "But you need to find a more diplomatic way of saying it."

"Agreed." Maybe we had more in common than either of us was willing to admit.

One afternoon we went to dinner as a battery, Drill Sergeants Eppinghaus and Belcher in the lead. When the former gave the command to go to parade rest, some of Wolfpack shouted "*Snap*!" having been conditioned by our (much more intimidating) drill sergeant.

Eppinghaus threw a fit, during which I heard him mumble something about the whole battery saying "snap."

Several minutes later, Belcher gave the same command; I belted out loudly and proudly: "SNAP!"

I was the only one. "Uh-ohs" rolled through the formation, and Belcher demanded to know who the idiot was. I forthwith presented myself.

"Go tell DS Eppinghaus," came the order.

I moved ahead of everyone in the battery to the entrance of the chow hall, where he was counting privates. After I entered my plea of "no contest," he ripped the APG patch from my shoulder. Then I went to the head of the line and ate my chow.

It seemed scandalous to everyone in our platoon that a drill sergeant from Third Platoon could fire me. Back at the battery Eppinghaus approached Jackson and gave him the patch, which had been neatly attached to my uniform when we had stepped off. Still outside, Jackson called me up. I ran swiftly up the steps prepared for a lecture on patience and drill sergeants with different styles. Without a word, DS Jackson handed the patch back to me.

One morning I discovered, despite my unusually long shelf life, that I wasn't completely above the law. We were preparing to go to another range, when DS Jackson shouted, "Everyone up front for chow!" We began to eat our cold meals on the balcony just outside the front doors of our barracks. Just as we were finishing up, Jefferson strode into the bay and made a comment about someone's locker being open. Half of the faces in our platoon sunk, mine included.

They called it a "tornado." It was a metaphor for what would happen to the bay when several lockers were left unsecured, in clear violation of the rules. To teach the point, DS Robertson once complained that someone had taken his campaign hat, for it had gone missing. He blustered about, harassing everyone and looking here and there. He finally conducted an inspection and discovered it was in PFC Ritenour's locker. Ritenour was a meek, mild-mannered kid from Texas who would never dream of taking someone else's property, especially a drill sergeant's. He shed tears when Robertson confronted him, pleading for mercy.

In short order Robertson admitted having planted it to illustrate the importance of locking our wall lockers. Now Jefferson would reinforce the lesson. It was only a matter of time before our platoon drill sergeant worked his way back to my locker. I had lost my appetite, and could only wait until we were invited back in to assess the aftermath. They didn't call it a tornado for nothing.

I was stripped of my stripes, as was Slater. Though disappointed at first, I was soon at ease. I don't remember who took our places, because I wasn't thinking about the platoon at that point. I could finally be just another private.

Even when I wasn't in fact APG, Jackson entrusted to me the duties of such. I ran errands, collected information, and relayed questions to our drills. I was also given the order to use "peer

181 | "A Master's Degree in Moronism"

pressure" to help some of our misfits find the value of conformity.

After what could have been construed as an apology for allowing Jefferson to fire Slater and me, Jackson made it clear that he fully expected us to maintain our informal authority in the platoon. We would need to clarify to the others that neither indolence nor insolence would be countenanced. Everyone knew that it wouldn't be by drill seargents, now it needed to be broadcast in no uncertain terms that fellow soldiers wouldn't tolerate it either.

The plan's details were passed around by word of mouth rather secretly. We wanted to keep them among those who were considered completely trustworthy and unflappable in the face of the kind of menacing interrogation seen earlier during BCT. There were eight of us.

At 0130 I was awaken and directed to the latrine, where we convened a strategy session. The excitement was reminiscent of those early morning romps in suburbia to play some malicious prank masquerading as innocent teenage high jinks. There was no such tomfoolery tonight. I was leading a group that was frustrated at the constant punishment inflicted on the many for the sins of a few. DS Jackson had effectively explained what to do and how to do it. We stole through the darkened aisles of the bay toward our victim.

Our target was Rogers—Big Rogers. He just couldn't shut his mouth. We all thought that he probably suffered from some emotional imbalance, but that didn't absolve him of guilt. It was a simple cause and effect relationship; his behavior often caused us misery and embarrassment. Perhaps a more powerful force could effect a change in behavior.

I relieved the fireguard, not telling them exactly what was happening and explaining that they wouldn't want to know come morning. At the agreed upon moment, I killed the few lights that illuminated the desk and front doors, and the action began.

I didn't see what happened next, but I can imagine the panic and frustration that engulfed him when several eerie figures wearing gas masks and enrobed in wool blankets smothered him with fists. One person spoke to him, admonishing that he improve his behavior and attitude.

On attitudes, mine was that Rogers only needed to be aware that there was a significant set of soldiers bold enough to resort to secret violent tactics in the middle of the night. Pain need not be inflicted, and the matter needn't have been unduly prolonged for the message to resonate in his rather thick skull.

Sometime during the next few days DS Jefferson caught wind of what had happened. Rogers, whose grievances had fallen on Jackson's deaf ears, went straight to the platoon drill sergeant.

"Who assaulted PVT Rogers?" demanded our platoon drill sergeant.

We were all standing around our bunks, and Jefferson was losing patience quickly. Finally, Zaccardi stepped forward. Knowing that the drill sergeant knew there were more, more stepped forward. I never did. I justified it partly because I had stood behind the wall. Plausible deniability was the name of my game, call it cowardly if you like. Slater, who was also significantly older than the average private, and I felt an ethical impediment to our participation in the assault of minors. Nevertheless, we also felt duty-bound to our drill sergeant and the well-being of our platoon, so with some reluctance, I had agreed to help plan. Only to plan.

Feeling a little betrayed that our midnight rendezvous was exposed, I approached Jackson and asked him if anything dire would come of those who admitted participation in the affair.

He was surprised to find that Jefferson knew anything about it, proof positive of my suspicions that drill sergeants rarely communicated effectively. Assuring me that nothing would come of it, he called Rogers into his office to have a little chat.

"A Master's Degree in Moronism"

"Why'd you tell platoon sergeant about the code red?"

Yes! He actually said the words, "code red!" I was an enthusiastic fan of the silverscreen classic, *A Few Good Men*, and thrilled to hear a reference to its plot.

Rogers, far from being overjoyed, looked consternated. He fumbled with a few explanatory words about why he felt like Jefferson could help him. He was under the impression that a rogue few were out to get him.

"You know I ordered it, right?"

Dumbstruck replaced consternated. Nothing more had to be said. Rogers knew he was an unmistakable problem in Wolfpack.

If Jackson trusted me to help maintain discipline in the platoon, Robertson mocked my competence. I was coming to realize more assuredly that it was only an act, or a management technique, for he continued to rely on me to conduct routine business. Helping him with some computer task, I showed him a handy shortcut in MS Outlook, to which he replied contemptuously, "I may not have a *masters degree*, but I can read my email!" His insults were a way of acknowledging the fact that I was his intellectual superior.

Somehow, no matter how smart I thought I was, I managed to convince Robertson that I was not. When he fired another set of squad leaders *en masse*, I was among them (having been rehired at the lower position by Jackson after only a few days off). He subjected us to a PT session and went in his office with the bidding that each leader leave his patch in front of the office door.

I was so frustrated that I stopped short of where I could reasonably throw the patch so that it would land appropriately. When he came out, he saw that only three patches were where they should have been, while mine had gone errant in my toss of disgust. I couldn't bring myself to dignify the drill sergeant's outrageous hiring and firing practices. He correctly interpreted it as a form of disrespect.

"You trying to be smart, Stowell?" Knowing where the blurry line gave way to a bolder boundary, I admitted to nothing and said that it must have got brushed aside.

There was a bit of give and take between my drill sergeant and me, though I never forgot who was in charge. In formation one evening, while we were waiting for a few straggling privates, he began to make fun of me in his usual way, going after my strengths.

"You think you're smart?" He asked in front of the whole platoon. "I could kick your ass in anything, Stowell."

Having thought about it for a while, I called his bluff. "We could have a competition, then, drill sergeant," I suggested.

"Oh yeah? What? You name five things that you could beat me in."

"A math competition; Let's see, I ought let you have one, so I'd include a combatives competition. A race—I could beat you in any length of race. A shooting competition (knowing that I would get throttled by an E6 Infantryman); and…you pick the last one."

"A pussy-getting competition. I can get more chicks than you can."

"Don't be so sure about that, drill sergeant," I warned him. "You might be able to get some ugly Lawton girls, but when it comes to quality, smart gets the goods."

We never had that competition.

Towards the end of July, something happened that caused me to rethink my own IQ, and it wasn't playful at all. On a road march back from the FOB, where we had done training on capturing enemy prisoners of war, a loud crack broke the silence near our battery.

My rifle had fired a blank round. More accurately, *I* pulled the trigger when a blank was loaded. My heart sunk just before Robertson demanded accountability.

"A Master's Degree in Moronism"

"Who was that?"

I immediately stepped out of formation and took responsibility. DS Belcher, who was 30 meters ahead, also approached.

"It's OK, Belch," said Robertson. "I got it handled. Then he came close to me, so that nobody could hear. "Why'd you do that, Stowell?"

I was grateful for Robertson's discretion. I had done one of the most idiotic things a Basic Training soldier could dream of doing. Due to an accounting error, I assumed that there was no more ammunition in my weapon. Apparently, another soldier had extra rounds that somehow mingled with my pile. I never checked the chamber, something that was standard operating procedure anytime rounds had been loaded.

I was preparing for the clearing procedure that we completed every time we reentered the battery after using weapons at the range. It really was a matter of safety. Two long lines of trainees formed at the clearing barrels, a sand-filled oil drum, and followed the steps:

Remove the magazine.

Place the weapons on "safe."

Lock the bolt to the rear (which opened the chamber for viewing).

Visually inspect the chamber.

Let the bolt slide go forward.

Place the weapons on "fire."

Pull the trigger

On the road march I was reviewing the steps in my mind and got carried away. Without inspecting the chamber, and my weapon on "fire," I stupidly squeezed the trigger.

I became a legend, not because I was a specialist, or because I had a masters degree. I was now known by everyone in the battery as the jackass who fired off a round during a march.

A perfect display of "moronism," if you will.

WEEK 7

"Win Me A Streamer"

DRILL SERGEANT JACKSON rolled up the flag on our guidon as we stood in formation watching him seethe. He secured it tight as a public display of dissatisfaction. All platoons had guidons: banners attached to the end of a palisade. The guidon was a symbol, since time immemorial, of a unit's unity and willingness to go forward in the face of a challenge. It was an emblem of our honor, which drill sergeants could denigrate with some manipulation of the banner.

Platoons moved through phases at BCT, beginning in Red Phase. Only after demonstrating its ability to accomplish elementary tasks and behave more like soldiers than teenagers would it advance to White Phase, marked by the ceremony in which we formally changed out the red banner to a white one. In Foxtrot, all platoons graduated from Red to White on the day we qualified in BRM, nearly halfway through our training.

Aside from announcing our progress through Basic and leading our marches, the guidon displayed any streamers we had won. Streamers are the notches on drill sergeants' belts, absolving

"Win Me a Streamer"   187

our leaders of any weaknesses in their training abilities. They are simple ribbons attached to the top of the pole, just below the finial, and hung like awards won at a state fair. The more the better. One each was awarded for major components of our training, such as rifle marksmanship.

Another opportunity for a streamer came in Week Six, when we ran the Combat Conditioning Course. The CCC was the Army's obstacle course, and it was the funnest thing we had done in weeks. The course was a quarter mile loop that included a variety of obstacles that would test the fittest among us. After, not surprisingly, a safety briefing, we set out to attack the obstacles as quickly as we could. First was the low wall, which most privates hopped over fairly easily. After negotiating some balancing beams and a higher wall, at a 150-meter mad sprint, we arrived at a cargo net climb to the top of a tower. No time to rest and we were on monkey bars before rounding a corner to head back to the beginning.

We high crawled through a concrete tube and then were sifted through the final major obstacle: a mud pit with a low, barbed-wire ceiling. The final portion was a 100-meter sprint which would weed out the weakest soldiers.

I decided who the weakest were even before we got there. DS Robertson had asked me to help him choose the members of Wolfpack who would represent us in the intra-battery competition, and chance to win the streamer. Eager privates sucked up to me in an attempt to curry favor in the quasi-patronage system. I remained above it, primarily because they had nothing to offer me. We settled on the fastest, strongest, most motivated, and craziest privates to run the gauntlet.

Jefferson was looking desperately for a reason to not hate us quite so much. The morning we stepped off to go to the CCC Range, he had given us the closest thing he could come to a pep talk. After sufficiently motivating us through such techniques as not demeaning us with every breath, his final words to us were, "Now win me a fucking streamer."

It would have got us into the lasting graces of our drill sergeants. Those of us not running the competition cheered on our platoon mates as if our lives depended on it. Realivasquez, fueled by his modest desire to be the best soldier in the history of the United States Army, anchored the team. Most did very well, but one soldier lagged behind, unable to muster the energy to get through the low-crawl. He was spent, and crossed the line seconds behind the winning time.

The streamer eluded us, and we were crestfallen. There were several other opportunities for us to earn the prizes at Foxtrot, the CCC being only one. Additional competitions included High BRM, 1SG Inspection, Drill and Ceremony, and Honor Platoon.

Though our platoon was leading Week Three's BRM competition (scored by counting the number of soldiers who qualified on their first attempt) most of the day, we came up just short of the best. It very well could have been—had I struck one more target my initial time through—that our platoon would have won the first streamer of all. As it turned out, as is always the case with the second-finishers, only we knew how close we had been to glory.

Glory and bragging rights were in store for the victors; disrespect and disgrace for the losers. We had our share of the latter after BRM, and still in White Phase by Week Seven, our guidon was bare, with the appearance of a sock having been pulled over it.

We had Drill and Ceremony in the bag. Wolfpack was the only platoon that had worked on D&C since Week One, having spent precious hours after dinner chow in the parking lot learning basic movements. Other platoons were nowhere in sight in the sunlit evenings of late June and early July. It wasn't until about the

"Win Me a Streamer"

week before that we discovered why. Next to the door of the CQ was a giant whiteboard with the day's schedule posted. For the first few weeks of BCT, nobody paid much attention to it. Then, as we got slightly more relaxed soldiers would roam up close enough to it to make out what it said. We finally realized that our schedule was public information despite what drill sergeants indicated to the contrary. Most of us in Fourth Platoon seemed incredulous that there were items called, "soldier time" and "drill sergeant contact time." The only contact we had with our training NCOs was our dear PT time, and those extra hours of D&C that other platoons never got.

By now, all that time added up to confidence. I was also personally more confident, because of my new assignment. Earlier in the week, DS Jackson walked a lap around our bay, passing me by as I stood near my bunk talking with some privates. After he passed, my comrades pointed out a patch on my shoulder that wasn't there before. I was now a squad leader. So I had served the gamut: from PG down to squad leader, House Mouse and everything in between. My newest calling was as the leader of First Squad, an incredibly important position from the standpoint of drill and ceremony.

That entire week we practiced as we had never practiced before. While the others had soldier time, poor old Wolfpack was on the blacktop rehearsing elementary movements for marching as a platoon: the columns-left and right, about-face, and the counter-column; as well as more advanced moves: left- and right-flanks, and rear march. There were commands regarding how to stand in formation: at close interval, normal interval, and open ranks; as well as a host of movements with our weapons: port arms, order arms, right- and left-shoulder arms, present arms, and the most difficult of all, inspection arms.

When done in unison, the movements were spectacular. Spectacles were rare with us, however, as one or two soldiers always managed to move out of step. DS Robertson sent his hat into the air often in disgust, but we made good progress and our hopes were high as the weekend's competition neared.

Though we couldn't brag about any streamers, our platoon was feared by the rest of the battery for one thing—combatives. Ever since our training on the jujitsu-style fighting, we performed combatives once a week formally, and many more times off the record.

Our morning PT regimen was supplemented every Thursday with combatives. After forming a giant platoon-sized circle and practicing drills with partners, NCOs would call pairs of soldiers to the middle of the ring for a bout. The fights were tiring, but provided us endless entertainment. Drill sergeants would make sure that every private had a chance to engage with someone.

"Come on, grandpa!"

Knowing DS Robertson was talking to me, I feigned excitement and went center circle to meet my foe, Reyes, who made short work of me. I never liked wrestling much, and I wasn't any better at combatives, especially against younger soldiers who looked to the opportunity to beat up a high school teacher, legally, as the chance of a lifetime.

We didn't always fight amongst ourselves, though. As a way to settle inter-platoon feuds or affronts, drill sergeants would arrange a foray between representatives from separate platoons. Fat Walker, who was a self-proclaimed state wrestling champ, had a permanent bit in his mouth to chomp at when combatives was announced. Tapp, too, was a very efficient fighter. Those two, along with Slater, Reyes, and Ray often embarrassed soldiers from the other platoons who insisted on disparaging us.

A combatives bout didn't end until a drill sergeant said it ended. Presumably, that would be when one soldier tapped himself out, admitting defeat. Normally, he could only tap if his life was in peril, such as when he was choking and gasping for

191 "Win Me a Streamer"

air. Effectively, the winner would have to choke out the loser. Jefferson, however, made it very clear that neither tapping nor choking was a signal to stop a round, a rule Jackson and Robertson were more than eager to follow.

"Choke him out!" We followed our drill sergeants' orders, which became the mantra for any fight. The corollary was "he who didn't choke got choked."

One afternoon, Jackson gathered us around the great seal on the floor in the front of the barracks. Floor mats were brought from the dayroom to lay down for a few hours of combatives. He paired up soldiers on the spot and when it came to my turn, I was told to fight PVT Volpe. Now I didn't know if Volpe was any good, but it wasn't worth the risk of testing one's opponent. Rather, wiser was the fighter who overwhelmed his foe as quickly as possible. So I did. The adrenaline rushed through my body as I clawed at Volpe's body parts. I was getting coached from everyone watching, screaming, and eventually I was able to lock him in an insurmountable position. I cinched my elbow around his throat and applied as much pressure as I could. He choked and tapped, but I couldn't let go. Just when I thought I might cause permanent damage, Jackson declared me the winner. We began the second of a two-of-three series, which ended the same way as the first. I had won my first real combatives match.

NCOs watched for the mere sport of it, it was the dog fighting of the Army. More legitimately, it was also a chance to motivate troops and get them to let off steam. Most of all it was an important aspect of hand-to-hand combat. We daily swore an oath to "deploy, engage, and destroy the enemies of the United States of America in close combat." We settled for our battle buddies.

Drill Sergeant Jefferson was an apostle of that attitude. He was so proud of us one morning when several of our privates embarrassed challengers from other platoons, he promised us a trip to Taco Bell. Our morale skyrocketed. If we were fighting dogs,

Taco Bell was our Milkbone.

The epitome of a close combat weapon is the bayonet.

"What is the spirit of the bayonet?"

"To kill! Kill! Kill without mercy!"

The entire battery was formed on the PT field adjacent to our starship. We had been issued bayonets, which were essentially knives to affix to the end of our rifles. Otherwise, they hung in a holster from our pistol belts, and we only attached them once for practice.

"What makes the green grass grow?"

"Blood! Blood! Bright red blood!"

Drill Sergeant Martinez followed a script throughout the training, which highlighted the time-honored offensive thrusting, jabbing, and slashing maneuvers with the bayonet. It also contained Army legend about Lawrence Chamberlain, the Union commander of the 20th Maine, who led a bayonet charge on the second day at the battle of Gettysburg in July, 1863.

LTC Chamberlain, who was also a teacher[1], was tasked with holding the high ground on the far left flank of the Union forces that day. His unit, posted at the base of a hill called Little Round Top, was as important as it was tenuous. Manifesting the value of the hill as the stepping stone to the higher hill to its south, Confederate troops fired on Chamberlain's position relentlessly hoping to gain the high ground where they could place guns to fire down the Union line with impunity.

As his men ran out of ammunition, Chamberlain made the decision to attack with that most elemental of weapons: the blade. Sounding the order, "Fix, BAYONETS!" he led the charge that successfully drove off the attackers. His heroism, tenacity, and courage could very well have saved the Union that day, for

---

[1] Chamberlain taught rhetoric and oratory at his alma mater, Bowdoin College in Brunswick, Maine.

the federal troops held the high ground and forced The Southern generals to make the ill-fated charge at the center of the line that next day, where they met stiff resistance. Gettysburg was the confederate high tide. After the summer of 1863, the Union victories began to mount, and the Confederates' resources dwindled in the face of continued federal strength. Chamberlain has rightly been lifted to hero-status, and his bayonet charge central to his legacy.

"What is the spirit of the bayonet?"

"*To kill! Kill! Kill without mercy!*"

Two-hundred of us stood in our positions on the field, in extended lines a dozen rows deep, plunging and swiping our rifles in unison—a perfectly choreographed display of deathly obedience.

"What makes the green grass grow?"

"*Blood! Blood! Bright red blood!*"

If the spirit of the bayonet was the kill without mercy, I had to ask the question, "Did I have what it took to kill?" Could I abandon all mercy if the moment required? The Army didn't seem interested in employing men who make moral judgments in the middle of a fight. Rather, it needed soldiers who would destroy the enemies against whom the Army is sworn to defend America—at any cost.

To be sure, a certain amount of programming had to occur to breed soldiers capable of the messy business of warfare. But I realized, long before I enlisted in the United States Army, that our contemporary enemies had no mercy for us, and if our soldiers offered any to them, then the fight would be lost before we even had a chance to employ our Basic Combat Training.

I can certainly empathize with those who take a dim view of this line of thinking (I worked in the schools of the San Francisco Bay Area, after all). The other side of the coin, they say, is that violence begets violence, and that it is precisely the attitude of abandoning mercy for one's enemies that create and motivate them. We are feeding the fires of hatred with such indoctrination, they claim.

Perhaps, but the other side of the story is told by the Lawrence Chamberlains of the world, who were and are ready to sacrifice themselves for a higher purpose. I hoped I could grow into a fraction of the stature of those heroes, even if I had to repeat silly warmongering slogans while stabbing the air with the tip of my rifle to do it.

Presumably to practice the various moves we had learned in bayonet training, we next divided into platoons to fight with pugil sticks. More American Gladiator than US Army soldier, battling with the giant Q-tips was fun and draining. Again in a circle formation we sat as DS Jackson invited opponents to center ring. Two by two, we attired ourselves in the football helmet and brandished the sticks. A whistle blow started and ended the match.

A thrust from Ray sent his battle buddy to the ground. PVT Worm took a slash to the side of the head and almost went unconscious. Jackson called me up and the others started to shout out the name, "Umpenhour!" who had dissed me a day earlier. I promised I would kick his ass given the chance and had asked DS Jackson for that chance. Umpenhour it was.

I forgot all about the jabs and thrusts. All I could think about was "to kill without mercy," and made an important discovery: to kill without mercy, I had to stay alive. Yet, the fight was exhausting me faster than I could think to move the sticks into any type of position, offensive or defensive. As they got heavier and heavier, I threw them as hard and as fast as I could toward my enemy. My mind and body were losing energy quickly; the heat was rising, and I could barely stand. One blow from Umpenhour and I would certainly not be able to continue.

After the whistle ended, we were both miraculously upright.

"Win Me a Streamer"

It was exhilarating to use a weapon to beat someone's head as hard as I could. Those primal chants had their effect. Perhaps, of course, I felt freer to pummel another man knowing that it was perfectly safe. On the other hand, the Army tried very hard to turn me, and every other soldier, into a heartless fighter. If it became fun, it was all the easier for them.

According to TRADOC, our battery was supposed to have conducted an inter-platoon pugil tournament. As with so many other things, it never materialized. Thus, another opportunity for a streamer eluded us, and with it a chance to get into the good graces of our drill sergeants.

Though winning streamers was at the forefront of our collective mind, we still had essential training blocks. Midweek we stepped off once again to the FOB where our battery leadership taught us how to deal with enemy prisoners of war (EPOW). Obviously, the Army had had recent public relations disasters in the field of detainee operations, so this training seemed imperative. We were taught by the book, and the book was thick. There were many different roles in this stage play, and the choreography had to be flawless. In the real world it really could have been a matter of life or death. It was a perfect example of how doctrine—derived from lessons learned on the battlefield—composed a script that soldiers needed to master to deliver a rousing performance.

But then the cadre took a more creative view of teaching, which consisted of wildly dramatic scenarios whereby NCOs and our commander alike would toy around with us in scenes of improvisational theater. Only we didn't realize it was improv.

One team was assigned to guard the gate at the FOB; several soldiers stood guard while others were hidden behind barriers and camouflage ready for any type of attack. Our captain and a drill sergeant, dressed up in some makeshift Arab costumes, theatrically approached the vehicular checkpoint.

Whichever soldier was in charge did his best to follow the lesson plan: asking for ID, demanding that the individuals step out of the vehicle, calming down agitated actors. Of course, the actors hammed it up and made it as difficult as possible for those of us at the checkpoint. We followed the script that our teachers had already tossed out entirely. DS Robertson had ordered a group of privates to act as guerrillas—extras, if you will— to hide in the brush and ambush at a given time. There was a mock shootout. Cadre was shouting out lines to the play actors on defense, who had lost all hope of staying within guidelines. Brand new soldiers all, we ran about uncontrollably shouting and countermanding orders, trying to make sense of a scenario that abandoned what we were supposed to have been practicing.

It was messy and chaotic. It was as if we had just wrapped up a seminar on advanced Shakespearian theatrics and concluded it with a critical analysis of *Dumb and Dumber*.

DS Jefferson had promised the trip to Taco Bell, so when he told us he had arranged for us to go with a buddy of his we became giddy schoolgirls. The stranger showed up in the familiar campaign hat and loaded us into a truck. How many privates can you fit in a vehicle? One more.

It was all a cruel tease. This drill sergeant was expecting a new cycle in a few days and we cleaned up *his entire battery*! We were slaves, to be loaned out to other plantations. On the other hand, this was more prized time away from our battery and drill sergeants, so even though it was the same tedious work—dusting, mopping, polishing, scrubbing—the scenery was different. We were like teenagers who were happy to do chores for friends' parents, who always seemed cooler than one's own.

But even DS Jefferson couldn't go back on his word. At long last we were marched to Taco Bell, just across the street from our starship. There was an ominous feeling in the air. The group having been duly split into two, I went with half of the platoon to the Shoppette to buy some sundries, while the other half went to the restaurant. After I had paid for my items I was told to form up outside.

"Someone fucked up." I got the word as I exited the Shopette, sundries in hand. Those of us who hadn't already eaten were told that the party was over. PFC Shuster had fed the jukebox and others joined in lip-syncing. How embarrassing! Soldiers had the audacity to mouth the words to songs they had lived with and loved before BCT. We learned new rules of the game every time the referee called foul. Very rarely were expectations made explicit. Unacceptable behavior was like the elusive Supreme Court definition of pornography: they "knew it when they saw it."

The collective euphoria of our platoon morphed into disappointment which became anger projected at Shuster. I was irritated, too, but I soon realized that such resentment was irrational—clearly DS Jefferson was determined to find any justification for terminating our fast food binge. It was just too convenient. The only thing poor Shuster did was make that reason more difficult to scrutinize. If it weren't for the quarter in the jukebox, someone who refilled a soda or took too much hot sauce would have been the fall guy.

At any rate, I resigned myself to the fact that Taco Bell would have to wait for graduation. No big deal, really. But after reprimanding the group and humiliating Shuster, Jefferson rethought his position and reversed his edict. He, like I had done as a teacher many times, let the disappointment of sub-expectation behavior inflame the passions that guided his interpretation of good comportment. On reflection, he realized that he had probably overreacted and denying half of the platoon a tasty meal had little correlation to Shuster's ability to behave the soldier. At length we went in and stuffed our faces.

That meal tasted so damned good.

We had to pay for it later, though. In return for his amnesty, DS Jefferson put us through some severe PT once back in the barracks.

"I got games," he proudly declared. Thus commenced the most unusual correction session we ever had. Lockers and bunks were moved to one side of the bay to create a dance floor for a host of creative new exercises. In order to drive his lesson home, he referenced Shuster's boner that had got us here, and made up a ditty to help us remember:

"I put a quarter in the juke box, ohhhh yeah!
"*I put a quarter in the juke box, ohhhh yeah!*
"Do you like the rock music? *Ohhhh yeah!*
"Do you like the country music? *Ohhhh yeah!*
"Do you like the rap music? *Ohhhh yeah!*
"Do you like the soul music? *Ohhhh yeah!*

We syncopated the sarcastic reprimand as we clapped to the beat. It was hard not to laugh at 54 soldiers sweating and singing that ridiculous song, all the while DS Jefferson looking like he was guarding death row inmates at San Quentin. The effect was not trivial: our effort and morale increased. This PT—though clearly punishment—was not dreadful, it was actually kind of fun, as PT sessions go.

Jefferson was also skilled at illustrating the big picture. Prior to shipping, I had looked forward to spending considerable time with the drill sergeants, assuming that I would grow to know and like them, anticipating a mature mentor. Hopefully, the feeling would be mutual; after all, being so close (in so many ways) to any reasonable person is usually an opportunity to make friends at best, and appreciate good qualities about them at worst. Jefferson had no intention of getting to know me or any of the other privates, but he did want us to know who he was, and what he was up to.

"You should be studying right now," he said during our

"Win Me a Streamer"

vaudeville routine.

We had our 1SG Inspection upcoming, during which we would have to answer any number of potential questions posed to us. He was right, and we all understood in that moment that he wanted us to learn.

I overestimated drill sergeants' desire to forge any semblance of a personal relationship with trainees, but I suppose I underestimated their ability to teach simple lessons in unconventional ways. Jefferson had us in the palm of his hand. Our morale was up for having been allowed to make a run for the border, then he put us through a strenuous workout without making us feel manipulated, and we appreciated our drill sergeant even more for recognizing priorities. Our PT session was thus cut shorter than announced so we could begin our mental preparation for the all-important inspection.

Jefferson acted the benevolent despot like that at times. He effectively beat and robbed us, then made us feel grateful for giving back half our property. Part of his "charm" was that he took the time to put things into a clearer, broader context.

Each of our drill sergeants had ways of beating us, though, sometimes figuratively and sometimes not. Combatives, for instance, aside from being a tool to give us a good workout and morale boost, was employed as a means of conflict resolution. Conflicts abounded in our platoon, and so combatives flourished. Ongoing quarrels were a detriment to productivity and learning, so NCOs encouraged us to fight it out and then leave it on the mat. Getting problems resolved in this way was efficient and quick. There were other "messy" ways to deal with disagreements. Jackson, in fact, confided in me at one point how he resolved an issue that could have turned into a full-blown legal mess. One private had accused the other of bitch-slapping him (the other didn't deny it), which was tantamount to assault and a pile of paperwork. Instead of following protocol, Jackson mediated a therapy session in the laundry room, where the age old "eye for an eye" rule of justice was meted. One bitch-slap later and all was forgiven.

Robertson and Jackson preferred to stage tournament-like forums in which challengers would engage with problems in wrestling matches in the barracks with the rest of the platoon looking on, adding to the ambiance with oohs, aahs, and advice to the fighters. Jefferson, though more authoritarian, was not above getting his hands dirty, either. I never found out what happened to those soldiers who confessed to having assaulted Big Rogers, but Rogers continued to be a problem. Jefferson wanted to give his rivals a chance to show him—through physical contact—how vexed they felt.

In a somewhat tidier version of conflict resolution by means of combatives, he invited platoon members to express their objection to certain persons or their behavior. Several soldiers indicated that Rogers was still on their shit list. He asked me who I had a problem with, and I responded that, after I had laid the pugil sticks to Umpenhour's body and head, I had grievances with no man. I was the only one in the platoon that wouldn't be called a liar for saying so.

Nevertheless, something had to be done for the others who sincerely detested Rogers and his lack of improved behavior since the code red. Instead of the public, mob-fed, gladiator style bouts that Jackson and Robertson preferred, Jefferson had quarrelling soldiers go into the day room and fight privately with the lights out.

PVT Rogers had to defend himself against three or four privates during one such episode. Once out, he was forced to admit that he had it coming; his ass had clearly and convincingly been kicked. Our drill sergeant again wanted effective punctuation on the incident and told Big Rogers to express how he felt.

"I feel like a bitch," was his pathetic reply.

"Win Me a Streamer"

A few days after our Taco Bell outing, we noticed that DS Jefferson had not been around. I asked Jackson where he was, and the reply was that he had gone off to some Army school. "Is he going to be here for our graduation?" I asked.

"He'll try."

We never saw Jefferson again.

On my eighth Friday of Basic Training, we chowed and got ready for our Drill and Ceremony competition. I was confident that the streamer would be ours.

"The weight of the entire world rests on your shoulders, Stowell. Can you handle it?"

I think DS Robertson felt more comfortable with me in the first squad leader position than anyone else. I loved bearing the burden, and I looked forward to the performance. After a little more practice, we waited the rest of the morning for the competition to begin.

Each platoon went in turn, which meant that, as the last to compete, we would basically know if we had it in the bag or not. From the first command, "Fall IN!" to the complicated yet elegant arms-toting movements, I concentrated on my role and nothing else for the four minutes of the performance.

In my position at the head of the first file, I couldn't see anyone else, except during the rear march. I muddled one "inspection arms," but hid it well. There were several unidentifiable drill sergeants roaming about our element, monitoring and examining our slightest moves. Our handler led us around on an imaginary leash while judges recorded their opinions cryptically on clipboards, with the authority to lend to the prized "Best In Show." We performed our routine in silent reverence of their power to pronounce victors.

If Robertson could have spoken out during the event, we would have heard something like, "What the fuck are you doing

Shuster?" The same private who messed up at Taco Bell had committed the unpardonable. "Left flank, MARCH!" immediately sent four files of ten, previously marching in the direction of their length, on a perfectly right angle in sync so that ten files of four marched in another direction. Beautiful when done properly, downright hideous when one private breaks off. Shuster was like a car careening off the four lane freeway, on his way to some hideous crash.

We all made mistakes, like the one I hid during the inspection arms. Very minor imperfections could go forgiven or even unnoticed, but when Shuster took *seven full steps* in the wrong direction, it made Robertson nearly explode, and it did us in. Our best hope for a streamer was lost.

We had two other chances to redeem ourselves almost immediately: the APFT and 1SG Inspection. I held out little hope for the former; besides, there was nothing we could do fewer than 24 hours prior to improve our physical fitness test scores on our final assessment. The inspection, though, was a different matter. I could help in many ways, and our drill sergeants expected nothing less.

The inspection was unlike anything we had experienced or prepared for. Instead of simply organizing our lockers and assembling our gear in a uniform manner, we would be required to completely clean—from ceiling to floor and every nook and cranny in between—the entire bay. All of our lockers had to be exact replicas of the others, right down to which direction the toothpaste tubes faced in the second drawer. Finally, we had to clean and arrange our TA-50 on our made bunks, in a prescribed fashion.

The first challenge, cleaning the bay, was met by good old-fashioned delegation. I had spent a considerable time figuring out everything that had to be done and dividing it into 54 nearly-equal pieces—one for each private. With such an approach, the hefty task looked small. Our floors were still a major problem, but we couldn't spend valuable time on something that was never going to improve.

The second challenge was the locker arrangement. Again, there was an assigned place for every item to be displayed, the trick was for each private to arrange it accordingly. Sameness was more important than correctness, though, so I assigned a soldier from each squad to meet and decide on uniformity. Were the buttons fastened all the way up on all shirts? Which way would the hooks face on hangers? How many folds compacted the washcloth in the toiletries drawer? The first sergeant may have been a battle-hardened soldier, but he had a delicate side, and his penchant for neatly-arranged bars of soap and tubes of jock powder were not to be taken lightly. Once a consensus was reached, the four squad leaders inspected and corrected each locker in their row.

Finally, we had to arrange our gear on our bunks. DS Jackson provided us a photo exemplar, and we struggled to find and place everything with the precious-little quickly-passing time.

The job posed two problems: it was taking us into the morning, and once the bunks were covered they were unusable for slumber. The APFT was in a few hours, and we apprehensively stayed up trying to get ready for the inspection, knowing it would compromise our performance on the test.

DS Jackson was driving us to do more and more, while we were lobbying for a reprieve and the permission to get to sleep. We were already going to suffer having to sleep on the hard tile floor without a blanket. In a fit of rebellion, I hopped onto an empty upper bunk and tried to get some rest. No sooner than my head hit the pillow, "House Mouse!" Jackson called me into his office—there was highly important paperwork to be done at 2300 hours. It must have been bad karma for resting on the job (though others were beginning to do the same) that I now had the additional responsibility of some clerical task. It would be impossible to get it all done in one night. I worked for a couple of hours for Jackson before finishing my bunk. Tapp had been a good soldier and done most of the work, but it wasn't until 0100 that we finally all fell asleep, I in my long johns on one of the only empty bunks. Everyone else was on the floor.

Wake up came entirely too soon. We were administered the Army Physical Fitness Test the same as twice before, only this time it counted. No matter how well I did on the previous attempts, this one alone determined whether I would graduate.

I got personal high scores on pushups and sit ups, and I knew I had improved my cardiovascular fitness, so the run didn't intimidate me. I ran with the first group, 1SG Gulliksen giving the word to start. Again, I went in my even pace, letting enthusiastic privates pass me by.

I ran that first lap for myself—proud of how far I had come and what I had accomplished. The run around the starship typified my drive and resolve; I crossed the line at 4:20, knowing I would need to work harder on the next lap (a little longer since we started several meters ahead of the finish line) to maintain that speed.

The next lap was God's. I prayed as I ran and thought about the spiritual transformation that I was making. He had helped me immensely, and I wanted to prove to Him that I could work hard and sacrifice in such a way that He would be proud. I crossed the threshold at 9:00, slower than before, but still on a personal best-pace.

The final lap was for my wife. I reflected as I ran on the wonderful times we had together until we were forced to live apart. I thanked God for giving her to me and allowing me to be with her in a matter of days. I wanted most of all for her to be proud of me and have a stronger husband than the one that left her nearly nine weeks earlier.

"Win Me a Streamer"

As I rounded the third turn, LTC Pastore was there cheering us on. I was among the first of the soon-to-be finishers, and he reached out his hand for me to slap it. I picked my legs up even more, rounded the last turn and crossed the line in less time than I had run two miles, perhaps in my lifetime.

My drill sergeant, whom I was sure I had made proud as well, was there to congratulate me. "You run too slow for being the oldest man in the battery Stowell!"

"I run fast, drill sergeant!" It was the wittiest thing I could manage to think of with so much blood diverted from my brain to my legs.

After chow we headed up to the bay for final preparations for our inspection. While we were tidying up our bunks and doing some final dusting, 1SG Gulliksen walked in, had a few words with DS Robertson, then departed.

Whatever was said sent Robertson into apoplectic rage. In our unpreparedness, we managed to embarrass him for the umpteenth time. Instead of taking advantage of the extra minutes, he had us stand at parade rest while he berated us. Thus we waited. Of course Robertson knew that he severely decreased any chance we had of nailing the inspection, while increasing opportunities to punish us further.

In due course, the first sergeant reappeared and began the formal inspection. Down one row he moved, occasionally stopping in front of a private to check his uniform, his weapon, his gear, and his knowledge.

"What is your third general order?"

"Why is your muzzle dirty?"

"Who is the post commander?"

"What is the maximum effective range of the M16?"

Drill Sergeant Robertson accompanied him rendering approval of every insult the first sergeant had for deficient soldiers. He also absorbed quite a bit of the inspector's criticism, on which he ruminated for the duration of the ordeal. They went through the latrine and analyzed our cleaning job, popping out on my side of the bathroom.

I was sure he would pick on me, as the highest ranking trainee. Instead, he zeroed in on Zaccardi, who stood across from me. His weapon and gear were immaculate. Zaccardi's knowledge about weapons was impeccable, too. But when first sergeant asked him a question about our chain of command—silence.

While Zaccardi stood mute, the most extraordinary thing happened. My eye registered a green flash and I heard a crash. First Sergeant Gulliksen and DS Robertson turned immediately to see a collapsed PFC Vadney pulling himself up. Faintings were not uncommon early on in BCT, but near the end, and especially during an inspection, it was odd. Robertson had a feeling this wasn't a typical fainting spell.

"You fell asleep, didn't you Vadney?"

"Yes, drill sergeant."

Our lack of sleep the night before had certainly caught up with Vadney, in a dangerous way. The poor devil just could not withstand the assault of pure boredom during the inspection. A perfectly erect and unconscious Vadney fell forward, waking up the exact moment the bunk rail in front of him made contact with his face. The blackness and swelling was apparent almost immediately. We couldn't help but laugh, from the position of parade rest, of course.

"The Fall" typified our entire BCT experience: well-meaning and dutiful, but inadequate and prone to mockery. Vadney and Fourth Platoon would be the butt of many more jokes.

We didn't win the streamer.

"You Think You Already Graduated"

WEEK 8

My eyes popped open in the dark of the morning. Alert, something had nagged me out of my slumber. I usually slept perpetually fearful of waking up late. This morning I was the first one up, and I briskly hopped off my bunk to survey the situation and gather my wits. I had laundry downstairs—that must have been what bothered me—so I quickly made my way down to get it. As I exited the bay in my PT uniform, I noticed that no fireguard was on duty, but thought little of it. On my way down the stairwell I also noticed DS Robertson's Jeep pulling up. I thought I'd better hurry. I collected my laundered clothes and reentered the bay to a room full of soldiers in the front-leaning rest. I considered turning right around and heading to the laundry room, but then a wave of guilt and regret inundated me for not having woken up the platoon before I first went downstairs. I grudgingly joined in the collective punishment.

"You think you already graduated, huh? You don't have to pull fireguard anymore?"

DS Robertson was peeved at arriving to a bay full of sleeping soldiers. Apparently, someone had slept instead of relieving the fireguard shift.

"One, two, three..."

"*One!*"

By all accounts, there was little to redeem Wolfpack. Though we didn't know for sure, it didn't look as if we would win the APFT streamer, either. What we did know was that Week Eight would be our last of any substantive Army training, after which were out-processing and graduation drills.

Seven full weeks in Army Basic Training wore me out like an engine on overdrive for too long. The physical tasks overheated the motor, the dysfunction of our platoon contaminated the oil and clogged vital system parts. To extend the metaphor, the interior began to stink. Our drill sergeants thought that the pedal to the metal would purge the bodily engine of impurities and increase performance. I was out of gas.

We had hit the homestretch, and I knew that it would be a tough fortnight—mentally if not physically. My letter to Esther dated 28 July reflected as much. It was one of despondency and despair, in which I poured my heart out admitting to her that I cried again under the pressure: "The nearer I get to the day we will meet again, the harder it seems for me to cope and to persevere."

I also realized that in the grand scheme of things, it really didn't make a difference; my post script said, "Though BCT is frustrating, know that I am good at looking at the big picture. I realize that this is a great opportunity and will be over soon. Don't worry about me. Just plan our trip and we will celebrate beginning August 9," in reference to our reunion—she was going to come to Fort Sill to pick me up in just a couple of weeks.

For the time being I could rest a little from the extra duties assigned to the leaders who had replaced me. That desire was shattered when Robertson asked me if I wanted to be APG again.

"Is this a trick question?" I asked. He smiled to indicate that he understood my ambivalence, but that it was not.

"I will do my duty." That was to say, "No, I didn't want to be APG, but I wanted the consequences of saying so even less." Slater had been rehired as platoon guide just moments before, and he requested that I serve as APG. Robertson handed me the staff sergeant insignia without another word.

With the conclusion of BCT looming, the pace quickened. We moved ahead with training in advanced weaponry, more complicated urban operations, and convoy attack formations. In each case, our battery training cadre continued to flout any and all sound instructional principles. Ignoring "crawl, walk, run," our trainers told us to make a mad dash, and then they tripped us the moment we got going.

Now Week Eight, we thought it would be a little easier until the end. It was around this time that drill sergeants from all platoons started using the phrase, "So, you think you already graduated?!" *ad nauseum*. Part question and part declaration, the point was simple: though we were getting closer to graduating, we better not ease up and start coasting to the finish line. But if we really were following the "crawl, walk, run" philosophy, then we were clearly at the run stage by Week Eight, and the vast majority of us wanted to sprint as fast as possible to the end.

Drill sergeants were also sniffing the finish line. In their eagerness to rid themselves of the worst battery ever, they may have lost whatever remaining patience they had up until then. When I first fired the 240B rifle the week prior, for instance, I was in DS Lanka's line. I lay down as instructed, and placed my right hand on the handle near the trigger guard and my left hand on the muzzle, like I did for the other rifles. A swift kick to my left elbow stunned me. The pain told me I was doing something wrong, but habit took over until another swift kick, a little harder this time, reminded me that my left hand belonged on the butt stock. Who says corporal punishment doesn't work? I fired off two belts of ammunition with a sore arm.

In one day we fired dozens of rounds from fully automatic weapons, both before and after sundown. It wasn't until 0300 that we arrived at the battery. But we still hadn't graduated. There were plenty of requirements still unmet, and we continued to be, apparently, as ate up as ever.

One such requirement was our 10K road march that we were supposed to have done to get to the gas chamber way back in our second week. Since the floods had prevented us from using the water crossings to get there, we had taken buses. By now the summer heat had dried up the creek waters, and little rain fell in July to replace them, so the roads were wide open for any route that our NCOs chose for us.

In Foxtrot, everything was done the hard way, it seemed. During the march we passed by several other batteries who all looked like they were in Hollywood: sleeves rolled up, vests missing the heavy plates, chinstraps dangling undone, and wearing tinted goggles. The contrast made us painfully class-conscious. We were an oppressed group.

We certainly didn't think we had already graduated after seeing how the other half lived. The conventional wisdom was that Foxtrot 1/40th was the most dreadful battery to be in and every experience confirmed it. We lived in a cycle of despair, performing worse with every lowering of expectations.

Our platoon exemplified the inadequacies of the entire battery, and a handful of soldiers personified the sorriness of Wolfpack. One private could never keep up; another suffered from chronic fevers, coughs, and aches; a couple of others were overweight. We had a narcoleptic, another who couldn't ever shave his entire face, and a known thief. One soldier outdid them all, though. He suffered from most of the aforementioned flaws, but amazingly outdid even himself most days: he rarely wore clean clothes and he employed the same logic to his personal hygiene that he did to his equipment: unless it was inspection day, it wasn't worth cleaning. Other soldiers reminded him frequently of the common courtesy we referred to as "showering," but he didn't seem to understand its health or social benefits. His stench was beyond nuisance.

If that wasn't enough to frustrate us beyond belief, this poor fellow couldn't dress himself. It was a result of some unfortunate combination of low motivation or low intelligence. Drill Sergeant Robertson went with the latter and labeled the unfortunate private, "retarded." Robertson got so fed up with his tardiness to formation that he ordered his squad leader to personally dress him. If the humiliation didn't spur him to dress more quickly, at least the help would get him out the door sooner.

Though we knew we had to avoid serious infractions during our final two weeks, it was futile. The next few days would be spent at and around the FOB, where DS Robertson would have ample opportunity to punish us for any number of infractions, not least of which was our tendency to oversleep without a fireguard duly posted.

At the FOB, we went through more STX (Situational Training Exercises) and headed toward Liberty City, which was some distance away. It was one of the hottest days that July. The thermometer registered 94 degrees, and the long midday march baked us. The heat added to the realism of the situation—we were going to employ some maneuvers to engage enemies in an urban environment.

As we neared the site, DS Jackson pointed us toward a heavily wooded area and told us to meet DS Robertson on the other side for the commencement of our operation. We were to stage an attack on the community that was mocked up to look like a Mesopotamian village, complete with minaret. The Military

"You Think You Already Graduated"

Operations in Urban Terrain, or MOUT, was an exciting way for us to synthesize much of what we had been practicing, from weapons handling and tactical movements to communication and teamwork. We entered the woods and trudged through swampy marshes. Slater and I organized the 54 of us in an elaborate design to take advantage of cover and entrance points. Part of our emphasis was to designate certain teams for specific duties, like radio communication and casualty evacuation.

After all of our planning and rehearsing, DS Robertson came down and told us the whole idea was a bunch of shit, and imposed his own plan on us. Happy to be off the hook, we executed his plan, attacking by teams. I acted as a squad leader and moved two teams in position to move on the village. As we began to make our move, blank rounds rained on us from every building in sight. Two by two soldiers ran to closer cover as those left behind covered them with their own rounds. We each had four magazines of blanks and began to use them with enthusiasm. My team cleared the first building easily.

Moving up to the second story was more difficult, since the enemy had the high ground. Drill sergeants loomed like the Grim Reaper, pronouncing privates dead without warning. We fought back, collected casualties, and tried to regroup under incessant rifle fire, with grenade smoke swirling the compound.

We practiced many things we had learned up to that point. Aiming and shooting, communicating under stress and noise, moving and treating casualties, and rallying at an operations center. Yet the rapid adjustments to the plans of attack and conditions of battle caused missteps and mishaps. In the end, our performance was rated poorly. DS Robertson had nothing good to say about it—it was completely unacceptable.

"You think you already graduated?!"

Slater and I were fired, not surprisingly. The other platoons did no better, yet the revolving door on their leadership was locked. A simple lecture and an appropriate AAR did the trick... they learned.

No such luck for us. Every activity brought with it the surety of rebuke and criticism. Sometimes it was justified, but often it seemed the inevitable consequence of simply being there. Effort was irrelevant. We never fancied ourselves above criticism, but we hoped that it would sometimes be constructive. Again, no such luck.

There was one soldier who may have had a bit of luck after all. For the second time, PV2 Scott was named platoon guide. He had been fired earlier by DS Jackson, but Robertson saw fit to reinstate him. Jokes (in various versions) about the vicinity of Scott's face to DS Robertson's midsection abounded. Scott was probably the only one aside from Real, for whom being a soldier in good standing with the NCOs was the absolute most important thing in the world. He had been lobbying for the position of PG—something any sane person would perceive as a burden more than a privilege—ever since I was tagged as the office's first occupant. I felt more than a little awkward when he promised me, in a very flattering way, that he would take my job. Congratulations, soldier.

Now everyone hated him.

It seemed that our drills were more concerned about who was left with the buck than in truly teaching us military tasks. With the MOUT operation at Liberty City, for instance, there was just too much to accomplish. War (and wargaming) is a complicated thing, particularly in an urban environment. How any novice to the craft could keep up with all the demands of managing a team in such a dynamic and stressful environment, while meeting a difficult and dangerous objective was beyond me. But like our EPOW simulation, cadre seemed more interested in proving that we were not up to the task.

I absorbed it all. In an effective classroom, teachers are

concerned first and foremost with student performance, not in assigning blame for shortcomings. This curriculum design would be thrown out by any self-respecting educator. A few simple changes could have added much more value. First, dry runs of an attack formation and the initial charge against enemy fire would have prepared us for the larger operation. Once we had that sufficiently choreographed, they could introduce additional layers of complication. They're called drills! The more precise and narrowly defined they are, the more beginners will learn from them. Surely they didn't expect 54 new recruits to take a town that rivaled an Iraqi insurgent stronghold on their first attempt. In retrospect, they probably didn't. It was more entertaining to watch us fail, and they were more justified in treating us like incompetents when we did.

Besides, what did I know? I was just some trainee who probably thought he had already graduated.

On the march back to the FOB, DS Robertson showed us just how ate up we were by marching us at breakneck speed. The temperature had gone nowhere but up, and we were exhausted from the earlier march and operations of the day.

I tipped my proverbial hat to the soldiers in Iraq because after a full day of work, I could just barely keep up, and I was one of the fittest. I never doubted Robertson's stamina, but he was going to prove just how steadfast it was, at the expense of some of our slower and weaker privates. By then we were so broken and defeated that privates weren't even embarrassed or afraid to strike. They just stopped. It wasn't worth feigning grit and determination, it was too damned hot. Our fearless leader could have this win. And he did—Wolfpack straggled into the FOB not as a team, but as the sorry band of buffoons the drill sergeants always claimed us to be.

The next day, after shooting off rounds from a moving open-bed truck at pop-up targets, we had a quaint little family meeting during which PV2 Scott harangued us for not being less ate up than our drill sergeants estimated. Scott and Realivasquez, his right hand, berated us in true drill sergeant-style. They hurled curses at us that would have made our NCOs cringe, and warned, in very unspecific terms, that unless we mended our ways, we would not enjoy any more privileges (Gatorade aside). Mostly, though, our honor was at stake.

While these two wannabes had our attention, I decided to steal the spotlight and pose a question that was really meant for our drill sergeants: "Why should we? Why should we stress ourselves out any more?" I was speaking truth to power. No matter what we did at this point, we were douche bags and pussies, and if Real and Scott wanted to defect to the drill sergeants' side, then they could delude themselves into thinking that the label didn't apply to them.

"I don't really expect that to come from you," offered Real.

Mine was the more legitimate concern. Far from getting more bearable, our treatment had been worsening over the past few weeks. Worse than physical punishment was the psychological distress of not ever being good enough; just drill sergeants' bitches. Our platoon leadership was only perpetuating the dynamic. In Week Eight they had revived the timed shower policy, for heaven's sake. Who could possibly find motivation when he couldn't' even relax in the shower for more than 90 seconds?

We had been immersed in Army ways for at least eight weeks, and to our drill sergeants we had learned nothing. They said as much.

The "you think you already graduated" mantra got old before it got started. The ironic part was that we would have performed much better if only we thought there was some recognizable progress. Perhaps there was, but no drill sergeant of ours, or their current lapdogs, would ever let us know it. The self-fulfilled prophecy was thus realized.

It was hard to earn anything at Basic Training. The day after our Convoy Live Fire, we conducted more urban training at Freedom Town (Why we were attacking the namesakes of our democratic ideals was an irony lost on everyone). As we prepared to march on our objective, DS Jackson called out from across the field, "Let's go privates!"

We all did a double-take. Who was this mysterious person and what had he done with Drill Sergeant Jackson? The mystery was soon unraveled when we noticed that our battalion commander was on the range. LTC Pastore wasn't too keen on his drills verbally abusing the trainees. That's sooo officer, to expect NCOs to treat soldiers with respect.

And it was so drill sergeant to scoff at the idea. As I did some routine business in the drill sergeants' office one day, DS Eppinghaus came in. He was of the same feather as Robertson: young, cocky, and prone to cite irrelevant accomplishments like how many miles he had driven without rest, and how fast he could eat an MRE. Robertson took the opportunity, after demeaning me for a spell, to brag about how he had dropped the f-bomb on some privates during the APFT. Apparently, there was a zero tolerance policy on swearing, though they wouldn't have had to worry about any whistleblowers from the battery because we weren't privy to the policies governing our training. I just happened to be in the room during their gripe session. Robertson mentioned how the commander gave him a look of disapproval.

"Fuck that guy!" screamed Eppinghaus, as he stuffed a Golden Oreo in his mouth. "I fucking hate him!" Nuggets of saliva-moistened cookie sprayed out in his disgust.

They bonded for a moment in their dissatisfaction with a superior officer. It was tender.

Just when we were getting relaxed in our tents on the FOB again (this would be our last trip), we got word that Robertson wanted to see us under one of the canopies by the NCOs' quarters. The sun had long ago set, so we gathered informally on the concrete pad and wood tables to listen to another tirade. He was in a surprisingly jovial mood, amplified by energy drinks. Mail call was usually Jackson's act, and he performed it with vaudeville histrionics. With us seated, paying nominal attention to him, he regaled himself with our personal correspondence. There were absolutely no secrets at Basic—Jackson ordered soldiers to stand in front of the group and read aloud the letters. Often, he'd tear them out of the privates' hands and read them himself. He never failed to thumb through pictures, just to make sure there was nothing in violation of Army policy. Even I wasn't immune, just lucky enough to have a boring enough life to avoid embarrassment.

Robertson would also conduct mail call, but he usually dispensed with the fraternal jokes and intrusive queries about our mail that his superior loved so much. On this night, for some reason, he was milking it.

The mail call was long and arduous. I was simply enervated, and not in the mood for Robertson's repartee. It was a good thing that it was past nightfall, so Robertson couldn't see me. I slept for at least an hour until I heard my name. Reflexively, I jumped up and approached the man with my mail.

My wife had sent me a couple of packages, and Robertson was curious what was in them. The first one had two white tee-shirts, which he snatched from my hands. They were religious undergarments, and I had requested them to wear with my class As. Robertson had long ago given up on questioning me about my underwear, so he took a humorous course this time.

"I like my men hard," he said holding up the blank tee as if reading a print. "What the…?"

He earned a few chuckles from the tired crowd with that,

"You Think You Already Graduated"

admittedly, clever joke. He made the amateur comedian's mistake of trying the same thing again.

"I'm a homo..."

"—Yeah," I interrupted, "my wife said she was sending one for you, too, *drill sergeant.*"

My joke garnered an equal share of laughter, along with several cringes. I was sure to get smoked for the flagrant insult, but Robertson seemed not to notice, or didn't want to acknowledge the touché.

The second package was in honor of my birthday, just two days away. The most prudent policy at Basic was to keep one's birthday private; I ran a bigger risk getting dusted off with this sensitive information. To my luck, when I opened the package he didn't notice the giant card that said, "Happy Birthday." He was more interested in my gift—a Tide spot removing pen.

The marketing geniuses at Proctor and Gamble knew how vital it was to be clean in the Army. In an ad that aired over the summer I was away, several soldiers were shown finishing up lunch when their drill sergeant announced that break was over. As he assembled his troops he noticed one private had left some of his meal on his tee-shirt.

"A stain Vaughn?! A ketchup stain?! How dare you disrespect me, your country, and your mama!" As he hoots, hollers, and dances in disgust of his troop's disregard for personal appearance, his battle buddies pass him a "Tide ToGo" stain remover, which he employs quickly and stealthily. The drill sergeant returns and asks, "Do you have something to say about the stain, Vaughn?"

Vaughn replies, "Sir! What stain?!"

By now the stain is history, the drill nearly goes into convulsions. "Ohhh! What'd they do, send me a dag-gonned Houdini?!"

The apparition of the little marvel from my box rendered Robertson equally amazed, and he took it as a premise to play the part of the commercial actor.

"Is your wife trying to make fun of the drill sergeant? I see how it is. Well, let's see if it works!"

He forced me to play my part of the ad. Following his instruction, I put a Sharpie stain on my tee-shirt. Then, DS Robertson examined me and yelled verbatim the part of the television drill sergeant.

I scrubbed quickly with the stain pen, and, if the testimonial be forgiven, it actually worked!

"Ohhh! What'd they do, send me a dag-gonned Houdini?!" Cheers of laughter all around.

After mail call, Robertson still had to deal with our dereliction of fireguard a couple of days earlier. He had two words that would help us think about our failure: sleep deprivation. Scott and Real were just too eager to go along. Their orders were to organize and supervise fireguards comprising half of the platoon. One hour on, one hour off. We had to bed down by 2300. The rest of my shift and I were snoozing comfortably when a grenade explosion woke us up.

"*Hurry up! Hurry up!*"

I decided that I'd rather die than get out of bed. If I didn't want to defend myself against a surprise enemy attack, wasn't that my prerogative? I realized that it wasn't, having surrendered my agency upon my enlistment in the United States Army: "*I am a guardian of freedom and the American way of life!*" The oath didn't include caveats for waking hours.

So grudgingly but dutifully I got dressed, grabbed my weapon, and put on my pro-mask to help set up a security perimeter. Eventually we got word that the drill was over. Finally, back to sleep, except no—DS Robertson wanted us in formation, fully dressed in battle rattle wearing our masks. His point was not yet proven, so I marched with my mates to the road where our fearless leader was waiting to rebuke us anew in the darkness.

"You think you already graduated?!"

His sentiment was that we had no idea what the real Army was like, and probably couldn't make it if we did. To follow his logic, he had to make the rest of Basic Training as unbearable as possible.

Fat Walker gave him another reason to do so. "Private Walker doesn't have his pro-mask?"

I mentally surrendered. Just a few weeks before, the sweaty mask fogging up around my face and slowly suffocating me would have been torturous. Now, it provided some sort of protection from the verbal onslaught of my drill sergeant. His words rang in my ears, but I couldn't see, and felt hidden from his view. It couldn't protect me from the sentence, though: a nearly all-night fireguard. By the time we were dismissed, it was well after midnight, and my next shift was just beginning. For the rest of the night we would alternate between hour and a half patrols and equal amounts of sleep—in theory. Under conditions of sleep deprivation, every annoyance is exaggerated into a matter of life or death; every slight an injustice of epic proportions. Privates Scott and Real managed the other 52 privates and their infinite complaints.

It was the night of the living dead. We circumnavigated our tents like zombies—it was all I could do to stay upright. I saw several soldiers falling asleep mid-stride. The groans and grumbles added to the ambiance of an underworld of armed men, chasing themselves in circles until the taskmaster gave them reprieve.

I had never been more tired in my entire life. We had been up 20 hours straight, most of the time filled with tiring tasks in drowning summer heat. Now we had to fight the most evasive temptation, Scott and Realivasquez hovered over us like cruel overseers.

The anguish didn't escape me, but I wasn't as affected by it as others. PVT Thomas was ready to fight anybody who crossed him. Someone had to pay for his pain.

Thomas was a very public Christian. A bit of a hypocrite at times, not unlike most of us, he claimed discipleship but often acted contrary to the Word. I reminded him of the story of Christ's betrayal, as told in the Gospels. Jesus was at the precipice of the greatest, most momentous event in the history of humankind as he prayed in the Garden of Gethsemane, and all he asked of his disciples was that they stay awake. It was only one night. They may not have known the import of the moment, but they failed Him in that seemingly slight way.

I tried to get Thomas to see a parallel. Though our drill sergeants were far from model Christians, what they asked was simple. Not easy, but simple. The shortcoming of the twelve was discipline. They became disciples through trials, and the proverbial refiner's fire.

Could this have possibly been such a trial? Could I let it refine me and make me a stronger, more patient, more understanding man? How could I help the younger soldiers see the same opportunity? I was groping for lessons here.

I had other trials, too. DS Robertson still had to deal with me for a certain safety breach. Perhaps he knew that I could self inflict more mental trauma if he left me alone to ruminate about my dim-witted mishap on the road march. If so, he was correct. I thought of all the terribly frightening possibilities of my oversight. It could have been deadly.

One morning several days later Robertson called me in to the office and made me pay. I ran in place while I recounted the idiocy that I had put on display. He could tell I was truly penitent, but threatened an Article 15 anyway. He should have given me one, as Jackson half-heartedly suggested, but he knew I had learned my lesson.

That I did learn lessons made me a consensus choice as

"You Think You Already Graduated"

Liaison to the Drill Sergeant. Though I didn't like to bother DS Robertson for anything, I knew that some things were important to the soldiers. He let me know that he was bending over far backwards to accommodate my irritations.

"What is it?!" he would ask in such a way as to remind me that it better meet some arbitrary standard of importance. I selflessly communicated my platoon mates' concerns that never did quite rise to that standard.

On one Sunday afternoon, he ordered me out.

"I gotta get out of this place." he grumbled, hoping I'd hear. I couldn't have agreed more, but now it was my turn to be annoyed. Robertson took pleasure in highlighting our weaknesses, and for the past eight weeks I was one of his targets. I missed home, I was exhausted, and I didn't want to give him the satisfaction of thinking that I felt sorry for him.

I bit, but added as much sarcasm as I thought I could safely get away with: "Why would you ever want to leave beautiful Fort Sill?"

The reason BCT last nine weeks is because it takes that long for young soldiers to learn warrior tasks and to hone the unit cohesion necessary for advanced training and combat. It doesn't last longer because even the dimmest soldiers start to realize that drills aren't that cool or that scary. Their grip of authority can't stay tight forever. My moment of realization was now. From this moment on, Robertson was going to be my inferior in everything but rank and title.

Toward the end of the week we went *back* to Liberty City for another round of urban operations. Again, if the Army was preparing us for war, they must have already conceded defeat, for the instructors' emphasis was on getting us there and back, rather than teaching us anything that we could execute with any degree of proficiency.

It betrayed a "check the box" mentality. As long as they went through the motions to say that we had completed a given task, then they had fulfilled their duty. Checking the box wasn't metaphor, either. Nearly every activity in the Army has, at a minimum, a packet of forms associated with it. It often has reams.

The drill sergeant is a consummate professional—in the paper drill. He knows that an officer will hold him accountable, not for the proficiency of the soldier, but for the boxes that were or were not checked. The failings of the instructional system won't be felt until many months and years later on the battlefield of Iraq or Afghanistan, and by then there will be many layers and middlemen to blur the ill-effects of Initial Entry Training.

Thus, the non-commissioned officer will ensure that his bosses don't ever have to worry about that. They will go through the motions, shuttle the basic trainees back and forth from task site to task site, and check the boxes. It is doubtful that they are trying to fool anyone. To them, this is how it is done. As long as we went to Liberty City once, twice, the prescribed number of times to complete the prescribed number of tasks, we had met the standard.

The standard, at Basic Combat Training in Fort Sill, Oklahoma in the summer of 2007, was to check the box.

Perhaps the problem is that nobody did know who "they" were. Our drill sergeants were cogs in the machinery just like we were. They took their marching orders from the Chain whose immediate link above was First Sergeant Gulliksen in Foxtrot 1/40th. Above that, they may or may not have known who was calling the shots.

Ultimately, it did not matter. It was Army Doctrine…infallible. To question it would have been tantamount to heresy.

Besides, by this time we could let just about anything slide. We were short timers, and like seniors in high school whose level of interest tapered off steadily toward the end of the school year, so we cared a little bit less with each passing day.

"You Think You Already Graduated"

Our NCOs' interest grew in direct proportion with our declining concern—their interest was to get the boxes checked and get us the hell out of there. The first step was to get us out of Liberty City and to the battery, but the bus wasn't there, and no sign was had of its arrival. So DS Rodriguez organized a shuttle service using the small fleet of pickup trucks and the deuce and a half at our disposal.

Shuttled we were back to the barracks to take a bit of a rest and prepare for the climactic event in our nine-week Basic Training.

We were bused out to a site that we had never before laid eyes on. It was quite nice: a park surrounded by thick woods. Our drill sergeants were less than oppressive this afternoon. I couldn't decide whether they had resigned themselves to the nearing conclusion of our cycle, and had chosen to save their rants for the next group, or whether they just began to treat us like the soldiers that the Army had molded us into. Either way, we were glad for the change.

If the drills pestered less, the insects didn't. I brought plenty of repellant, which my wife had sent me, and applied it liberally. It was the evening of 3 August, and the temperature was dropping into a fairly comfortable zone that the mosquitoes were enjoying just as much as we were. After a "Pre-Combat Inspection" of our gear, we lay down in formation to take a brief nap. At the precise time (to which only the drills were privy) we shoved off. The beginning of our 15-kilometer road march was nice and easy. Everyone seemed eager to complete it cheerfully.

The sun was settling down along a ridge in the west, a ridge we were quickly approaching. We stayed on an asphalt road that curved lazily up the foothills, green pastures to one side, rising slopes to the other. Over 200 soldiers strong, we marched past grazing cattle and galloping deer, a sight that reminded me that there was certainly more to life than Army Basic Training.

Everyone—including the drills—seemed to be in high spirits. The countryside was beautiful, and the feeling of nearing the end was euphoric. It was a tough march—we were already gaining altitude quickly—but the kind of work that was satisfying.

As daylight faded, I began to tire. We were now high enough to see the hills cresting in the distance, the hazier ridges creating a soft canvas for the more colorful hills in foreground. Who knew which one was our destination?

By this time, I had already gone through my four quarts of water. The drill sergeants marched down the center of our two column formation, reminding us to hydrate and keeping us apace. It kept them in control, as they had an eye on our discipline and health. They encouraged us to drink water and read the signs of faltering soldiers. DS Jackson made jokes with Wolfpack troops, in a sort of lighthearted way that may have betrayed a hint of pride.

We stopped every hour or so for a mandatory rest. The first one was a luxury, after that they were necessities. Within two hours, the many quarts of water I drank were covering my body, having drenched my uniform in sweat. My feet started to ache. My hands and arms burned holding my rifle at the low ready for so long.

Several hours into the march, night fell upon us. The temperature dropped, but I kept drinking water at the same rate. We took our scheduled rests and continued along, making turns through a network of mountain roads that seemingly led to nowhere.

As fatigue began to set in, I wondered how far we had marched and how much farther we had to go. A marching column can distribute information or rumors through its length like pulses of electronic information speeding through wires. During our march, the information we all wanted was, how much farther?

"You Think You Already Graduated"

How long was 15K? Besides the fact that most soldiers hadn't the faintest idea of the true length of a kilometer, they probably never walked 15 of them consecutively. And, even if we were familiar with the distance, the perception of it could so easily be distorted by the darkness, our heavy loads, frequent breaks, and stepping up zigzagging inclines. Our leaders certainly weren't giving us updates.

Come to think of it, our leaders never told us how far we'd have to march. We had all heard 15 kilometers from the sages of Reception—the venerated AIT soldiers, who we now knew were only slightly less idiotic than the lot of us. And they were probably more prone to exaggeration as information gatekeepers than a drill sergeant would have been. So all we could do was walk and wonder.

Abruptly, we arrived at what we knew had to be the end of our march, and filed into a fenced camp to form up by platoon. Drill sergeants continued the information blackout, so we waited and rested. After some time, we were led to the inner portion of the range, where we stood under the brightness of mobile generator-powered spotlights. It felt darker and later under the artificial illumination.

It was probably after midnight by the time we got in a single file line and rushed through forested path. I had grabbed the handle on the armored vest of the soldier to my front, and a good thing. Before long, the train had picked up pace and we were whipping along the trail in the darkness. I halted to the sounds of gunfire and the smell of smoke.

WEEK 9

"We'll Cancel Family Day and You Won't Graduate"

MY NINTH WEEK at Basic Combat Training came in with a bang. I was crawling, with my weapon, through sand gritty enough to remove skin. At a command I'm sure was given, but didn't actually hear, I had prostrated myself and began the ascent up an embankment about 10 feet high. As protocol dictated, Wolfpack was the last in the queue, so I trailed behind dozens of other soldiers wriggling in the night. The ground was especially hard, and I found myself surprised at the difficulty of the movement.

The Army low crawl is not a hands and knees affair, but something altogether more complicated and painful. According to the Army Field Manual (of course there is a manual that explains how to crawl) you are to "keep your body flat against the ground. With your firing hand, grasp your weapon sling at the upper sling-swivel." It's an awkward position, and that's before the movement even begins.

"Let the front handguard rest on your forearm (keeping the muzzle off the ground), and let the weapon butt drag on the ground. To move, push your arms forward and pull your firing

229 | "We'll Cancel Family Day and You Won't Graduate"

side leg forward. Then pull your arms and push with your leg."

I might as well have done it without any legs, because in the low crawl they create more drag than propulsion. Almost all of the force of movement is from the upper body, which is also the part of the body that has to keep the muzzle off the ground. I had trouble completing five pull-ups on my own. The equivalent of five

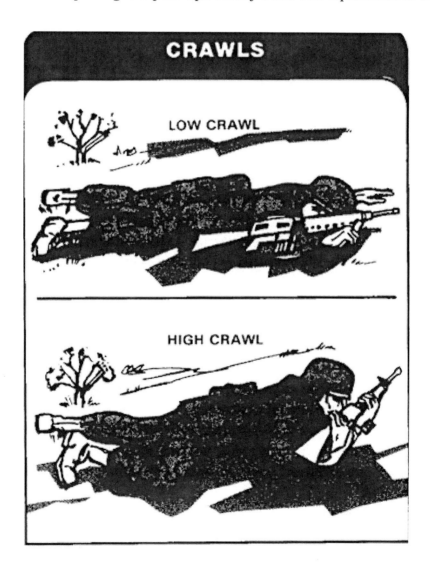

lateral pull-ups on the ground got me about three and a half feet. In dirt.

So by the time I had gone about five meters to the top of the embankment I was exhausted. Only 150 meters to go. Rockets flew overhead. Grenades emitted plumes of smoke and belched thunderous booms. Live rounds whizzed above us.

I dropped down about a five-foot precipice, and looked ahead toward the end of the course. All I could see were bodies slithering along in the soil and smoke, but I judged the rest of the terrain to be relatively flat.

Much of the sound was pumped out through huge speakers around the course, but the effect was still overwhelming. The rounds, mortars, and rockets soaring above were all genuine; the smoke…there's no real way to fake smoke. And it all added up to stress. I wanted to quit, but my options were pretty few at that point. I couldn't stand if I wanted to take the risk (not that it ever crossed my mind), but barbed wire prevented even that. I figured the sooner I got to the end, the sooner it'd be over.

I slogged along in the dark, the sounds and smoke disorienting me and the rounds keeping me earthbound, sweating as much as I had all summer, barely able to muster the upper body strength to continue. The gritty earth found its way through my uniform with every move, and it mixed with my sweat to form a cakey mud on my skin in places that I couldn't itch. Whatever was in my pockets was digging in to my body, but that was the least of my worries. I passed some soldiers, got passed by others. In the end it didn't matter. No one was keeping track of who finished; when an NCO awaited me at the end of the line, he told me to exit the course.

I felt, for perhaps one of the last times at Basic Training, exhausted. I *had* almost graduated.

Again we formed up by platoon after the ordeal. It was getting

231 | "We'll Cancel Family Day and You Won't Graduate"

late, and exhaustion aside, we were all getting sleepy. Our drill sergeants thought it the perfect time to get cuddly.

Since Reception, AIT soldiers had told us of this moment. One who had gone through it promised that we would cry, but wouldn't elaborate further. To him and his comrades who had also graduated from BCT, it was a sort of fraternal initiation that they would not dishonor by revealing.

To me it sounded like a bunch of sophomoric frat guy antics aimed at explaining away weeks of arbitrary maltreatment as an initiation into an elite society. Indeed, it was an over-glorified attempt to cast solemnity on what was otherwise a lame attempt to spartanize a bunch of immature guys who, though there for many different reasons, hadn't realized *how* lame the process was going to be until it was all over.

No matter what it was actually supposed to be, when the sophomoric frat guys are put in charge of the solemn ceremony, the ceremony becomes nothing more than tacky melodrama.

Na na-na naaaa na-na naaa na...Thun-der! Na na-na naaaa na-na naaa na...

Fire spit out of a barrel as a portable radio wailed AC/DC as loudly as the three-inch speakers could. If a poll had been conducted to decide the tackiest song, they couldn't have come up with a better choice. Angus Young and Brian Johnson would usher in the pinnacle moment of our United States Army Basic Combat Training.

Thun-der! Na na-na naaaa na-na naaa na ...

As the song reached its opening crescendo, one drill sergeant lit a smoke grenade to give the formation area a 90s rock appeal. Apparently we were to celebrate the entire affair at parade rest. Not to worry, though, our nurturing drills had a special surprise for us.

In our traditional four-rank formation, we stood as DS Jackson and DS Robertson came through and shook our hands one at a time. Jackson handed us a token to commemorate our grand accomplishment—a dog tag with the Army Values!

We had been obliged to study them throughout BCT. The Army Values became part of the initial training program in the late 1990s. The addition coincided with the moment the Army started to become "soft," according to the many NCOs who would have rather beat us into compliance on their grumpy old man rationale that that's how it was done "in my day." It was, of course, a constant complaint of the drill sergeant corps that the Army was too worried about things called "feelings," which worry prevented them from training young soldiers according to a much more efficient model, one that did not include impediments like "respect." As it was, however, the trainers at boot camp were compelled to follow TRADOC's program, values and all.

This is what I learned of the Army Values.

Loyalty: *to bear true faith and allegiance to the U.S. Constitution, the Army, your unit, and other Soldiers.* Drill sergeants never once made mention of the Constitution, most of them probably had no idea what it was exactly, or what relevance it had to an army.

Duty: to *fulfill your obligations.* Obligations, by our NCOs' reckoning, was whatever they decided.

Respect: *to treat people as they should be treated.* This was violated with nearly every single cadre-trainee interaction. Respect ran only one way.

Selfless Service: *to put the welfare of the Nation, the Army, and your subordinates before your own.* Any mention of this would have been well-remembered, but I don't remember it at all. The notion was lost among the important business of making bunks, and getting dressed and undressed in 45 seconds.

Honor: *to live up to all the Army Values.* As long as we didn't get the urge to learn what they were, this was easy.

Integrity: *to do what's right, legally and morally.* Our drill

"We'll Cancel Family Day and You Won't Graduate"

sergeants were men whose definition of honesty was to tell them whatever they needed to know. Adultery, drug abuse, excessive drinking, cussing, sacrilege; these were all minor blemishes on the profiles in morality of F 1/40th.

Personal Courage: *to face fear, danger, or adversity.* It could have well been that the very last phrase was the only one that drill sergeants remember from their training, because it was perhaps the only value that they taught, albeit indirectly, with any regularity. Adversity was to be found in spades, and they made sure we faced it often and in great quantities.

TRADOC had a fairly good concept in mind when they began to integrate values training into the curricula for accessions. Each major range had an associated Army Value with a soldier profile that exemplified the value. The exercise at Treadwell Tower was a good example, but our mentors only paid lip service to personal courage, as they did all the values. At the tower, 1SG Gulliksen had indicated that we could go read about 1LT Treadwell, with no further mention of who he was, or the extraordinary gallantry he displayed.

The most respect our trainers paid to the Army Values was to pass out the dog tags on which they were inscribed. That tag meant as much to me as what it represented to them. I gave it to my niece a few days later.

DS Robertson wasn't to be left out of the ceremony. He graced each soldier in formation with a handshake—the first one any of us ever received from a drill—and the kindest words he could muster. To me he simply said, "I couldn't have done it without you."

As much as I despised him, the words actually did mean a lot to me. I was probably deluding myself thinking that they meant anything to him, and I certainly couldn't convince myself that he was the least bit sincere with any other troop. At the time, though, I had to agree with him. At least in one respect. Of course he *could* have done whatever he wanted without me, but I think he hit the mark, even if accidentally, in that I spent much energy blunting the drill sergeants' cutting approach. Though it probably wouldn't have been much different had I not been there; maybe a few more fights, and more jockeying of position for PG and APG, certainly more headache on the paperwork side. But cycles come and go, and each one is a big, insignificant pain in the butt in the grand scheme of TRADOC's Basic Training model.

We had our coins and our congratulations, and this thing was nearly complete.

It was after 0200 hours, and we lined up on the road outside SPOTC, exhausted, wet, and getting cold. The buses were running late, not surprisingly, but I didn't mind. As if to celebrate by living dangerously, our entire battery lay down in the dark along the side of the road, using our rucksacks as pillows. Staring at the brilliant sky and trying to ignore the wet sand inside my uniform, I fell asleep content for the first time in weeks.

The bus ride home was equally pleasant. Drills left us alone and we knew that a hot shower and our bunks awaited us at our destination. When we did arrive, we had a quick accountability formation, and then headed upstairs.

The stairwell leading up to our back door was calm for probably the first time during our cycle. When we trudged up them on the morning of 4 August, we found our bay door locked tight. We were all patient, though. Chalk it up to our fatigue, or to our joy at the realization that it was quickly ending, but we just sat there, without complaint.

PV2 Scott, who was possibly the most motivated platoon guide in the history of the Army, was responsible for getting us in. But DS Robertson had split. A cell phone call brought him back to the battery, and Scott was fired before the keys were handed over. He was completely broken up about it.

Relieved of the responsibility, Scott should have slept like a

"We'll Cancel Family Day and You Won't Graduate"

baby, the rest of us sure did.

From that point on, all we could think about was Family Day, when parents would arrive much more appreciated, to a group of boys much more developed. It was the dénouement of our training.

During this last week, we finally got our official APFT scores. They determined, for many privates, whether they would graduate BCT or not. Drill Sergeant Jackson handed out our score cards, and we checked them against our own recollections.

"Stowell," he came upon my card and said my score: "226."

"Drill sergeant," I said to get his attention. "The drill sergeant messed up my score." According to the time recorded, 13:30, I earned a 98 on my run. "He only gave me 96."

"Lemme see that." Sure enough, I was right. "228, then, drill sergeant," I said proudly. Jackson acknowledged my pride with a chuckle.

Realivasquez exceeded all standards and scored a perfect 300. He had cranked out nearly 90 push-ups and sit-ups in two minutes, and a blistering 12-minute two-mile. There were several outstanding performances, but not enough to make our platoon the best. We came in second yet again.

By now, most of us in Fourth Platoon had developed a healthy apathy, veritable Captains Yossarian, were we. We were on our way out, no matter what. Even if our drills testified under oath that they could keep us, orders had been signed, parents notified, trips planned. They must have been bluffing. I had certainly bet on it.

Perception counts for a great deal in the Army. Following a corollary to Sun Tzu's maxim, Foxtrot battery made every attempt to appear stronger (more cohesive, disciplined, motivated, and happy) than we were. The graduation rehearsal at the post theater was clearly given primacy to any warfighting technique. If we could look sharp enough, who would want to do battle with us? Uncle Sam could save a lot of money if we nailed this ceremony.

Countless run-throughs of speeches, formations, presentations, and standing in unison on the "key word" drove us to madness. Our excitement to participate in the milestone event wasn't enough to keep us awake. It was the August version of our CLS class, only with plush seats and air conditioning.

NCOs did their military best to encourage us. "Have some pride!" was supposed to somehow magically overcome the physical effects of sleep deprivation. If calls to our military or family honor wouldn't do the trick, maybe a good old-fashioned threat would.

"If you can't do this, we'll cancel Family Day and you won't graduate!" Gulliksen warned more than once. After a nearly complete Basic Combat Training cycle getting young minds and bodies ready for war that may require the ultimate sacrifice, his creative powers failed him. He resorted, as always, to the lowest type of motivation—fear. It was no wonder that we tuned him out, he was ruining our naps.

Part of the rehearsal and imminent ceremony was the presentation of diplomas. Each soldier stood in line and walked to the stage. It was typical of any high school commencement ceremony, drill sergeants stood in for teachers, 1SG Gulliksen was the principal. SGT Stevenson was the Master of Ceremonies, an odd choice since he had neither a face nor a voice that impressed. He read from his script, which included the alphabetized roster from each platoon. As House Mouse, I had made our list.

"Private Strangler," Stevenson said in his ugly voice, face to match.

"It's *Stangler*," the private mumbled. Stevenson, no matter how many times he was corrected, couldn't help but to mispronounce the soldier's name.

"Private Richard Stowell."

"We'll Cancel Family Day and You Won't Graduate"

"Drill Sergeant," I whispered to Robertson. "You didn't tell me to include ranks on the roster I submitted." It was very important to me to be recognized as an E-4, after nine weeks as just another private.

"Don't worry about it, Stowell. You're all privates anyway."

After Scott's ouster Realivasquez had been placed back in charge, the Casey Martin of Wolfpack. Not surprisingly, he tapped me to be his APG. Though we were only days away from freedom, there were still important tasks to be accomplished. We didn't mind, because they seemed mere formalities that only underscored the reality of our imminent departure. Our Battalion Commander's Inspection was on Tuesday, 7 August—the last performance and our final chance at an elusive streamer.

We pulled out all the stops for this one: taking our TA-50—which had been through nearly nine weeks of soil and sweat—outside for some deep cleaning. It was all scrubbed, rung, sprayed, and hung to dry. Canteens were sanitized, cups polished. The Army could have learned some things from Wolfpack about mobilizing for a common effort. We marshaled our time and talents on an unprecedented scale for this one final chance to make a good impression. One soldier stayed up all night ensuring that our rucksack frames were reassembled correctly.

We even skipped trips to the D-Fac to make sure we got this one right. The first time, DS Jackson ordered me to collect $20 from each soldier for the pizza fund. The mental math quickly yielded a result of $1000, which I was uncomfortable handling.

"That's a lot of money, drill sergeant. I don't think we'll need that much."

"Well you figure it out, then."

I gathered $10 from each member of Fourth Platoon, well more than enough to get everybody a large pizza and a two-liter of soda to split with a battle-buddy. In fact, the trust bankrolled two more pizza meals and a trip to Taco Bell.

It wasn't all fun and games, though. Pizza tasted good, but they were working meals, often cut short so we could get back on task. We worked hard in every way—the administrative demands were increased. I learned about the PMCS: preventative maintenance checks and services. Our pro-masks needed such attention according to some manual, and soldiers were assigned to pay it by looking for cracks in the goggles and missing parts in the filters. Of course the heftiest part of the PMCS was the paperwork. Meaningless in its essence, it satisfied the lords of compliance, and seemed proof of industry when there was, in fact, very little.

I had paperwork of another sort, too. Documentation needed to be furnished to show that trainees had, in fact, completed tasks that proved them battle-worthy. I had to manufacture the documentation. For each private, I gave a "go" next to no fewer than 108 tasks in their official files. In many cases, I had to sign DS Robertson's or DS Jackson's name. All the threats of not graduating melted away as I passed every single one of the soldier's on every single warrior task.

Another sleepless night turned into another disappointing morning, first when our first sergeant appeared instead of our battalion commander, and then when the former pronounced victory on another platoon. Our major offense this time was the toilet water, which betrayed some soldier's completely unbattle-worthy, but environmentally friendly practice of letting the yellow mellow. We weren't as heartbroken this time; the habit of falling short had made us accustomed to seeing things from our lowly station.

We were, however, a little irked about what happened next. Within two minutes of Gulliksen's departure from our bay, and without warning, the order went out to pack up all of our TA-50 for its return to CIF—*within two minutes!* We scrambled to change into ACUs and pack the goods—rucksack, sleeping bag, sleeping

239 | "We'll Cancel Family Day and You Won't Graduate"

mat, poncho, chemical suit, mud boots, protective vest, body armor plates, helmets, canteens, cups, and dozens of associated bags, straps, and parts, into a duffle, onto our backs, and out the door.

What was the hurry? The hurry was that we had to get out into the parking lot before the bus arrived...25 minutes later. Hurry up and wait.

This pilgrimage to the Central Issue Facility was worse than the first. The heat may have been the same, but the stress level was much higher. For one, it was like getting mustard back into the bottle. All this equipment had been duly issued from clearly labeled bins and boxes almost nine weeks ago, then dragged to the four corners of Fort Sill, tossed about bays by unhinged drill sergeants, and sent every which way before we tried to gather it all up in a matter of minutes. Needless to say, it didn't run as smoothly as these military planners had hoped.

"We'll cancel Family Day and you won't graduate."

Privates were frantic trying to present the equipment they had signed for. Piles of extra boots were here, soldiers missing ponchos stood over there. We were all engaged, to one degree or another, in a pit, clandestinely trading commodities before the familiar man in the same USMC cap declared the market closed.

Meanwhile the government regulators stood sentry over the whole enterprise. I was lacking my horse collar—an attachment to the armored vest that protects the neck. The collar was neither used in training nor displayed during inspection, so we had all stowed it deep in our wall lockers out of the way. In my rush I neglected to stuff it in the duffle. The auditor, a soldier I had never met, dutifully noted its absence in a notebook. Uncle Sam could collect his money before I saw my next paycheck.

Some privates had hundreds of dollars worth of charges leveled against them. I had to complete the paperwork for it later on in the office. Never mind that we collected most of the missing gear the next day as we cleaned and organized the rest of our belongings. Another trip to CIF was too much trouble for our leaders, especially when they had a perfectly compliant House Mouse who could solve the problem with statement of charges.

Even if our illustrious drill sergeants were sympathetic to privates incurring charges, they must have believed that we were truly accountable. They had preached for two months about our irresponsibility and unreliability, so they would have to have done a mental about face to see things from a different angle. It was too late in the game for them to make that move. To paraphrase Sydney Smith, "Drill sergeants cling to their delicious tyrannies, and to their exquisite nonsense, like a drunkard to his bottle."

Up until the final moments of BCT, like a tyrant who sees liberty's promise in his subjects' eyes, our NCOs seemed to become more despotic and ruthless in their attempts to quell the hope.

The standby way to quell just about anything but frustration was a smoke session. We had one the next morning as we prepared mentally, emotionally, and physically for seeing our loved ones.

On our way to chow, I asked Real if he'd let me drive the platoon. He consented, and Wolfpack marched along happy as could be from the dining facility to our battery, singing louder and prouder than ever before, eager to show off our newly acquired poise to our families, who were lying in wait on the drillpad. We needed it, too, as they closed in on us for a reunion hug, photo-op or just to register the differences that time at Basic had imposed on our bodies. Scantily-clad teen-aged girls floated like groupies to see their brothers and boyfriends. Starved of such sights for so long, it was a wonder anyone stayed in the formation at all.

From there, the entire battery marched to a field a few hundred yards away, where our families would watch the

"We'll Cancel Family Day and You Won't Graduate"

Cliffs Notes version of BCT. One group performed a weapons demonstration, another group showed combatives drills. A small team came out and played the part of goofy, slovenly privates clueless in the ways of a PT drill, to be replaced by sharply disciplined soldiers who breezed through an exercise routine. A few words from our battery and battalion commanders tested our resolve to stand still in the sun. The thought of impressing our guests proved to be much more powerful than any motivational scheme a drill sergeant could devise.

In due time we had arrived back on the drill pad, those last few moments before being released to the custody of my wife growing more excruciating by the moment. As I stood there in the early August Oklahoma heat with my 53 battle-buddies, I knew my wife was within mere feet of me for the first time in over ten weeks. I was unable to look her way; the sense of discipline and propriety that had been drilled into me scarcely defeated my urge to catch a glimpse of her.

DS Robertson stood before us, at the ready to bellow out the command to move us out. As an assistant platoon guide I stood at the far left of the group, so that the civilians were scattered on and about the bleachers to my immediate left.

"Left, FACE!" came the command.

During the past nine weeks I had stood countless times in this very spot. A thousand times before, the order was given to face to the right. Our bodies had been programmed. Now, at the crucial moment when friends and family from all over the country had come to see us perform, we had been given a different instruction.

Or had we? Time slowed down long enough for me to think about the devastatingly embarrassing consequences of hearing it incorrectly. Or of making the wrong movement. The moment lingered; did I hear properly? Maybe Robertson had said it wrong, expecting us to compensate by doing what we had done countless times before. All the options and their consequences flashed through the circuitry of my mind in a microsecond. It was stage fright at its worst.

When it came down to it, left was left, and right was right. I performed the movement with exactness and speed, facing my wife, still dodging her gaze.

"What?!" came the angry and incredulous reprimand. "YOUR MILITARY LEFT! Nine weeks and you still don't know your left from your right? You're an embarrassment to the Army!"

For a moment I thought my snap decision had been wrong. Many other soldiers in our formation undoubtedly thought the same. But to my relief, another poor soldier was singled out for ridicule. Our drill sergeant broke ranks, grabbed PVT Ritenour's cap, and threw it on the ground ablazed.

We were summarily ordered out of sight and up to the bay to laugh it off. We broke down and analyzed our performance, amusedly congratulating one another. I mentioned to Zaccardi that I was, in fact, hesitant when the command to face left was given. DS Jackson overheard me and asked "Why was you nervous?"

"Even when you're right, if you're the only one, you still look like an ass" was my reply. He couldn't disagree.

After switching from ACUs to the Class Bs[1]—the Army dress uniform minus the coat and tie—we were off with families. It was a strange feeling, euphoric, but awkward in a way. I was programmed less than most, but I still acted like a soldier more than a husband. My wife confessed to me later how upset she was that she couldn't get a kiss. Nevertheless, the moments spent with my dear wife, the woman to whom I had spilled my heart and soul every day, will forever be among the most treasured of my

---

[1] While there are many dress uniforms in the Army, the main one is commonly called "Class A." It consists of matching forest green blazer and trousers, a mint green dress shirt, black tie, belt, socks and shoes, and the black beret. The Class B uniform composed all of the above minus the blazer and tie, with a short-sleeved shirt substituting for a long-sleeved one.

life.

    My parents, two brothers, a sister-in-law, a niece, and a nephew were along for the ride. The few hours allotted to spend with them passed quickly, and in an instant I was back in my bunk, for the last night I would ever spend in it.

    The morning of graduation was the only time we didn't go to breakfast chow. Instead we cleaned, packed, and got ready for the big ceremony. My battle buddy, Yeitter, was in physical therapy for a broken ankle. The fact that he appeared one day toting crutches and wearing a cast wasn't enough to convince Jackson and Robertson that he wasn't malingering, but they still had to make sure he was packed and ready to go to a new platoon as a recycle.

    "Where the hell are Yeti's Class As?!" DS Jackson took his responsibility for Yeitter very seriously, ordering any non-specific soldier within earshot to "get the fuckin' things packed up." Nobody seemed to know where they were at, so no one paid much heed to his command. I had a strange recollection, though, of having placed Yeitter's uniform in *Drill Sergeant Jackson's locker*, though Jackson wouldn't hear of it. He wouldn't admit that they could be anywhere in his office.

    "We're gonna do pushups until that uniform shows up!" he warned, losing patience. I reminded him again of the possibility that they may be in his office. No, they weren't.

    Robertson came to add weight to the order, offering to dust us off on graduation day. I suggested to the younger NCO that his colleague might have the missing uniform in his locker, offering to check.

    I needed permission to start digging through Jackson's personal effects. Even if I had discovered Yeitter's Class As, I would have been smoked for violating the drill sergeant's personal space. So armed with Robertson's go-ahead, I peered into Jackson's locker. Lo and behold…

When I revealed to him that they were under his nose all along, DS Jackson said, "Oh, okay." Not yelling at me was his way of saying thanks.

Meanwhile, everyone else had gussied themselves up in their own Class B uniforms for one more rehearsal. Foxtrot's corps of drill sergeants had managed to get us to stand on cue and pivot correctly on stage—two key parts of the winning formula of a successful ceremony. We still had the Army Song to contend with, though, that musical enigma that befuddled us from the beginning. The *Soldier's Handbook* lists an intro and three verses:

March along, sing our song,
With the Army of the free.
Count the brave, count the true,
Who have fought to victory.
We're the Army and proud of our name!
We're the Army and proudly proclaim:

First to fight for the right,
And to build the nation's might,
And THE ARMY GOES ROLLING ALONG.
Proud of all we have done,
Fighting till the battle's won,
And THE ARMY GOES ROLLING ALONG.

Valley Forge,
Custer's ranks,
San Juan Hill and Patton's tanks,
And the Army went rolling along.
Minute men from the start,
Always fighting from the heart,
And THE ARMY KEEPS ROLLING ALONG.

"We'll Cancel Family Day and You Won't Graduate"

Men in rags,
Men who froze,
Still that Army met its foes,
And the Army went rolling along.
Faith in God,
Then we're right,
And we'll fight with all our might,
As THE ARMY KEEPS ROLLING ALONG.

Then it's hi! hi! hey!
The Army's on its way,
Count off the cadence loud and strong (TWO! THREE!)
For where e'er we go,
You will always know,
THE ARMY GOES ROLLING ALONG.

Anything beyond the first verse and the refrain (Then it's hi! Hi! Hey!) remained unsung and unknown. And despite many smokers, we couldn't seem to omit the parenthetical "Two! Three!" It just felt so natural, but for some reason it was declared *verboten*. Our troubles were more pronounced, and more amplified while trying to perfect our performance for the big show. Soldiers often pushed for blurting the offending line during a rendition, and since the stakes were higher, it naturally followed that the pushing would be more severe.

Half a dozen attempts yielded half a dozen prohibited utterances of "*Two! Three!*" Drill sergeants fumed anew with each failed effort. Each time, novel threats were issued, and each time the anticipation of success filled the air rising to a hearty crescendo as we neared the third line of the chorus. A couple of dozen errant voices were whittled down to four or five, but the progress was not sufficient for our overachieving cadre. More threats. Then some advice: "If you just can't control yourself, and you know you're gonna sing, 'Two! Three!' then don't sing at all! Lip sync!" They really didn't want us to pollute their otherwise sacred hymn with the scandalous numbers.

Another try, this time only two privates exclaimed the forbidden lyrics.

DS Rodriguez, Foxtrot's Drill Sergeant of the Cycle, assumed the mantle by giving us an utterly Patton-esque speech.

We had one more chance. We had been under the tutelage of our drill sergeants for nine full weeks, and in the waning moments of our cycle, we still hadn't learned a damned thing about discipline, respect, or pride. If we couldn't sing the simple words—only the authorized words, that was—to a song, then we weren't worth their valuable effort.

We began to sing optimistically and determinedly.

First to fight for the right, and to build the nation's might!

We would walk the stage tall and proud that very day. Our families would be there to witness it, and our drill sergeants would shake our hands admiringly, esteeming us as equals for having endured.

And THE ARMY GOES ROLLING ALONG!

Their calculated insults were designed and delivered for our own good, to achieve something only they understood. Until now. The words reflected our confidence:

Proud of all we have done, fighting till the battle's won!
And THE ARMY GOES ROLLING ALONG!

The sound was beautiful, and our confidence spilled and swelled and swallowed up the seasoned sergeants who had stood by us, training us patiently, and with dedication to our well-being and learning.

Then it's Hi! Hi! Hey! The Army's on it's way!
Count off the cadence loud and strong!

We were going to do it! This one moment represented our ultimate triumph over all the trials at Basic, and we—

"We'll Cancel Family Day and You Won't Graduate"

"Two! Three!"

The discordant words pierced the air and shattered the good will and our good spirits. A soldier from Third Platoon who was persistently insurgent, had sabotaged our performance. I'd like to think that it was his rage against the machine that impelled him to belt out the solo. Like Tommy Smith on the '68 Olympics medals stand, holding his fist in defiance of the system, this private sent the message that he guarded his agency jealously, even if he exercised it to his own detriment. It was a perfect little protest.

And it earned us one final smoker. Just moments before we were bused to the theater for our moment of glory, the drill sergeants of Foxtrot Battery dropped us in our Army dress uniforms for a last reminder that they could.

"They break you down so they can build you up," is the mantra that I grew up hearing about military training. It is a reasonable proposition; indeed, many enlistees come with excessive baggage of all types: mental, emotional, and not least, physical (i.e., girth). Yet there is no grand plan that I could see to strip away the baggage in exchange for something better. They broke us down all right, right up until the last day. We were doing push ups in our Class As moments before we caught the bus to our graduation ceremony, for goodness sake. If ever there was an appropriate time for the NCOs to "build us up," it would have been then: young men standing tall, donning neatly pressed uniforms with ribbons, pins, and brass. Building us up was apparently going to require just more sweat.

I was the only one to shower after the smoker, determined to be clean for the moment. While my platoon was gathering downstairs, I was adjusting my tie like I had done for so many privates who had no idea what a Double Windsor was.

We packed into the front third of the Post Theater; families and friends were already seated in the rear. The stage was set: flags in the background, podium on the right side. The wall to the left of the stage bore huge gold letters: THE KING OF BATTLE.

During the ceremony, nobody fell asleep. We sat straight and stood snappishly. We bowed our heads in unison and lifted them to a chorus of amens that would move the angels. Our movements were perfect. The Soldiers Creed sent tingles down the collective spine. The battery sang the Army song brilliantly. SGT Stevenson mispronounced Stangler's name a final time. The paparazzi flashed photos and pressed up against the day's celebrities. It was a stirring ceremony: dignified, grand, poignant.

One at a time, the 48th class of 2007 at Fort Sill walked across the stage and shook hands with 1SG Gulliksen and the platoon drill sergeants. After the speeches, presentations of awards, and message to families, we exited in formation as we sang to DS Rodriguez's cadence.

Everywhere I go...
There's a drill sergeant there!
Everywhere I go...
There's a drill sergeant there!
Drill sergeant!
Drill sergeant!
Why don't you leave me alone?!
Why won't you let me go home?!
When I go to chow...
There's a drill sergeant there!

It continued as we filed out, the volume tapering off as the last soldier exited the building.

Before being released to our families, we had one final classroom formation. Jackson handed us our travel orders, training records, and airline tickets, and issued final instructions. Robertson took

"We'll Cancel Family Day and You Won't Graduate"

the opportunity to give out some awards. Slater and Realivasquez got a piece of candy each for motivation and hard work, respectively.

"And to the brains of the operation," he said looking in my direction, "Stowell." A can of Chef Boyardee was mine as a keepsake of the bond that was forged with this giant of men.

Then, a new face appeared in the back of the bay. Someone's father had come up, then another, a girl, and a mom. The fortress walls had been breached, the fight was over. Drill sergeants gave up the defense and let us go.

A few awkward goodbyes, including DS Robertson playing the sycophant to my wife, and I was gone. My brother carried one of my duffles, I had the other and a garment bag slung over my shoulder, now wearing the ACU. We exited the same back door that I had gone through hundreds of times as a tired, stressed, angry, motivated, fearful, excited, proud soldier.

I didn't look back.

EPILOGUE

I returned home from Basic Combat Training on a Tuesday. That Saturday I was at my National Guard drill. RSP, as it was called, stands for Recruit Sustainment Program, and is the Guard's way of getting warriors prepared for BCT and AIT.

As excited as I had been to get back to my teaching position, I was also eager to expand my opportunities. I was offered a job the day I got back working as a consultant for a firm that sells contracts to schools and districts in California for academic services: teacher coaching, technology implementation, and assessment building. In my new position I had the opportunity to visit many different classrooms, see many teaching styles, and watch thousands of students engage in the learning process. In the back of my mind was often the question of how effective the Army training model was.

An enormous amount of money is spent by schools, districts, and states to answer that question for their own organizations. I wonder how often Army teachers have asked it introspectively. The stakes are too high not to, yet I don't believe there is a serious effort to improve Army instruction. It is far too grounded in tradition and doctrine.

During this time I met my future permanent unit, the 69th Public Affairs Detachment (PAD), and discovered what my military job would actually entail. To give away the punchline, nothing like I had expected.

Of course I had more initial training to complete. After a full school year consulting and teaching at the University of San Francisco, I was off to my 13-week Advanced Individual Training (AIT) course at the Defense Information School (DINFOS) at Fort Meade, Maryland. From making the rounds through stimulating learning environments across the state of California, teaching aspiring, idealistic future teachers at USF, and collaborating with some of the best minds in education, going back to the Army way was a real downer. A sugar crash. DINFOS, somewhat like Basic, was a place where they thought the best way to make you learn was by yelling. To be fair, the schoolhouse was less painful, though the teaching no less deplorable. But the training cadre for our student company were drill sergeants and former drills themselves, so wielded their self-described godlike powers clumsily and blatantly.

Those were good times, though. I met some creative, smart, compassionate, and all-around wonderful people, many of whom I still keep in touch with. Towards the end of my AIT I found out I'd be deploying in support of NATO's Kosovo Force (KFOR) with the 69th PAD, and began preparing for fatherhood and an overseas tour at the same time.

Three days after I returned from training in Maryland, my son was born. I got to know Joseph Aniefiok Stowell for about ten weeks before I had to ship out for the KFOR mission.

It is now a year later, and serving overseas as a full time professional Soldier has been truly rewarding. My understanding of the Army continues to expand, and I meet so many exceptional people, Soldiers and civilians alike. It hasn't been without challenges, though. For one, being away from my family so much has a tendency to make me look forward to our reunions. I struggle to relish the moment. It's also hard to watch my son grow up without me.

On the military side, I continue to be frustrated with the way many Army leaders communicate and treat each other. I have found an outlet for these frustrations in blogging. That's another book, though.

I look eagerly forward to getting back into a high school classroom like the one I left behind almost two and a half years ago when I began my military adventure. I also look forward to many more opportunities to grow in the Army.

Perhaps one day I can take my civilian teaching experience and apply it to train younger troops. Now *that* would make some story.

APPENDIX I:
ACRONYMS

Week 0
MEPS: Military Entrance and Processing Station
WTC: Warrior Transition Course
BCT: Basic Combat Training
MOS: Military Occupation Specialty
AIT: Advanced Individual Training
IET: Initial Entry Training
NCO: Non-Commissioned Officer
PT: Physical Training
PX: Post Exchange (military-operated department store)
BCG: Basic Combat Glasses
BAH: Basic Allowance for Housing
TRADOC: Training and Doctrine Command
LDS: Latter-Day Saint
IPFU: Improved Physical Fitness Uniform
ACU: Army Combat Uniform

Week 1
DS: Drill Sergeant
ASVAB: Armed Services Vocational Aptitude Battery
AAR: After Action Report
CQ: Charge of Quarters
CLS: Combat Life Saver

Week 2
FM: Field Manual
TA-50: Table of Allowances [chapter] 50
TMC: Troop Medical Clinic
CLP: Cleaner, Lubricant, Protector

Week 3
D-Fac: Dining Facility
MRE: Meal Ready to Eat

Week 4
CD1: Conditioning Drill 1
AGR: Ability Group Run
BC: Battalion Commander (sometimes Battery Commander)
CSM: Command Sergeant Major
D&C: Drill and Ceremony
APFT: Army Physical Fitness Test

Week 5
BRM: Basic Rifle Marksmanship
E-Gas: East Gas Range
EST: Engagement Skills Trainer
FOB: Forward Operating Base

Week 6
PG: Platoon Guide
APG" Assistant Platoon Guide
SPOTC: Squad/Platoon Operations Training Center

Week 7
CCC: Combat Conditioning Course
EPOW: Enemy Prisoner Of War

Week 8
STX: Situational Training Exercise
MOUT: Military Operations in Urban Terrain

Week 9
PMCS: Preventive Maintenance Checks and Services
USMC: United States Marine Corps

Alphabetically
AAR: After Action Report
ACU: Army Combat Uniform

AGR: Ability Group Run
AIT: Advanced Individual Training
APFT: Army Physical Fitness Test
APG: Assistant Platoon Guide
ASVAB: Armed Services Vocational Aptitude Battery
BAH: Basic Allowance for Housing
BC: Battalion Commander (sometimes Battery Commander)
BCG: Basic Combat Glasses
BCT: Basic Combat Training
BRM: Basic Rifle Marksmanship
CCC: Combat Conditioning Course
CD1: Conditioning Drill 1
CLP: Cleaner, Lubricant, Protector
CLS: Combat Life Saver
CQ: Charge of Quarters
CSM: Command Sergeant Major
D&C: Drill and Ceremony
D-Fac: Dining Facility
DS: Drill Sergeant
E-Gas: East Gas Range
EPOW: Enemy Prisoner Of War
EST: Engagement Skills Trainer
FM: Field Manual
FOB: Forward Operating Base
IET: Initial Entry Training
IPFU: Improved Physical Fitness Uniform
LDS: Latter-Day Saint
MEPS: Military Entrance and Processing Station
MOS: Military Occupation Specialty
MOUT: Military Operations in Urban Terrain
MRE: Meal Ready to Eat
NCO: Non-Commissioned Officer
PG: Platoon Guide
PMCS: Preventive Maintenance Checks and Services

PT: Physical Training
PX: Post Exchange (military-operated department store)
SPOTC: Squad/Platoon Operations Training Center
STX: Situational Training Exercise
TA-50: Table of Allowances [chapter] 50
TMC: Troop Medical Clinic
TRADOC: Training and Doctrine Command
USMC: United States Marine Corps
WTC: Warrior Transition Course

APPENDIX II: RANK ABBREVIATIONS

<u>Enlisted</u>

E1, PVT, Private
E2, PV2, Private Second Class
E3, PFC, Private First Class
E4, SPC, Specialist
E4, CPL, Corporal
E5, SGT, Sergeant
E6, SSG, Staff Sergeant
E7, SFC, Sergeant First Class
E8, MSG, Master Sergeant
E8, 1SG, First Sergeant
E9, SGM, Sergeant Major
E9, CSM, Command Sergeant Major
E9, SMA, Sergeant Major of the Army

<u>Officer</u>

O1, 2LT, Second Lieutenant
O2, 1LT, First Lieutenant
O3, CPT, Captain
O4, MAJ, Major
O5, LTC, Lieutenant Colonel
O6, COL, Colonel
O7, BG, Brigadier General
O8, MG, Major General
O9, LTG, Lieutenant General
O10, GEN, General (four star)

APPENDIX III: PICTURES IN ORDER OF APPEARANCE

NCO Rank, from *IET Soldier's Handbook*, TRADOC Pamphlet 600-4, October 2006

ACU, from "United States Army Uniform January 2009," taken from us.army.mil/publications

Army Emblem, from "Department of the Army Seal, and Department of the Army Emblem and Branch of Service Plaques," Army Regulation 840-1 19 February, 2009

Officer Rank, from *IET Soldier's Handbook*, TRADOC Pamphlet 600-4, October 2006

M16 Parts, from *IET Soldier's Handbook*, TRADOC Pamphlet 600-4, October 2006

Army Values, taken from http://www.bragg.army.mil/18ABN/army_values.htm

The Squat Bender, from "TRADOC Standardized Physical Training Guide BCT," 5 November 2003

Rifle Firing Position, from *IET Soldier's Handbook*, TRADOC Pamphlet 600-4, October 2006

Crawls, from "Field Manual 21-75, Combat Skills of the Soldier," Department of the Army, 3 August, 1984

ACKNOWLEDGEMENTS

There are many people who have helped me complete this project. First, my wife, to whom it is dedicated, motivated me to continue writing on those days when it seemed like I had nothing to say. I also need to mention my son, Joseph, who has been an inspiration to me ever since he joined our family shortly after my graduation from AIT.

Many of my family, friends, and colleagues were instrumental in *Nine Weeks* taking shape. My battle buddies from the 69th Public Affairs Detachment, Nevada Jack Smith and Joseph Samudio, who read and reread drafts, were diligent and encouraging. If there are any mistakes left, I blame them.

My commander, CPT Jonathan Masaki Shiroma (a network news reporter for 25 years) gave me much support and helpful criticism. Safely back in California, Kara Greene, who made the jump from the enlisted ranks of the Army to become an officer, gave me some of the best insight I could ask for.

On the family side, I'd like to particularly thank my aunt, Kay Gaisford, whose meticulousness was invaluable, and who passed some initial drafts to her friend, Jeni Grossman. My cousin Rebecca Miles had amazing suggestions that I valued highly.

Lauren Campbell, a splendid writer, also gave me much appreciated feedback. Working as a teacher gave me access to other great writers and critics, as well. Rachael Maves and Hallie Han come to mind. Any students who have them for teachers should count themselves lucky.

My good friends Morgan McKeown, Tyler Harris, Maneeza Jaan, and Ruth Hochman also gave great advice that I appreciated very much.

ABOUT THE AUTHOR

Rich Stowell currently teaches Education Technology at the University of San Francisco and works as a math and technology coach for a California education consulting firm.

While he was teaching high school math in the San Francisco Bay Area he got an itch to serve his community, and joined the Army National Guard in 2007. Part-time soldier quickly became a full-time job. After his initial training Rich mobilized with the California's 69th Public Affairs Detachment and deployed to the Balkans in support of NATO's Kosovo Force.

He has written extensively about his military experiences and how they relate to teaching on his military blog, "My Public Affairs" (http://my-public-affairs.blogspot.com).

As a civilian, Rich has taught and coached at several Bay Area schools. He attended California State University East Bay (previously Hayward), where he met his wife, Esther. He earned his California teaching credential from CSU East Bay and his M.A. in Teaching Mathematics from Western Governors University.

A Californian for the past decade, Rich grew up in Salt Lake City, Utah. He lives with his wife, Esther, and their son, Joseph Aniefiok, in Oakland.